NEW YORK FREE SCHOOL NO. 1.

THE NEW BUILDING OPENED IN 1809 IN TRYON ROW.

PUBLIC EDUCATION

IN THE

CITY OF NEW YORK:

ITS HISTORY, CONDITION. AND STATISTICS.

AN OFFICIAL REPORT TO THE BOARD OF EDUCATION.

BY THOMAS BOESE,

Clerk of the Board.

NEW YORK:

HARPER & BROTHERS, PUBLISHERS,

FRANKLIN SQUARE.

1869.

TO THE BOARD OF EDUCATION.

In accordance with the request of your Honorable Board, I hereby transmit a report upon the origin, progress, and condition of Public Education in this city, to which are added statistics and other information in reference to the educational facilities provided by religious, charitable, and private means.

The difficulty of obtaining material for the early history of education in this city was very great, owing to the fact that no attempt had heretofore been made to gather information on that subject. As the duties of my office take most of my time, it would have been impossible for me to obtain the necessary knowledge and properly compile it without assistance. This has been rendered by Thomas F. Harrison, Esq., Assistant Superintendent of Schools, who has been of much service both in obtaining the information, and in the literary labor requisite to the preparation of this report.

THOMAS BOESE,
Clerk of the Board of Education.

New York, *December* 30, 1867.

PRINCIPAL AUTHORITIES USED IN THE COMPILATION OF THIS REPORT.

Reports and Documents of the Board of Education.

Reports and Addresses of the Public School Society.

Minute-books of the Public School Society and its Committees.

Minute-books of Public Schools.

Sketch of the New York Free School. Collins & Perkins, 1807.

Lancasterian System. Collins & Perkins, 1807.

Dunshee's History of the School of the Reformed Dutch Church. N.Y. 1853.

Brodhead's History of New York.

History of the New York African Free Schools. Mahlon Day, 1830.

Valentine's Manuals of the Common Council.

Mitchell's New York in 1807.

Francis's Early New York.

Hardie's Description of New York. 1827.

New York as it Is. 1837.

New York Past, Present, and Future. 1851.

Life of John Griscom.

Manuals of the Free School Society.

Manuals of the Public School Society.

Manuals of the Board of Education.

Longworth's City Directories.

Newspapers of various periods.

Barnard's American Journal of Education.

Reports of Legislative Committees. 1857 and 1866.

Special Report of Superintendent Rice. 1867.

New York Code of Public Instruction, by Superintendent Rice. Albany, 1868.

Charities of New York.

Batchelor's History of Teachers' Associations of the City of New York.

Personal reminiscences of various teachers and school officers (oral).

CONTENTS.

HISTORY OF PUBLIC EDUCATION

IN THE CITY OF NEW YORK.

I.

SCHOOLS OF NEW AMSTERDAM.

1614–1664.

Public Schools in Holland, 1585.—West India Company bound to maintain Schools.—First Common School in America.—ADAM ROELANDSEN.—Stuyvesant.—Luyck's Latin School, 1659.—Large number of Schools.

THE settlers of New Amsterdam did not neglect to provide for the education of their children. In their native land they had themselves been participators in the advantages of public instruction, furnished by the first system of common schools ever established in Europe. The thrift, energy, and bravery of the citizens of the little republic were early co-ordinated with a wise regard for the cultivation of intelligence, and legal enactments sought to protect the state from the evils inseparable from an ignorant population. "Neither the perils of war, nor the busy pursuit of gain, nor the excitement of political strife, ever caused them to neglect the duty of educating their offspring. Schools were everywhere provided, at the public expense, with good school-masters to instruct the children of all classes in the usual branches of education."[1]

With the same forethought, the national authorities bound the West India Company to maintain, in their distant colony in the wilderness of New Netherlands, "good and fit preachers, *school-masters*, and comforters of the sick;" all of which

[1] Broadhead.

functions seem at first to have been exercised by the same individual. The exact date of the establishment of the first school on this island can not now be definitely ascertained; but enough is known respecting it from the official records of the town to warrant the assertion that it had the honor of being the first on the continent of America which was maintained at the public expense, and was open to the children of all classes of society. It is true that, like the schools at home, it was under the direction of the Established Church; no people having yet advanced so far in their conceptions of religious liberty and mutual right as to place the public secular instruction of youth under the control of the civil authorities alone.

As the Government bound the Company, so they, in their turn, obliged the patroons to support, in their several agricultural colonies, a minister and a school-master. It was not till 1633, even in New Amsterdam itself, that the two offices were practically separated; but at this date, and with the advent of Wouter Von Twiller as governor, we find that Dominie Bogardus is the officiating minister, while ADAM ROELANDSEN is at the same time mentioned as the *school-master*—the first of that long line of instructors steadily increasing in numbers, and now amounting, in the public and private schools of the city, to over four thousand persons.

The school was long without a permanent home, being kept in such premises as could from time to time be obtained. The first efforts to build a school-house were made in 1642; but the financial difficulties of the colony were so pressing that the funds collected were again and again diverted to other uses, chiefly to defense against the Indians, so that the building was probably not erected till after the English occupation. Small private schools were also early established for the children of the more wealthy portion of the community, but, even in these, no one could teach without a license from the civil and ecclesiastical authorities.

The range of study must have been very limited, as appears from a remonstrance from the colonists to the Government in consequence of the irregularity of the school, especially of one interregnum of three months. They demanded that the school should have at least two good masters, and that there should not only be instruction in reading and writing, but also in the religious doctrines of the Church—an early indication that sectarian had a natural tendency to separate itself from secular instruction, and can only be kept in combination with it by making the minister the school-master, or the school-master the minister. As to other subjects of study, the simplest forms of arithmetic and the keeping of accounts were not taught to youth till the next century, geography not being added till within the last eighty years.

The interest manifested in the schools by Stuyvesant, the last Dutch governor, seems to have increased their number throughout the colony. At the close of his administration there were, in New Amsterdam alone, three public schools and a dozen or more private schools, besides a Latin school of such high reputation that pupils were sent to it from Fort Orange, from the Delaware, and even from Virginia. So great an attention to education is certainly very creditable for a town numbering at the most only some fifteen hundred inhabitants, struggling with the privations of a distant colony, and surrounded by a generally hostile Indian population which still roamed over nearly all of the island, and in times of peace were found in the streets of the settlement itself.[1]

The school first established as the Public School is still in existence. It is known as the "School of the Reformed Protestant Dutch Church," its peculiar public character and support terminating with the Dutch Government. Fully participating in the advanced views of our time, it is yet in good and thriving condition, and seems likely long to continue, as

[1] In 1658, the schout, or sheriff, Nicasius D'Sill, complains of the trouble he has had with the "shouting of the Indians," at the same time venting his wrath upon the boys of the town, who, by "*cutting of hoekies*," caused him much annoyance. Many juvenile Manhattanese of other than Dutch extraction still keep up the ancient custom, and play "*hookey*" as in times of yore.—*Valentine.*

probably the oldest educational institution in the United States. A few years since, on the occasion of the transfer of the school to its present commodious building, its principal prepared a sketch of its history, from which the greater part of this and the following section has been compiled.[1]

[1] History of the School of the Reformed Protestant Dutch Church, by H. W. Dunshee.

II.

SCHOOLS DURING THE ENGLISH COLONIAL PERIOD.

1664–1776.

Schools remain Dutch.—Lord Cornbury's efforts to anglicize them.—Trinity School, 1710.—Effects of Immigration.—King's School, 1754.—Struggle of the Dutch for their Language.—Whelp imported from Holland, 1755.—Revolution closes all Schools.

DURING the century following the transfer of the colony to the English, education received but little attention from the Government. The great majority of the people were Dutch. The tide-waves of immigration that were to set in from the British islands had, as yet, scarcely begun to move; Dutch customs and the Dutch language long prevailed, and were but slowly supplanted or modified by the national peculiarities of the new-comers. A glance at the names of those who were associated with the English governor in the conduct of public affairs shows that wealth, power, and influence continued to be held by the descendants of the original settlers of New Amsterdam. Their churches and schools went on in the old way, though receiving no governmental support, except that the excellent Latin school of Luyck, established in 1659, was continued by the English authorities for eight years longer.

By the terms of the surrender the people were guarantied "liberty of consciences in their divine worship and Church discipline, with all their accustomed jurisdiction with respect to the poor, and orphans;" the last phrase being understood to involve the care of the Church schools. This was made more definite by the charter granted by William III., who naturally favored the Dutch settlers, in which it is expressly stated that "Our will and pleasure further is, and we do hereby declare that the ministers of said Church, for the time being, shall and may, by and with the consent of the elders and deacons of said Church, for the time being, nominate and appoint a *school-master*, and such other under-officers as they shall stand in need of." Notwithstanding this, several of the English governors, whether actuated by zeal for the English Church, or by the enlightened policy of gradually securing uniformity of language and greater homogeneity of the people, endeavored to break up the distinctive Dutch schools throughout the province, Lord Cornbury even "claiming the direct appointment of the school-master." Though partly successful on Long Island, through the severe measures used to effect his object, yet the resolute front presented by the sturdy Dutch burghers of New York thoroughly defeated his plans in the city, and secured for a while longer a continuance of the old customs.

Meanwhile new schools were established by immigrants from Great Britian and the neighboring colonies. In 1710 the school still existing under the name of Trinity School was opened by William Huddlestone, under the direction of a society connected with the English Church. A few years previous to this a free Grammar School had been founded and built on the King's Farm; an Episcopal missionary, William Vesey, had opened a school for blacks, and numerous additional private schools had been established under English or Dutch masters.

But a power mightier than a governor's edicts was soon to be at work, slowly gathering a force that would in a few more years overcome all the resistance of the conservatives. The great immigration was about to begin. As late as the census ordered in 1754 at the outbreak of the French and Indian War, the population of the entire province was less than 97,000, the English settlements being chiefly on Long Island and along the river.[1] Within little more than

[1] The population was distributed in a way that now seems very singular. The City and County of New York returned 10,768 whites and 2272 blacks; while the City and County of Albany reports 14,805 whites, and 2619 blacks:

forty years after this the population of the city alone had advanced from thirteen thousand to more than sixty thousand, or nearly fivefold; while its cosmopolitan character was already indicated in the many dialects of English, Welsh, Irish, Scotch, and Dutch spoken in its streets, and greatly impairing the purity of the English tongue that was finally to prevail. In the opinion of Smith, the historian, "the language was hopelessly corrupt," there was no uniform standard as in the New England colonies, the schools were in general badly conducted, and good and competent instructors were only to be found in the private employ of those families whose hereditary wealth enabled them to secure the best advantages for their children.

The year 1754 also claims notice in the educational history of the city for the establishment of King's College—the Columbia College of post-Revolutionary times. Its charter was granted by Governor James Delancy, previous to which acts had been passed authorizing lotteries to raise money for its establishment.[1] Till nearly the close of the century it had to struggle for its existence, one of its first difficulties having been a controversy as to the character of the special religious influence which should control it, finally terminating in the adoption of the forms of the English Episcopal Church.

Meanwhile the Dutch battled vigorously against the extinction of the language and customs of their fathers. As late as 1755 the Consistory of their Church sent expressly to Holland and imported a genuine Dutch school-master and chorister, one John Nicholas Whelp, who, for what was then thought the generous salary of two hundred dollars a year, the use of a small house and garden, and the payment of the expenses of his voyage, was induced to bring out with him his wife and family, and continued to serve acceptably until his death in 1773. But they were fighting the irresistible.

total population of the province, 96,765.—From census of 1754, as quoted in "*Mitchell's New York in 1807.*"

[1] Mitchell.

Even before the end of Whelp's time English seems to have been introduced into the school itself. The Church had already in 1764, just a century after the transfer of the province, been forced reluctantly to alternate its Dutch services with one in the English tongue. This change had been wrought against the most strenuous opposition, but was finally acknowledged necessary, to prevent the young people from abandoning the religious connections of their fathers. The necessity was quite as great for the further continuance of the school; and the successor of Whelp, appointed in 1773, was expressly directed "not only to teach reading, writing, and arithmetic, but to instruct the children in the English as well as in the Dutch language."[1]

But the fierce excitements of the Revolutionary period were already upon them. The city was the scene of some of

[1] In the memoir read by Judge Benson before the New York Historical Society in 1816 occurs the following passage, which is worth preserving: "There was a day always kept here by the Dutch, and the keeping of it delegated by the mothers to their daughters still at school—*Vrowen Dagh* (Woman's Day); the same with the Valentine's Day of the English, and although differently, still, perhaps, not less salutarily kept. Every mother's daughter, furnished with a piece of cord, the size neither too large nor too small; the twist neither too hard nor too loose; a turn round the hand, and then a sufficient length left to serve as a lash; not fair to have a knot at the end of it, but fair to practice for a few days to acquire the sleight; the law held otherwise, dueling. On the morning of the day, the youngster never venturing to turn a corner without first listening whether no warblers were behind it, no golden apples to divert him from the direct course in this race. Schoolboy Hippomenes espied, pursued by charmer Atalanta: he, encumbered with his satchel, still striving to outrun, and, to add to his speed, bending forward, thereby giving the requisite roundness to the space between the shoulders; she, too swift afoot for him, and overtaking him, and three or four strokes briskly and smartly laid on; he, to avoid a further repetition, stopping and turning; she looking him steadfast in the eye, and perceiving it required all the man in him to keep back the tear; not all the fruit in all the orchards of the Hesperides, and in their best bearing year, to compensate for the exultation of the little heart for the moment.

"The boys requested that the next day should be theirs, and be called *Mannen Dagh* (Man's Day); but my masters were told, the law would thereby defeat its own very purpose, which was, that they should, at an age and in a way most likely never to forget it, receive the lesson of manliness;—he is never to strike."—Quoted in *Dunshee.*

the most memorable events of its early stages. "Here the Provincial Congress met in 1765, and passed the famous Declaration of Rights. Here the stamped paper had been destroyed, and the lieutenant-governor hung in effigy. The assembly had refused to provide quarters and provisions for such troops as England wished to march into the colony, and, on the arrival of a cargo of tea in 1773, the Sons of Liberty destroyed it. These and other like measures, when the crisis arrived, led to the early subjugation of the city, which, as the head-quarters of the British army, was under martial law. Many of the citizens fled, all the churches and schools were closed, and naught was heard save the accidents of war."[1]

[1] Dunshee.

III.

FROM THE REVOLUTION TO THE ESTABLISHMENT OF THE FREE SCHOOL SOCIETY.

1776–1805.

City during the Revolutionary War.—Governor Clinton.—Act of 1795.—Rise of Benevolent Societies.—Educational Societies.—Manumission Society, 1785.—Female Association, 1802.—Teachers' Association.—Common School Fund established.

DURING the seven years that New York was the head-quarters of the British army, the schools and the college remained closed. The business of the city was annihilated, no other portion of the country being so long and so completely isolated and cut off from all commercial relations with the rest. To add to the poverty and distress incidental to such a state of affairs, the two disastrous fires of July, 1776, and August, 1778, swept away a large part of the dwellings and stores, and there were neither means nor inducements to rebuild them. The school history of the period is a complete blank.

But the surrender of Cornwallis in 1781 assured the people that their redemption was at hand. Before the signing of the Treaty of Paris many of the inhabitants had already returned; while four days previous to that event, and months before the evacuation of the city in November, 1783, the school of the Dutch Church was already opened. It had lost not only its distinctive language, but even its ancient name of "free" or "public" school, which was thenceforth exchanged for the term "Charity School," received in common with all schools supported by the voluntary contributions of religious societies.

Though the condition of education was one of the first subjects to claim and arrest public attention, no definite action was taken by the Legislature till 1795. Previous to this, the subject of public instruction had been frequently discussed in the public journals, in the pulpits, and in popular assemblages, and its paramount importance to the future stability and prosperity of the young republic felt and acknowledged. Under this growing interest, the leading schools had so far recovered from their previous prostration as to receive commendatory notice from the governor in his annual message of 1792: "As the diffusion of knowledge is essential to the promotion of virtue and the preservation of liberty, the flourishing condition of our seminaries of learning must prove highly satisfactory; and they will, I am persuaded, be among the first objects of your care and patronage, and receive, from time to time, such further aid and encouragement as may be necessary for their increasing prosperity."

In 1795, he distinctly recommended the "establishment of Common Schools throughout the state," and, from his language, we may infer that the subject had already been introduced into the deliberations of the Legislature: "While it is evident that the general establishment and liberal endowment of academies are highly to be commended, and are attended by the most beneficial consequences, yet it can not be denied that they are principally confined to the children of the opulent, and that a great proportion of the community is excluded from their immediate advantages. The establishment of Common Schools throughout the state is happily calculated to remedy this inconvenience, and will, therefore, re-engage your early and decided consideration."

Pursuant to this recommendation, the Legislature passed, April 9, 1795, "An Act for the encouragement of Schools," which appropriated $50,000 a year for five years, "for the purpose of encouraging and maintaining schools in the several cities and towns in this state, in which the children of the inhabitants residing in this state shall be instructed in the English language, or be taught English grammar, arithmetic, mathematics, and such other branches of knowledge as are most useful and necessary to complete a good English education.[1]

Until toward the close of the eighteenth century, efforts for the establishment of systems of public instruction so as to benefit the masses of society by the blessings of education, had been chiefly the work of individuals. About this period, both in this country and in Great Britain, a memorable change took place in the nature and method of these efforts, and in the efficiency of the means adopted to render them successful. Voluntary benevolent and philanthropic associations were formed, having for their chief purpose the extension of the knowledge of things human and divine among all classes of society. Sunday Schools, the work of which was at first necessarily directed in a great measure to the instruction of neglected children in reading, sprung up and multiplied about the close of the American War, and were soon introduced into the United States. At no previous period had religious and legislative bodies manifested so much of intelligent interest in the advantages and necessity of furnishing at least an elementary education to the masses of the people. Bell and Lancaster were just entering upon the work that was to give so great, and wide spread, and permanent an impetus to the cause of popular instruction, by presenting a plan rendered practicable by its thorough organization, and the comparative smallness of the expenditure involved. Other benevolent societies also, for the amelioration of the many evils of the social system, appeared in rapid succession.

Among the earliest of these in this country was an association formed in this city as early as 1785, and soon after incorporated by the Legislature for the purpose of "mitigating the evils of slavery, to defend the rights of the blacks, and especially to give them the elements of education." This organization was known as the Manumission Society, and enrolled among its members a considerable number of persons of the highest social standing in the community, including a

[1] Gov. George Clinton's Messages for 1792 and 1795, as quoted in the valuable and comprehensive report of Superintendent Rice.

large representation of the Society of Friends. Governor Jay was its first President, and its first school was opened in 1787 in Cliff Street, and numbered about one hundred pupils. It seems to have been conducted on the plan usual in mixed, or ungraded schools, until after the introduction of the Lancasterian system. There were then in the city about 4000 colored persons, more than half of whom were returned as slaves by the census of 1805.[1] Several schools were established and maintained by this society, and subjected to frequent and vigilant inspection by its officers and members, the funds being supplied by voluntary contributions. The schools were continued, in a state of greater or less efficiency, through a period of about forty years, when, upon the solicitation of the Society itself, the Legislature of 1834 authorized the transfer of the schools and their considerable real estate to the Public School Society; and these are now the Colored Schools of the Board of Education.

In 1802 a school for white girls was opened by a Society known as the "Female Association for the relief of the Poor," which had been established some years previously, and consisted of benevolent ladies connected with the Society of Friends, popularly known as Quakers. "It was the original promoter of Free Schools in the city of New York," and so it extended its influence as at one time to have several large elementary schools under its direction and control, the last of which was extinguished in 1846 in consequence of their loss of further state and municipal aid. Besides the other permanent good wrought by this vigorous association during the half-century of its existence, it is definitely known and acknowledged that it was the success and advice of these ladies which induced a number of gentlemen, connected with them by domestic and social relations, to attempt the same kind offices for the neglected boys of the city, thus leading to the establishment of the "Free School Society," which afterward became the Public School Society of the City of New York.

[1] "Whites, 71,762; free colored, 1960; slaves, 2048."—*Census of* 1805.

Private schools also had largely increased in numbers with the increasing population of the city.[1] At least as early as 1798 a Teachers' Association was in existence, its meetings being held at Federal Hall every Saturday evening. The President for 1798 was Mr. John Woods, and for 1799, Mr. John Campbell.[2] In 1805 there were in the city 141 teachers, 106 of whom were males, and 35 females, including those of the Church schools, supported by the Dutch Reformed, Episcopal, Presbyterian, and Roman Catholic denominations, the last of these having the largest, numbering about 100 in attendance.[3] The schools of the Orphan Asylums were not yet in existence; the New York Orphan Asylum, the first established of these, and the oldest one in the United States not being organized till the following year, 1806.[4]

This was the general condition of school affairs at the beginning of the new and important era of 1805, a year rendered memorable in our local educational history by the law first establishing the Common School Fund of the State, and by the act of incorporation of the Free School Society of the City of New York.

[1] "There are many private schools, but these are not generally under as good regulations as in Connecticut and other New England States."

The population in 1756 was 10,881.			The population in 1791 was 33,191.		
" "	1771	" 21,863.	" "	1801	" 60,849.
" "	1786	" 23,614.	" "	1805	" 75,770.

Longworth's Directory for 1805.

[2] Directory 1798, 1799.

[3] Ibid. 1805.

[4] This year is further marked by the first course of scientific and popular lectures ever given in the city of New York. They were by Professor John Griscom, and were well attended.

IV.

ORIGIN AND ESTABLISHMENT OF THE FREE SCHOOL SOCIETY.

1805.

Free School Society.—Its Origin and Purpose.—Memorial of 1805.—Lengthy Title.—Lancaster.

THE Free School Society was founded in 1805. The results that have flowed from the successive stages of its progress have had so marked and lasting an influence on the condition of public instruction in the great city of the continent, that the history of its origin and development contains much matter of permanent interest. From the humblest beginnings, it gradually extended the field and advanced the character of its operations, until in the direction of the educational interests of the masses of a vast community, it held a trust such as probably never before was confided to a body of private citizens.

The original purpose of the Society was strictly charitable. The one hundred and forty-one teachers of the city were all engaged in private schools, excepting the few who were employed in the parochial charity schools of the several churches, in those of the Manumission Society, and in the school for poor white girls which was supported by the Female Association. There yet remained a large number of children not connected with any religious body and attending no school, their parents being either too poor or too indifferent to their interests to afford them even the simplest rudiments of an education. The condition of these children, and the final effects of their ignorance upon the community, had long been a subject of consideration among the philanthropic.

The success of the school of the Female Association showed the feasibility of organizing a similar society on a broader basis for the benefit of the neglected poor. An incidental conversation between two or three individuals, one of them for many subsequent years the vice-president of the society,[1] led to the call of a private and informal meeting of citizens of influence, and without respect to denominational lines, who would be likely to favor such an enterprise. Twelve attended. A committee was appointed to mature a plan and call a larger and more formal meeting, which, convening a few days later, passed a resolution to memorialize the Legislature for a charter. The memorial was signed by about one hundred citizens, whose high social position and influence, diversity of religious views and connections, and unanimity in philanthropic effort, gave promise of wide usefulness to the proposed society. The memorialists urged the importance of their subject, "and the multiplied evils daily resulting from the neglected education of the children of the poor. They alluded more particularly to that description of children who do not belong to, or are not provided for by any religious society, and who therefore do not partake of the advantages arising from the different charity schools established by the various religious societies in this city."[2]

In response to the memorial, the Legislature promptly passed an act of incorporation on the 9th of April, 1805, the lengthy title of the Society defining at the same time its field of usefulness—"The Society for Establishing a Free School in the City of New York, for the Education of such poor Children as do not belong to or are not provided for by any Religious Society." The list of names mentioned in the act begins with De Witt Clinton, and ends with Dr. Samuel L. Mitchell, and includes a representation of the best elements of the old English, Dutch, and other families. The same instrument appointed thirteen trustees for the year 1805, who elected Clinton president. Besides those thus mentioned by name, the mayor, recorder, aldermen, and assistant aldermen were declared *ex-officio* members of the Society, which was also open to any citizen upon his subscri-

[1] John Murray, Esq.

[2] Memorial, Feb. 25, 1805.

bing and contributing eight dollars for the benefit of the Society. At an annual meeting in May a report was to be rendered by its thirteen trustees, and a new board elected.

On the 5th of May, and immediately after their organization, the trustees published an address to their fellow-citizens, setting forth the nature of their enterprise, and appealing "to the affluent and charitable Christians of all denominations" for the necessary assistance. A full year was spent in raising money enough to make a practical beginning by opening a school.[1] During the interval, a member of the society being in England, had visited the school opened by Joseph Lancaster in the Borough Road, near London, in 1801, and was so impressed with the advantages of Lancaster's plan for giving elementary instruction to large masses at a small expense, that he urged and procured its adoption in the new enterprise.

This famous system, then entirely new, was drawing great attention in England, and finally spread over a large part of Europe and this country. In the brief space of three or four years its claims had been so widely and so energetically advocated, that thousands of intelligent men believed that a final and immediate remedy had been found for the evils of popular ignorance, and that the era of universal intelligence had begun.[2] A plan by which it was claimed that five hun-

[1] The original subscription-book, with the names of the donors, may be found in the archives of the Historical Society.

[2] The following extracts will show the extent of this delusion: De Witt Clinton, in a speech on opening the enlarged free school at New York, 1810, says: "I confess that I recognize in Lancaster the benefactor of the human race. I consider his system as creating a new era in education, as a blessing sent down from heaven to redeem the poor and distressed of this world from the power and dominion of ignorance.

Again, in his message as governor to the Legislature of New York in 1818, he says: "Having participated in the first establishment of the Lancasterian System in this country; having carefully observed its progress and witnessed its benefits, I can confidently recommend it as an invaluable improvement, which, by wonderful combination of economy in expense and rapidity of instruction, has created a new era in education. The system operates with the same efficacy in education as labor-saving machinery does in the useful arts."

dred or a thousand children could be profitably instructed under the care of a single teacher, with no assistance except what should be rendered by the children themselves, might well fill with hope all that wished well to their race.

President Nott, in an address to the students of Union College, July 11, 1811, exclaims: "Where is Lancaster, who has introduced, and is introducing a new era in education?" etc. John Adams writes to a friend in Cambridge, "I have heard friend Lancaster with pleasure; he is an excellent scholastic and academic disciplinarian. I was really delighted and enlightened by that lecture."—*From Barnard's Am. Journal*, 1861.

V.

FREE SCHOOL SOCIETY.

1805–1824.

First School.—Its Removals.—New Charter, 1808.—No. 2.—Effects of the War.—No. 3.—Apprentices.—Mr. Picton, of No. 4.—Arrival of Lancaster.—Separate Departments for Sexes.—Manual.—First Vacation.—Controversy with Baptists and others.—No. 5.—Pupils not restricted to special Districts.

THE Society took prompt measures to put the new plan into operation. "Happily a teacher[1] who had already adopted it with success, and who in other respects was well qualified for the undertaking, was found. Under his superintendence, therefore, the school was first opened on the 17th of May, 1806, in a small apartment (in the old Mission House) in Bancker Street—now Madison Street—near Pearl. Its appearance was in every respect as humble as were the unhappy objects whose improvement in it was contemplated."[2]

The school was at once a success. The little room was soon overcrowded, its numbers reaching sixty-seven. A new enterprise, and in such energetic and benevolent hands, it wanted neither visitors nor friends. Contributions in money, cloth, stockings, shoes, and hats were freely given for the physical comfort of the needy pupils, and Colonel Henry Rutgers, afterward the second President of the Society, donated a valuable lot of ground in Henry Street as a site for the school-house.

"Having, however, fully ascertained that an entire reliance on the benevolence of individuals for the support of the

[1] Mr. William Smith.

[2] "An Account of the New York Free School," published by Collins & Perkins, 1807.

institution would not place the funds in a condition to meet the expenses which must necessarily arise, the trustees naturally turned their attention to those sources whence adequate assistance could alone be expected. The Corporation, as guardians of the city, and especially of that part of it which the views of this society particularly embrace, were early addressed with a memorial soliciting their assistance. In consequence of this representation, a committee from that body visited the school, who appeared fully convinced of the usefulness of the establishment; and the result was an appropriation of the workshop adjacent to the almshouse for the temporary accommodation of the school, and the sum of five hundred dollars toward putting it in repair; the Society agreeing to receive and educate fifty children from the almshouse."[1]

In April, 1807, the school was removed to the new quarters, its number soon increasing to one hundred and fifty, including the fifty pauper children, the limit of accommodation being about two hundred. Application for assistance was meanwhile made to the Legislature, resulting in a grant of four thousand dollars toward erecting a building and an additional thousand dollars each year, all from the excise funds of the city, "until aid could be regularly afforded from the interest of the School Fund of the state."[2]

In a very short time the new quarters also became too strait for the expanding school, and sufficient funds for a new building of proper size not having yet been accumulated, the Society again applied to the Corporation for assistance, and received the liberal gift of the building known as the "Old Arsenal," conveniently situated on Chambers Street and Tryon Row. The property was valued at ten thousand dollars, and was accompanied by the sum of fifteen hundred dollars in money, to assist in preparing the building for a school. The condition attending this liberal grant was that the Society should educate *all* the children of the almshouse. Exten-

[1] Second Annual Report, May 4, 1807.

[2] Report of the Legislative Committee, Mr. Clinton, chairman.

sive changes were made in the building, costing about $13,000, and providing not only a school-room for five hundred pupils, but also apartments for the use of the Board and for the teacher's family.

While these changes were in progress, the Society had again applied to the Legislature for an extension of their powers, and a new charter, granted in April, 1808, changed their title from "the Society for Establishing a Free School," to "the Free School Society of the City of New York." In December, 1809, the new school building, long known as No. 1, was opened with interesting ceremonies, the President, Mr. Clinton, delivering an appropriate address.

A site having already been provided by the munificence of Colonel Rutgers, the Society again raised some $13,000 by subscription from the citizens, and on the 13th of November, 1811, school-house No. 2 was opened, having cost about $11,000. The same year the Society received a donation from the Corporation of Trinity Church of several lots on Christopher Street, and a further grant of $4000 from the Legislature, with an annuity of $500 during its pleasure, the number of trustees being at the same time increased to nineteen.

The war with Great Britain, 1812-'15, greatly interfered with the prosperity and growth of the city, and the Society, while contriving to keep open its schools, was not able to increase their number. In 1815, $3708.14 was opportunely received, being the quota of the School Fund under its first apportionment. With the return of prosperity, and the vast increase of immigration after the war, the operations of the Society began again to expand. Among other measures, and in order to secure the utmost efficiency in the internal management of their schools, a committee was appointed to obtain from England, and through the agency of the British and Foreign School Society—the very centre and fountain-head of improved Lancasterianism—a person completely competent to teach the system in its most perfect form. A salary of eight hundred dollars was offered, together with the expenses of the passage.

Some months before the arrival of the expected model teacher, Mr. Shepard Johnson, a young man who had received his entire education in the schools of the Society, and had passed through the successive stages of monitorship with great credit, was sent to Philadelphia at the expense of the Society to inspect the results of the monitorial system in that city, into which it had been introduced soon after the first experiments in New York. Upon his return he was appointed to take charge of School No. 3, which was first opened in May, 1818, in a public building on the corner of Amos and Hudson Streets, the use of certain rooms having been granted by the Corporation. Mr. Johnson was the first of the thousands of teachers who have been educated in the public schools of the city, and continued for many years in the employ of the Society, and was of great service not only in his own school, but in assisting and directing at the organization of other new schools intrusted to parties of less experience.

So well satisfied were the trustees with the results in Mr. Johnson's case, that about the time of his appointment in 1818, they introduced a plan for the regular training of future teachers, it being a peculiar feature of the system to have but one teacher to each department, however large. Three of the most promising lads, one for each school, were selected from the monitors-general and apprenticed to the Society. They were to be boarded and clothed, to reside, if possible, with their principals, and at the end of three years' satisfactory service were to receive one hundred dollars each. The experiment was never renewed, it being supposed that as good results to the system could be attained in another way. The expense, about two hundred dollars each per year, was thought so great that means were found to terminate the engagements, and monitors-general were supplied at the rate of fifty cents a week.[1]

In 1818, Mr. Charles Picton, the expected teacher, arrived

[1] One of these three lads is still connected with the city schools, being the Principal of a highly-successful Ward School in the upper part of the city.

from England, bringing with him a supply of slates and books, and other school material, for the use of the Society. He was appointed to take charge of a new school, No. 4, then in process of erection in Rivington Street, and which was opened on the 1st of May, 1819, Mr. Picton being employed in the interval by permission of the Board, and at the same salary, in reorganizing, on the Lancasterian system, the parochial school of St. Peter's Church in Barclay Street.

No. 4 was the first school-house specially constructed with separate departments for boys and girls.[1] No. 1 had no girls, they being taught by the Female Association. No. 2 had a few girls, but in 1818 it was stated in a hand-bill circulated in that neighborhood by order of the Society that the teacher was forbidden to admit any more, those already enrolled being transferred to the schools of the Female Association as fast as boys, who were specially invited, could be found to take the vacated places. On the organization of No. 3 in its temporary quarters, it was found impossible to exclude the girls entirely, as the Female Association had no school in that vicinity. They had no separate department till the completion of the new building on the corner of Grove and Hudson Streets, in 1821. In No. 4, Mrs. Picton was appointed teacher of the Female Department, at a salary of three hundred dollars, her husband receiving eight hundred dollars for the Boys' Department, with two hundred dollars additional for house-rent, the teachers of the other schools living in the school buildings. In order to obtain the greatest possible benefit from his training and experience, Mr. Picton, of whom great things were evidently expected, was entirely emancipated from the by-laws

[1] In the Minutes of the Trustees for 1820, No. 4 is referred to as "the only school having an exclusively girls' department;" and the gentlemen being evidently puzzled with so delicate a novelty, the ladies of the Female Association were solicited to appoint a committee for an occasional visit of inspection, and to report; but they declined "for want of time," but more probably because this new department was an incursion into their own special field, which had hitherto steadily expanded. Commencing with a mere handful, in 1817 they had three schools and 400 girls; in 1819, 600 "little girls;" and in 1820, 700 girls; the register of the Free Schools being at the same date 2589, of whom by far the greater part were boys.

and Manual, and directed "to conduct his school in any way he thought fit until further orders from the trustees."

In December, 1818, Mr. Lancaster himself arrived in New York, being on a visit to the cities of America for the purpose of advocating the advantages of his system, which he found already established, not only in the schools of the Free School Society, but also in those of the Manumission Society, the Female Association, and in the Dutch Reformed, Catholic, and some other parochial schools. He met with a warm welcome from De Witt Clinton and other prominent citizens, and his lectures, given in one of the school-rooms of the Society, were well attended, and did much to strengthen the hands of the friends of public instruction. A new energy seems to have been infused into the Society itself. The teachers were directed to compile a new manual of the system as practiced in the schools, in which work they were assisted by the teachers of the Manumission Society.[1] It was published in 1820, and was accompanied with a historical sketch.

The plan of separate departments for the sexes was carried out, small libraries, consisting chiefly of works on history, voyages, and travels were introduced into each school, and an address to parents was widely circulated, urgently soliciting their assistance in securing the regular attendance of their children both at the schools of the Society and at the various Sabbath Schools, and abounding with advice as to their religious, moral, and sanitary training, and the effects of parental example. At the same time the Board memorialized the Legislature for assistance in finishing the new school building, No. 4, laying great stress upon the effects of the rapid immigration which had again set in from Europe, consisting, to a great extent, of those whose means did not enable them to pay for the education of their children.[2] The annual ex-

[1] Each of the compilers was remunerated with a gift of twenty-five copies of the Manual, which, as the minutes of the Society itself soon pronounce the book unsalable even at 75 cents, was rather light pay for the embodiment of so much of personal experience and labor.

[2] They asked for $10,000, but received only $5000; but their funds were further increased by an act in relation to lotteries, directing that the $500 to

aminations, which up to this time had been simultaneously conducted in all the schools, were now changed into a more formal visit of the whole Board, with their invited guests, to each school in succession, with a systematic record of the results in the minutes. The citizens generally were also invited to visit and inspect the schools, and an invitation was extended to all who were disposed to do so to come in and "learn the system" with a view to teaching it elsewhere.

In August, 1820, at the united request of the teachers, the first vacation, extending through three weeks, was granted, and continued to be given annually by resolution for several years before becoming an established part of the by-laws.

The year 1821 was marked by no event of importance, except the opening of the new school-house No. 3, and an earnest though unsuccessful effort for a law levying a special tax upon the city and county, and raising $5000 a year for ten years, for the purpose of building five additional school-houses.[1] The next year, however, is rendered memorable in the history of public education in this city, by the opening of the first serious controversy in regard to the distribution of the school money to religious sectarian schools, a settlement not being effected till after much excitement and the lapse of two or three years.[2] An important step in increasing the direct influence exerted by the trustees upon the efficiency of the several schools was also taken, in the assignment of each member of the Board to one of five "sections," one for each school-house, No. 5, in Mott Street, having been opened on the 28th of October; and, girls being now admitted in both

be paid for each license, together with all fines incurred, should be equally divided between the Free School Society and the new Asylum for Deaf Mutes, which had begun with four pupils in 1817. Four lotteries gave the free schools $1000 the first year, and they had $1500 additional from the excise.

[1] The city contained at this time about 130,000 inhabitants. Its real estate was assessed at $50,619,720, and its personal property at $17,666,350: total, $68,286,070. Total taxes for 1821 were $299,225. It was proposed to add one-sixtieth to this amount.

[2] This will be considered more at length in the section on the Religious Question.

No. 1 and No. 2, five committees of ladies were nominated, and invited to inspect the several schools at their discretion, and to furnish a quarterly report to the Board of Trustees on such points and with such suggestions as they might think proper, the sections themselves also reporting quarterly to the general Board. For some reason which does not appear in the records of the Society, the plan of securing the assistance and counsel of the ladies does not seem to have been successful. The Board also appointed a special committee of their own body, to correspond with parties in the United States and in Europe, to gather information in regard to elementary instruction, and especially in relation to the means found most effectual in reaching the children of the poor.

An important proposition for dividing the city into school districts was also reported upon and then debated, it being the intention of the advocates of the measure to establish definite boundary-lines, restricting the attendance of the pupils to the school-houses situated in their respective districts. The final decision was adverse to the proposition, the uniform policy of the Board being to locate new schools so as best to accommodate the steadily increasing population. The result of this policy is still to be seen in the present organization of the schools of the city, there being neither ward nor district lines for pupils, every school being open to all citizens, whether residing at the Battery or at Kingsbridge.

VI.

FREE SCHOOL SOCIETY.

1824–1826.

No. 6.—Improvement in Character of Attendance.—Visit of La Fayette.—Bethel Baptist Church.—Proposition to introduce "Pay Scholars."—Sanguine Anticipations as to the Results.

In 1824, the Almshouse having been previously removed to Bellevue, the Common Council invited the Society to resume at that place its care of the pauper children, and a new school, No. 6, was opened, being the same that is now located on Randall's Island.

Several circumstances conspired at this time, with all these active measures, to elevate the general standing of the several schools of the Society, and to render them more truly the schools of the people. The withdrawal of the large number of pauper children from No. 1 had removed the natural objection felt by many parents as to sending their children to the same school, and the vacated seats were soon filled with a better class of pupils. The same was particularly the case with No. 2, to which a teacher, who had just previously taught a large and successful private school in the same vicinity, was about this time appointed, leading to the introduction of many of the children of his former patrons. No. 3, in its new building, and under the efficient management of Mr. Johnson, was highly popular; No. 4 was in charge of a gentleman whose special training and association with the fountain-head of Lancasterianism gave him the advantages of a high reputation; No. 5 had been intrusted to a teacher[1] whose powers of organization and firm yet gentle character,

[1] Mr. Joseph Belden.

and skill in teaching penmanship, soon made him one of the most popular of teachers; while his brother,[1] who had been educated to the medical profession, in a spirit of true, self-devoting philanthropy, and for a trifling salary, took charge of and lived with the neglected little ones of the city's charge at Bellevue, No. 6, having first "learned the system" for that purpose with Mr. Johnson in No. 3.

The exciting controversy with the Bethel Baptist Church and several other Protestant organizations that conjointly sought the distribution of the school money to sectarian schools, had also done much to attract public attention and sympathy to the schools of the Society.[2] This was still further developed in a skillful and somewhat dramatic way on the occasion of the visit of La Fayette in 1824. In October of that year, after visiting, in company with state and city officials and other distinguished citizens, the school No. 3, where, besides being presented with a certificate of membership of the Society, he was addressed by one of the pupils in behalf of the five hundred boys and two hundred girls there assembled, and listened to a poetic address by a class of girls in concert, the illustrious visitor at 2 P.M., and in the presence of an immense and delighted multitude, reviewed the children of all the schools of the Society, assembled, to the number of three thousand or more, in the City Hall Park, officered by their teachers and monitors, and bearing banners with appropriate inscriptions, conspicuous among which was one proclaiming "Education the Basis of Free Government."[3]

The popularity and manifest progress of the schools, and the principles developed in the discussions incidental to the controversy already alluded to, together with a proposition received "from a number of middle-class citizens" to be al-

[1] Dr. Charles Belden, who died, after two years' service, Aug. 5, 1825.

[2] See section on the Religious Questions.

[3] A sweet little girl recited an appropriate and touching poetic address, conveying, in the name of the children of America, their gratitude to this friend and associate of Washington, and ended by gently laying a beautiful floral and laurel wreath on the revered head of the nation's guest. The grave and affectionate kiss bestowed in response on the little spokeswoman touched all hearts.

lowed to send their children as pupils "for pay," seem about this time to have suggested to the trustees the expediency and feasibility of essentially changing the character of their organization. The grand idea of EDUCATION AS A RIGHT was not yet developed except in the minds of a few isolated individuals. To have their children educated without direct payment was by very many felt to be closely akin to acknowledging themselves paupers; a notion traces of which, absurd as we know it to be in the present condition of things, still linger in some benighted minds that can not keep pace with the grand march of modern democratic ideas.

The Society began to consider the possibility and propriety of converting their schools, excepting No. 6, into pay schools, so as to conciliate and attract those who were not willing to accept gratuitous instruction for their children, placing the rates so low that none need be debarred, at the same time retaining their original plan of "no pay" from those whose circumstances did not permit any contribution whatever. An extensive correspondence with schools abroad was immediately opened, and a great amount of testimony collected, setting forth the excellent results which had arisen from such an arrangement.[1]

A study of this period in the history of the Society is of importance, as the irrevocable steps which were finally taken led, however reluctantly, yet by an unavoidable necessity, through their unexpected results, to broader and juster views of the wants, and rights, and mutual relations of all classes of society in the matter of education. The results of the Bethel Church controversy had thrown all the school money

[1] The Irish Schools for the Poor, conducted on the Lancasterian plan, were in great part supported by the payment of a penny a week, and similar results were reported from the British and Foreign School Society. The schools of the Female Association had long been successfully conducted on the same principle by collecting from each pupil one or two cents a week, and it had only been abandoned from the fear of losing, in consequence, their portion of the School Fund. The largest school of the Manumission Society also, in the same way, had once been nearly able to pay the teacher's salary.—*Minutes*, 3d of March, 1825.

into their hands excepting what was paid to the "Mechanics' Society, the Orphan Asylum Society, and the Trustees of the African Schools." They had also caused a school census of the city to be taken, and reported about four hundred pay schools of all grades, most of them small and miserably conducted, and held in poorly-lighted and badly-ventilated apartments, the expense per scholar being several times as much as in the Free Schools. They therefore felt certain that, by revising and greatly extending their course of study, and at the same time asking a small amount of pay for instruction, they would secure the patronage and personal interest of a large part of the important class of citizens who supported these private schools. As a part of the plan, it was proposed to consolidate the schools of the Free School Society, the Manumission Society, and those of the Female Association, under one organization, which should be known as the "Public School Society," and receive the entire amount of the school money, and pay over to the Orphan Asylum and the Mechanics' Society schools their usual amount per pupil.

Among the beneficial results anticipated from the scheme they especially enumerate "a more truly democratic principle in the schools, where the rich and the poor should meet together;" "a more general attention to the subject of education by the citizens; harmony among religious sects; that all citizens would contribute, and be entitled to the benefits; a great increase in the amount expended for public instruction, and a greater economy secured by having the disbursements all made through the same channel;[1] a uniform system in all elementary schools, and therefore no loss by removals to other parts of the city," and more especially, "the cultivation of a proper feeling of independence among the poor and laboring classes."

[1] They anticipated a favorable balance of $10,500 even the first year.—*Minutes*, 3d of March, 1825.

VII.

PUBLIC SCHOOL SOCIETY.

1826–1827.

Third Charter, and new Title.—Schools become Pay Schools.—Preparations for great Increase of Attendance.—No. 7.—No. 8.—No. 9.—Establishment of Executive Committee.—Great Extention of Course of Study.—Central School.—Application for Assistants refused.

IN furtherance of these views, an application was made to the Legislature for another alteration of their charter, and in January, 1826, they were authorized, under the title of THE PUBLIC SCHOOL SOCIETY, to receive pupils at low rates of payment, from twenty-five cents to two dollars per quarter—according to the subjects of study pursued. The act added fifty members to the Board of Trustees, and the premium of membership, which had been raised to fifty dollars in 1810, was reduced to ten dollars, so as to greatly enlarge the Society itself, and induce a more general participation of the citizens in school affairs, and at the same time to give more facility in filling the increased Board.

More school buildings were at once provided, so as to accommodate the expected influx of the new and popular element. The new law went into operation on the 1st of May, 1826; the same day a new building was opened in Chrystie Street, and organized as No. 7, a site for another, to be known as No. 8, having been purchased a few days previously in Grand Street: this building was pushed with such energy that on the 1st of November it was opened for the admission of pupils; two additional sites were also procured in Wooster and Duane Streets. A few weeks previous to the change of the title of the Society, a school situated in a rural district of the island, and known as the Bloomingdale School, was transferred to their care, and also on the 1st of May was opened as No. 9. This school was accepted somewhat unwillingly, as its limited numbers,[1] and the character of its location, indicated that it would long continue small, and pecuniarily unprofitable. It had been opened, and for years chiefly sustained by public-spirited and charitable residents of the vicinity, and had passed, by a natural process, to the care of a neighboring church, St. Michael's Protestant Episcopal. The ordinance of the Common Council in 1825[2] had deprived it of all the public aid it had hitherto received, the funds being transferred to the Public School Society. For some months it had only been kept from disbanding by the generous efforts of a young collegian, who voluntarily devoted to it all his spare time.

A change of the highest order of importance was now made in the general management of the affairs of the Board in the appointment of an Executive Committee, consisting of five trustees elected by ballot, together with the President, Vice-president, Secretary, and Treasurer, and the chairman of each of the several local sections, "with power to appoint teachers and take general charge during the recess of the Board of Trustees." This compact and energetic body, composed of gentlemen of experience, and representing all interests, soon became the right hand and working power of the Board, its decisions and reports seldom failing to receive the prompt approval of that body.

In the internal affairs of the schools also, changes quite as important took place. The pay system was introduced as provided by law, and extensive additions made to the course of study. Up to this period the subjects taught had been simply reading, spelling, writing, mostly on slates, and the simple elements of arithmetic; a few only of the more advanced pupils being reported as having entered reduction, rule of three, and, finally, "practice," which seems to have the extreme limit in this branch. To these were now added, after due consultation between the teachers and a special commit-

[1] 26 boys and 22 girls.

[2] See Religious Question.

tee, a higher class of reading-books, the more advanced rules of Arithmetic, Mensuration, Geography, with the use of maps and globes, English Grammar, History, Book-keeping, Astronomy, and Rhetoric.[1]

Another evidence of new and enlarged views was the appointment of a committee of three, to consider the propriety of establishing a "Central School for the instruction of tutors and monitors, and for the promotion from the general schools of pupils deserving distinction." A special meeting to hear their report was held on the 6th of October, 1826, and, after long and full discussion, the plan as presented was adopted, by a vote of sixteen ayes to thirteen nays. Only a brief outline of this report can be given. They assert the great and permanent importance of the subject; that the necessity for such schools was generally acknowledged by intelligent men, and that the Legislatures of New York and Massachusetts have recently had the matter under consideration; that a suitable building was wanted to accommodate at least four hundred students, and furnish proper rooms for the meetings of the trustees and the Society; "the course of study should be eminently practical, and should therefore involve a due proportion of Natural Philosophy, Practical Mathematics, Mercantile Arithmetic, Book-keeping, and the elements of Geology and Chemistry;" that the institution should be "conducted throughout on the monitorial system[2] in order to be expeditious as to results;" it would furnish at least one hundred teachers a year for the city and state; and, finally, that its effect upon the "general schools" would be highly beneficial if they were made the sole avenue to the Central School.

[1] The list of books recommended by the committee included, for the seventh class, Scripture Lessons and Moral Monitor; the eighth class, Murray's Introduction, English Reader, and New York Reader No. 3; for the ninth and highest class, Murray's Sequel, Power of Religion, Historical Reader, Willet's Arithmetic, Day's Tables, Hart's Geography, 2d Book and Atlas, Tanner's Maps, Goold Brown's Grammars, Tytler's History, Bennet's Book-keeping, Hawney's Mensuration, Blair's Rhetoric, and Alvah Clark's Astronomy.—*Minutes of* 1826.

[2] The term Lancasterian henceforth disappears from the minutes.

A memorial to the Legislature,[1] asking for funds to carry out the new project, was ordered from the same committee, who were directed to report at the next regular meeting.

Applications having been made for appointments as assistants in several schools, the Executive Committee reported strongly against the measure, as "abandoning the principle of the beautiful system" from which they had so long derived excellent results, and "they hoped to meet the real requirements of the schools by good paid monitors," of whom they anticipated a "full supply from the better class of children who are entering the schools." A report as to the expediency of appointing a "General Superintendent or Executive Officer" was also in the negative, and both reports were adopted by the Board.

[1] This portion of the original minutes concludes with a significant line: "N.B.—This report is not meant for the Public."

VIII.

PUBLIC SCHOOL SOCIETY.

1827–1828.

Failure of Pay System.—Disastrous Results.—Caste.—Reports of Committee of Investigation.—First Result.—Poor American Citizens will not be considered Paupers.—Second Result.—Failure of the One-teacher System of Lancaster.—Permanent paid Monitors-general.

ALL these high expectations were to be sadly disappointed, and the plans from which such advantages were anticipated, to result only in disaster. An alarming condition of things was beginning to develop itself, and threatened to strike from under the Society the very basis of its existence—the popularity of their schools, and the moral support of the people. In their comprehensive scheme they had made two serious miscalculations, each of which was to teach a lesson never to be forgotten.

Complaints first begun to come in from teachers and sections as to unexpected difficulties in collecting the tuition fees, small as these were. Some, having never before paid, were not now disposed to do so, and withdrew their children upon being solicited to give the smallest direct contribution to the support of the schools; many others insisted that, as the schools derived money from the School Fund of the state, the Society could have no right to enforce further payment from individuals; that is, they would not pay twice. Though some came in from the private schools, yet their number was far less than was anticipated, and the general attendance rapidly diminished. Out of the shrunken register[1] of 4654

[1] A previous report, August 1, 1825, gave a register of 5919; on the 1st of May, 1826, the very day the new law went into operation, it had already shrunk to 4654.

pupils, no less than 1690 were on the free list; while of the 2874 who were nominally pay pupils, a large part of the parents paid only one or two quarters at the most, so that their children should be known among their schoolmates as "pay scholars," and thereafter evaded all further demands. As the teachers were the agents for the collection of the money, and were held in some sort responsible for their proportionate amount, they were more or less urgent in their efforts to swell the income of the Society, and unpleasant altercations with parents, leading to the withdrawal of pupils, of course resulted.[1]

A far more serious evil, and one fraught with most disastrous consequences, was the *caste spirit* at once introduced into the schools, and gathering strength from day to day with the efforts made to collect the money. Children who *paid* looked down upon those who did not or could not. Each school divided itself into two classes; the pride and assumption of the one, and the mortification and indignation of the other, intensified as both were by the keen sensibilities and imaginative temperament of childhood, being a fruitful source of disturbance of discipline and harmony in school, and of wrathful and disparaging comment by the sympathetic parents and friends at home. The Roman Catholic, the Episcopal, Methodist, and other churches opened wide the doors of their free schools to the dissatisfied of the one class, and, by establishing cheap pay schools, drew off large numbers of the other.

The carefully-selected committee of investigation, to whom this alarming state of affairs was referred, in a report which they promptly rendered to a full meeting of the Board, give evidence not only of a conflict of opinion among themselves, but of a reluctance on the part of some of its members to accept the first great lesson of the occasion. In presenting their views of the cause of the failure of their plan, it is painful to

[1] Comparative statements of the amounts collected in the different schools appear in the minutes, and must have been felt, in some cases, as reflecting upon the teacher.

find, as the very first point in their report, a curt and bitter allusion to the existence in the community of "a large class of persons who are *poor, and yet too proud to confess it.*" They had yet to realize that it was the legitimate outgrowth and evidence of that free and healthful democratic spirit that, even in the poorest of our citizens, refuses to accept an inferior social position for themselves or their children on account of their poverty, and which causes every man and every woman, whatever their previous disadvantages, and come from whatever land of caste and tyranny they may, to stand erect as American citizens, and demand, as their "inalienable right," a recognition of their possession of every attribute and characteristic of a full and equal manhood. It was but a form of that spirit of freedom which instinctively refuses to accord special social rights or consideration to mere wealth or the accidents of birth, and which realizes that, in our system of society, the children of those who are the rich to-day may be as poor as the poorest to-morrow; and that the little one on the father's knee, though supported and caressed by hands stained and hardened with honest toil, may some day be counted among those whom their country honors with its most sacred trusts, or enshrines in its most grateful memories.

Another and juster train of thought is manifest in a concluding part of their report, and a principle is stated that went to the root of the matter, and became, after a year or two of delay, the fundamental idea of their organization, and the living source of their expansion and progress: "Your committee believe that the only true and legitimate system of our Public Schools would be to open our doors to *all* classes of our citizens free of any expense, and that all deficiencies should be defrayed by a public tax."

The second lesson derived from their experience, and one which they were slow to acknowledge, was a revelation of a radical weakness in the machinery of the monitorial system, at least in the form which it had so long presented in New York. So long as reading, writing, and the simpler rules of arithmetic constituted the whole course of study, with proper energy and vigilance in their single teacher, a whole department might be carried on in a mechanical way, and a certain sort of result obtained. But as soon as more advanced studies were introduced, involving a higher mental discipline, and demanding something more than mechanical ability in the teacher, and ability to read from the monitor, the system at once broke down.

It seems incredible too, that gentlemen of so much experience could have thought it possible for one man or one woman to superintend all the various old grades from the alphabet to the highest—receive and confer with the trustees, parents, and other visitors to a school sometimes numbering five hundred pupils—collect, receipt for, and pay over the many small sums demanded—keep the usual minute record of the pupils' names, ages, promotions, and the occupation and residence of their parents—look after the absentees—maintain in the department that peculiar discipline the very foundation of which was undivided attention and unremitting vigilance—and at the same time take up and teach the new studies of geography, astronomy, grammar, history, and book-keeping; and, besides so heavy a drain on the energies of any one who should attempt to carry out such a programme, to require that the best half of Saturday should be added to the full five days previously required, and all without any additional compensation.

It needed no prophet to predict the result. For these higher studies, necessarily demanding so large a part of the teacher's time, and forcing him to neglect a large part of his school, the charge was two dollars a quarter. The first quarter 107 paid; the next, 78; the third, only 13; the total income from this source, from which so much had been expected, being only $318, while the outlay for maps and globes alone was at least $800, besides other new expenses.

Besides the statement of the important principle already referred to, and which is first and prominent in their list of remedies, the committee recommended certain modifications which they hoped would restore things to a satisfactory condition. Both the monitorial and the pay system were retained, the charges being reduced to one-half—only the old "studies were to be pursued except as a reward of merit;" Saturday should be again a holiday, and teachers should receive a special allowance for all over a certain number.

In regard to the "Central School" the times were evidently not propitious, and their committee asked to be discharged, "not being ready to report," while the question as to a superintendent is not further heard of.

Although reporting against the employment of assistant teachers, the Executive Committee acknowledged the necessity of more efficient and regular help than had heretofore been given by the casual monitors paid by the week, and asked for and obtained the power to appoint two permanent paid monitors to each department;[1] and although these were only advanced pupils from thirteen to fifteen years of age already trained in the various duties of monitorship, they soon became, notwithstanding their title, to all intents and purposes, assistants; the chief oversight and management of the monitorial part of the department falling, in a few years, into their hands, and allowing the principal to perform for the advanced classes the ordinary duties of a teacher.

[1] Two boys, combined salaries, $300; two girls, combined salaries, $200. This was the *maximum*. The usual salary for the first year was $25.

IX.

PUBLIC SCHOOL SOCIETY.

1828–1829.

Infant School Society.—Junior Department in No. 8.—Infant Department in No. 10.—Comparison of the two Systems.—Lancaster *vs.* Pestalozzi.—Absurd Conceptions of Pestalozzianism.—Rejection of Lancasterianism for Infant Pupils.

About this period another innovation in education began to develop itself in New York, leading in time to most radical changes. Originating at nearly the same time with the systems of Bell and Lancaster, Pestalozzianism was much more liable to perversion and misapplication, because far more philosophical in its fundamental principles, and requiring in the teacher abilities the very farthest from mechanical. Its methods and principles, already widely adopted in Europe, were but vaguely understood or appreciated, and had made but slow progress in America. Early in 1827, an association of ladies was formed in New York, under the title of the Infant School Society, Mrs. Joanna Bethune being the First Directress. Similar societies were organized in Boston and Charleston in 1828, other cities rapidly following. With much that was sound in principle and excellent in practice, these schools presented some features which now seem not a little absurd.

In London, New York, and Charleston, the ages of the children ranged from two to six years; in Boston, from eighteen months to four years. From two to six cents per week were usually demanded; two sessions of at least three hours each were held each day; vaccination was required before admission; several female teachers, usually two, were employed in each school; and, the children being taught in masses, the monitorial system was not used.

Up to this time all the various grades, from the abecedarian of the sand-class to the highest, were, in the Public Schools, taught in one department; but, stimulated by the success of the Infant Schools, the Society now ventured upon the experiment of separating the younger children, both boys and girls, from the older pupils, at the same time admitting infants. A trial of this plan was made in the basement of No. 8 by organizing therein a "Junior Department," in charge of a female principal, assisted by a paid monitress.[1] Children of three years and even younger were admitted, the numbers soon reaching 300 or more. Apparently not even questioning the superiority of the Lancasterian system for such a school, this experimental department was organized by the trustees on their favorite plan.

Meanwhile the ladies of the Infant School Society, had organized a school of about 170 pupils in Canal Street and upon the Pestalozzian system as they understood it. The introduction of singing, especially of lively, pleasant, and appropriate songs for little children, the variety in the exercises, the discarding of books and lesson-boards, and the substitution of oral teaching, partly, though not intelligently, objective, soon made the system highly popular; while the tender age of the little ones, and their manifest interest, aroused the warmest sympathies. The matter soon arrested the attention of the Trustees of the Public Schools, and several successive committees were appointed in 1827 for the purpose of inspecting this school, and yet another in Greene Street, and comparing the results with those obtained in the new Junior Department in No. 8.

Whatever the previous convictions of these gentlemen, their reports were all greatly in favor of the new system; and, in order more thoroughly to test its merits, an Infant Department was opened in the basement of No. 10 in May, 1828, and the counsel and assistance of the ladies of the Infant School Society solicited in its organization and super-

[1] Naomi H. Reynolds and J. C. Andrews, the first public primary teachers, appointed 1827, at $200 and $75, respectively.

vision. They accordingly appointed a committee for the purpose, who were of great service; the only disadvantage being such as would naturally arise from the school and teachers having two independent sets of governors.

When time enough had been allowed to develop the results, a committee was again appointed to compare the Infant Department No. 10 with the Junior No. 8. The report was to the same effect as before, and proclaimed that the monitorial plan had been weighed in the balance and found wanting. In their opinion, it was "too dull and monotonous for the infant mind, while the other presented a judicious admixture of amusement and instruction; that since fully one-third of all the children in the schools of the Society were between the ages of four and six, the adoption of the system was highly desirable; that an inordinate amount of time was spent under the monitor in the sand-class or the draft in learning to print or to decipher a single letter, or to spell a few unmeaning syllables;" adding the surprising alternative, that "the time might better be employed in conveying to their minds some of the simplest notions of geography, astronomy, and natural history, and in exercising their memories with some of the simplest facts of history, and matters of information in common life; all of which may be done by an intelligent person in a style of conversation, by aid of a few pictures and other materials for illustration."[1]

[1] This sort of perversion and misconception of the methods and principles of Pestalozzi was by no means confined to New York or to America, nor is it yet entirely without remaining traces; and the trustees may well be excused for greatly preferring even so unphilosophical a system, with its many redeeming features, to the mindless, musicless, and dull monotony of the monitorial system, which it partly, and should have completely supplanted.

In all parts of the country the highest commendation was bestowed upon this perverted Infant School system by men of high culture and social position, although it is a relief to find it stated in one of the commendatory reports of the Public School Society that "many intelligent and benevolent persons look upon such infant schools as the temporary effect of a mistaken philanthropy." The Charleston Report for 1829, after stating that none will be admitted till they can walk alone, gives the general impression produced at the time by these schools in exclaiming, "How delightful it is to hear these little one's lisping

Another conclusion stated in their report refers to a matter which, however trite it now is, was practically a revolutionary novelty in the schools of our city, and marks the progress they were steadily making toward a better state of things. "Your committee are unanimous in the opinion that, in general, female teachers are much better calculated than male teachers for the instruction of small children of both sexes."

In consequence of the report, a resolution was passed, changing the title of Junior and Infant Departments to Primary Departments, and looking to the final establishment of schools like that in No. 10 in the basements of all the buildings of the Society. The condition of their finances, however, and the necessity of providing more new buildings, together with a legal difficulty as to spending the school money in the tuition of such young children, delayed the measure for several years.

Another important inroad into Lancasterian plans was the abolition of its peculiar and distinctive system of rewards and punishments, which was based upon the award or forfeiture of tickets of merit having a certain pecuniary value, and exchangeable for toys, knives, etc.

knowledge *much beyond their early age*, were they not taught on the plan pursued," etc., and the Boston Report for the same year has similar testimonials as to "astonishment and delight at their progress."

X.

PUBLIC SCHOOL SOCIETY.

1829–1832.

Efforts to abolish the Pay System and establish true Free Schools.—Origin of the half-mill Tax.—School Census.—Grant of *one-fourth* of the Tax asked for.—Efforts for the Remainder.—Common Council demands Control.—Catholic Orphan Asylum.—Tax granted, and Asylum admitted to participate.

THE unsatisfactory and evil effects of the pay system, even in the modified form in which for a year or two it had been continued, at last led to a complete change of policy. Profiting by their varied experience, the trustees from this time forth boldly advocated a general school-tax of sufficient magnitude to furnish a generous support for the schools, the throwing open the doors to all citizens as a matter of *right*, and not of charity, and such a modification of the course of study as should offer for every man's children the best attainable English education. After a series of interesting propositions, reports, and debates, in which their views took definite and practical shape, a bold and vigorous address was issued to their fellow-citizens, abounding with advanced ideas, and proposing a plan for carrying them into effect.[1] After presenting school statistics and plans, and referring to the steady

[1] A synopsis is subjoined: After quoting from a recent address of the Mayor of Boston, "Every school, the admission to which is grounded on acquirements not easily attained by the children of the whole community, must be considered as for the benefit of the *few*, and *not* of the many. The standard of public education should be raised to the greatest height, but it should be effected by *raising the standard in the Common Schools*:" they go on to say that no part of the state has more means, and in no part is public instruction so imperatively demanded—that the ratio of pupils in schools of all kinds to the whole population varied from one to five to one to three in other portions of the state, while in the city it was as low as one to seven—that of a school population of over 52,000, nearly or quite 25,000 between the ages of five and fifteen attended no

increase of immigration and the importance of general intelligence in this city to the affairs of the state and the nation, it adds: "In other countries it may be justly thought dangerous to their present rulers to enlighten the people. But with us the question of their political power is settled; and, if they are true to themselves, it is settled forever. We wish to keep that power in their hands, and to enable them to exercise it with wisdom. The laboring classes have justly been called the backbone and sinews of the republic. It is not enough that they know how to read and write and cast accounts. We wish to provide them better excitements than they now have. We wish them to enjoy the pleasures, as well as the other advantages of intellectual occupation. We wish them to be able to understand and admire the beneficence of the Creator in the works of his hands. We wish them to feel that *virtue* is the *first* distinction among men, and *knowledge* the *second;* and to be themselves the great exemplar of these truths."[1]

It was therefore of the first importance that the Public Schools should be made desirable to every class in the community; and one of the most important uses they could possibly subserve, would be to break down at the very outset of life that separative *caste* spirit, which under whatever form or specious pretext it may present itself, is ever the deadly enemy of practical democracy. In regard to the proposed tax, "We submit to the liberal consideration of the rich whether

school whatever; and supposing one-half of them to be employed, there were still from 12,000 to 13,000 who should be in school, exclusive of infant pupils—that the proper order of claims had been too long inverted, the sick and the destitute not having higher claims than ignorant youth—and that good schools are the very foundation of democratic society. They must offer higher rewards for qualified teachers, propose infant schools for children from three to six, and recommend, 1st, one or more high schools, teaching all branches necessary for an active business life; 2d, a classical school; 3d, a seminary for the education of teachers for common schools; and, lastly, a half-mill tax to carry out these measures.

[1] It was probably the last effort of the noble spirit that had so long stood at the head of the Society, and does full justice to his broad and liberal statesmanship. Clinton died suddenly soon after.

their contribution would not be a profitable investment for their children, and whether their bonds and mortgages and public stocks are altogether beyond the reach of public opinion, and of that which must ultimately depend upon public opinion, the *administration of the laws.*"

Promptly following up the good effects of this address, the trustees set on foot among the citizens a petition to the Legislature asking for a tax of a half-mill on the dollar of assessed city property, which was signed by nearly five thousand of the most respectable citizens, comprising the names of a large part of the tax-paying community. The plan was formally adopted by the Common Council, who memorialized for the tax, though not to the extent asked for by the petitioners; and a law, levying, not four-eightieths, but one-eightieth of one per cent., was passed by the Legislature in the session of 1829. Though, by the refusal of three-fourths of the amount asked for, their plan was shorn of many of its best features, especially the higher and normal schools, and the total abolition of the pay system, the trustees were enabled to advance materially the character of their schools and prepare the way for further progress. In this they were also assisted by an act giving power to mortgage their real estate, and legalizing other loans to the amount of $70,000, which in the same form had been found necessary to the support and expansion of their schools.

While the subject of the tax was still pending, a school census, more complete in its results than any previous one, was taken by direction of the Common Council. It was thus ascertained that 11,000, or nearly two-thirds of the whole number in private schools, were of nearly an equal grade as to advancement with those in the Public Schools, the cost in the latter being much less than even in the worst description of the former, and with far greater sanitary and disciplinary advantages. All the essential facts were fully laid before the community in the public prints, and in the annual reports of the Society.[1]

[1] An abstract is submitted for comparison. See Table on page 57.

After two years, the Board again early in 1831 applied to the Common Council for another memorial to the Legislature asking for the remaining three-eightieths of one per cent. tax, so as to meet the original proposition of the 5000 memorialists of 1829. The Corporation complied with the request, but inserted into the memorial a clause providing that this additional three-eightieths of one per cent. "shall be and remain under the immediate and sole control of the Common Council." This was a new and unexpected phase of difficulty. An earnest memorial of remonstrance was presented to the Common Council, reciting in brief outline the history of the Society, the important controversy in regard to religious sectarian schools which they supposed had reached a final settlement in 1825, and the impropriety of the demand of the Corporation in view of the fact that its members were all *ex officio* members of the Public School Society, and the mayor and recorder of the Board of Trustees; and further, that they now and for many years had held all reasonable

ABSTRACT OF SPECIAL SCHOOL CENSUS OF 1829.

	Private Schools.	Incorporated Schools.	Charity Schools.	Public Schools.	Total.
Number	430	3	19	11	463
Principal Teachers	432	6	25	21	484
Assistants	259	23	5	24	311
From 4 to 5 Years of Age	1,013	33	197		1,243
From 5 to 15 " "	13,631	1,008	2,297	6,007	22,943
Above 15 " "	676	40	50		766
Attend Sunday Schools	4,489	168	970	3,808	9,435
First Elements	6,907	220	2,430	6,007	15,564
Geography, Grammar, and Arithmetic	7,214	841	960	475	9,490
Higher Branches	1,869	270	15	....	2,154
Mathematics	492	52	12	....	556
Dead Languages	442	48	1	....	491
Foreign Languages	850	141	4	....	995
Males	7,922	633	1,305	3,112	12,972
Females	7,398	448	1,239	2,895	11,980
Whole Number of Pupils	15,320	1,081	2,544	6,007	24,952
Male Teachers	339	14	9	23	385
Female Teachers	352	15	21	22	410

Of the 430 private schools, 6 were for colored children, 3 of them reported as "excellent;" only 52 private schools not elementary; of the 24,952 pupils, 805 were colored; and there were about one-twelfth more boys than girls.

control over the expenditures and distribution of school moneys in the Commissioners of Common School Funds of the city of New York—a body consisting of one person from each ward, appointed, as provided by law, by the Common Council itself, to receive and pay over the moneys as directed by state and city laws, and visiting every participating school twice in each year to see that all legal conditions were complied with.

The necessity for the additional tax is then stated *in extenso*, and their alarm at the unexpected proposition that the proceeds should be placed under sole control of the Common Council, and not, as with the rest of the school moneys, under that of the commissioners, ending with a cautious reference as to the possible motives which have led to such a proposition, they having "no conclusive evidence that it is intended to divert the proposed tax from the customary channels." An offer was also made, as in 1825, to convey all their real estate to the Common Council, receiving in return a perpetual lease so long as the property should be used for school purposes.

While this matter was still pending, formal application was made to the Common Council by the Roman Catholic Benevolent Society for their Orphan Asylum, and by the Trustees of the Methodist Church in behalf of their charity schools for a portion of the school funds. After much excitement, the matter was finally settled by the passage of an act by the Legislature, granting the additional tax, and providing for its distribution in the usual manner, but the Asylum was at the same time admitted to the participation for reasons which can be better given in another chapter.[1]

[1] See Religious Question.

XI.

PUBLIC SCHOOL SOCIETY.

1832–1842.

Final Abolition of the Pay System.—More Primary Departments opened.—Primary Schools established.—Assistant Teachers employed.—Course of Study extended.—Evening Schools.—Transfer of Schools of Manumission Society.—Saturday Normal School.—Trustees' Hall.—Financial Embarrassments.—Application of Catholic Free Schools for Participation in the School Fund.—Exciting Controversy.—Governor's Message.—Act of April 11, 1842, extends the State System to the City.—Organization of the Board of Education.

BEING now assured of sufficient means, the trustees commenced with energy the work of reforming or transforming their system. The plan of payment for tuition, which in the last year of its continuance had produced only $839, was finally abolished February 3, 1832, and public notice given that schools were now open to all as a common right, and that every effort would be made to render them attractive and desirable to all classes of citizens. A full year was spent in preparing for and introducing the necessary changes, the time being somewhat extended by the interruptions resulting from the fearful visitation of cholera.

Primary departments similar to that in No. 10 were opened in various schools as rapidly as circumstances permitted. A special committee having visited Boston for the purpose of inspecting the system of public instruction, and especially the Dame Primary Schools in that city, presented a report which was adopted by the trustees, recommending a new order of elementary schools. These were to be known as the Public Primary Schools on a modification of the Boston plan, and were to be established throughout the city, each ward to form a primary school district, with such subdivisions as might be found expedient. The large and expensive buildings owned and occupied by the Society were separated by wide intervals, which were steadily filling with a denser population. It was therefore judged expedient to hire such suitable premises as could be obtained, and thus scatter small and good schools; so that, by having them brought, as it were, to their own doors, thousands who would not send their little ones to the distant Primary Department or Public School would be induced to let them attend the small schools in their immediate neighborhood. No step ever taken by the Society had a more beneficial result. It added greatly to their popularity and usefulness, and was a chief source of their financial strength during the remaining years of their existence.

The several classes of schools were now to be known as 1st. Public Schools, having the more advanced boys and girls in separate departments; 2d. Primary Departments, which were the modified Infant Schools; 3d. Primary Schools. As the plan of appointing sections could not well be applied, a large standing committee, known as the Primary School Committee, was appointed, with power to call upon the Executive Committee for teachers, and the Supply Committee for the necessary material. Each Primary School was to be conducted by a female teacher and a paid monitress, the number of pupils not to exceed eighty; boys admitted from four years of age to six; girls, four years and over. The course of study embraced " reading, spelling, and writing, with the simple elements of arithmetic and geography, to be taught orally, and, as far as possible, with visible illustrations by means of a map of the hemispheres, numeral frame, and black-board." A modification of the monitorial system was introduced, the monitor's duties devolving chiefly upon the teachers themselves. The simultaneous or concert system was largely employed. Both of the lower orders of the schools were to make regular promotions to the Public Schools.

In consequence of this step, the operations of the trustees expanded with great rapidity. The committee were at first authorized to open ten schools;[1] but the popularity of the measure, as indicated by the promptness with which these were filled and even overcrowded, soon led to arrangements for ten more, followed by yet others; some sixty or more being finally opened, many of them with numbers far beyond the original limit.

Radical changes took place in the upper departments. The course of study was extended so as to include astronomy, algebra, geometry, trigonometry, and book-keeping. Profiting by their previous experience, an assistant teacher was now provided in addition to the two monitors for each department, and separate recitation-rooms built.[2] The principal and his assistant were chiefly occupied with the advanced classes, while the lower, under a form of the monitorial system, were in charge of the paid monitors. The salaries of the several grades of teachers were at the same time somewhat advanced.[3]

Applications having been received from various sections of the city for the establishment of evening schools for apprentices and others, the trustees took the matter into consideration, but ascertained from the legal advisers that the law gave no clear right so to expend the public money, and that they had better "avoid the assumption of doubtful powers." On the 18th of January, 1833, they put in operation, however, a plan which in their opinion complied with the advice received, by directing "that evening schools for apprentices and others be opened" in certain buildings belonging to the Society, and "that all engagements with male teachers, assistants, and monitors are to include a condition that they are to teach evening school if ordered, and without any additional pay." Several principals and assistants of day schools were

[1] No. 1, in Orchard Street, opened in September, 1832.

[2] Though often asked for, these had been refused in the earlier years of the Society.

[3] The salary of the male principal was raised from $800 to $1000, of the female principal, from $350 to $400. The maximum for each of the others was $600, $200, and $100 in the male department, and $250, $100, and $50 in the female department.

"ordered" to each evening school as associate teachers, and being necessarily peers, there was no real head, and, consequently, no efficient discipline. As, under the circumstances, the teachers could not be expected to take much interest in their work, it is not surprising that the report of the next year modestly refers to these schools as an experiment; the next, that they "are not entirely successful;" and succeeding ones "regret the smallness of their numbers, and the great difficulties in regard to discipline."[1] After a few winters of forced and uncompensated labor, the teachers were finally relieved by the quiet abolition of the schools, no resolution to that effect appearing on the minutes.

In the latter part of 1832, the managers of the Manumission Society, whose schools, like those of the Public School Society, were supported by the public funds, applied for a committee of conference to effect a union. It was felt by the trustees that on many accounts it was better that the two sets of schools should remain separate; but fearing further diversion of the school fund, it was desirable that the number of societies participating should be as small as possible, and arrangements were accordingly made for a transfer of the schools and property of the elder society. After some delay, in consequence of legislative action being found necessary to give a title to their real estate, on the 2d of May, 1834, the transfer was effected, the price paid being $12,000. An unexpended balance of school money, amounting to about $9000, was also transferred, and the six or seven African schools were placed in charge of a special committee, with similar powers to the Committee on Primary Schools, and comprising several of the most active members of the Manumission Society.[2] The aggregate register of these schools was nearly 1400, with an average attendance of about one-half that number. Applications were also made by the man-

[1] Corporal punishment was "miscellaneously" inflicted, each teacher disciplining his own class. Those familiar with evening schools may easily imagine the occasional result.

[2] The Manumission Society continued its separate existence for the other objects contemplated in its constitution.

agers of the House of Refuge, the Manhattanville, Harlem, and other schools in the upper part of the island; but various objections, legal or prudential, prevented a similar result.

The schools of the Infant School Society, and, with the exception of their school in the basement of No. 5, the schools also of the Female Association, seem to have been silently absorbed into the Primary Schools and Departments, no legislation being necessary, as they held no real estate.[1]

The large buildings of the Society were now fourteen in number, and contained three departments in each. Besides these, were the numerous Primary Schools and Departments and the African schools. In each and all of these from one to two monitors were employed, all, excepting those in the male departments, being females. Appointed at a very early age, usually from fourteen to fifteen, but in many cases in the primaries even younger, they were cut off, by the elementary nature of the studies committed to their care, from all further opportunity for systematic advance in their own scholarship. Many of these, developing executive abilities of a high order, were in time promoted to the position of assistant, or even of principal, in the primaries, but the great advance in the order of studies precluded their appointment to corresponding positions in the upper departments without greatly increased mental culture.

In view of these facts, and of the certainty that the difficulty would increase with the numbers of the schools, the Committee on Teachers and Monitors, which was a sub-committee of the Executive, presented on the 1st of August, 1834, a special report upon the subject. In accordance with their suggestions, a school for monitors of the Primary Schools and Departments was opened in No. 5 on Saturdays. The sessions were five hours each, and the studies chiefly those of the higher classes of the upper schools; though soon called a Normal School, no normal instruction was given. Two teachers, both of whom must be principals in the Pub-

[1] The school in the basement of No. 5 continued in charge of the Female Association till March, 1845.

lic Schools, were appointed at small salaries; the original arrangement, which seems to have been of no long continuance, providing that the school should have a female principal and a male assistant. The attendance was compulsory, under penalty of non-increase of salary, loss of promotion, or even of position. The beneficial effects being soon manifest, the plan was extended so as to include the female monitors of the upper schools, and those qualified pupils of the ninth class of girls who were desirous of appointments. A similar school, though necessarily on a smaller scale, was opened for the monitors of the male departments, and a third for the teachers of the colored schools.

Up to 1841, the meetings of the trustees and the Society and of their various committees had been held in a part of one of their school buildings; but their widely extended and increasing operations requiring a permanent location and much greater facilities, a site was purchased on the corner of Grand and Elm Streets, and a suitable building erected, with proper office conveniences, a room for the meetings, and others for the Saturday Normal School and two Primary Schools, besides a "Depository" for the storing and distribution of supplies for all the various schools of the Society.[1]

Notwithstanding the apparent removal of all financial difficulties by the grant of the full one-twentieth of one per cent. by the Act of 1831, the trustees again found themselves embarrassed. The city continued to expand with greater rapidity than ever, and more and more schools had to be provided. The Common Council, instead of advancing the sum annually raised for school purposes with the increasing valuation of property, saw fit to interpret the law as granting a fixed sum, equal to one-twentieth of one per cent. on the assessed value of the year in which the act was passed. Some of those who

[1] This building, now the Hall of the Board of Education, has since been greatly enlarged and improved, and is the central point in the management of the school officers of the city. It contains the offices of the Clerk and Superintendent, and meeting-rooms of the Board, embellished with the portraits of many of its presidents, together with those of De Witt Clinton and Geo. T. Trimble, the first and last presidents of the Public School Society

had signed the original petition for the levy of the special tax now claimed that they had understood that it was to be levied only for a short period. Toward the close of 1834 the Board of Supervisors "wished to be informed whether it would be again found necessary to raise a similar sum to that raised last year," and also if the trustees were now ready to convey their real estate to the Common Council. In view of the apparent desire to cripple them by refusing adequate means, and of the possibly disastrous result of another controversy on the question of religion, which was now beginning once more to present itself, the trustees did not deem it expedient to comply with the suggestion as to the property. In 1839, having become more and more embarrassed, and in order to secure the advantages of the increased value of city property, they made a vigorous though unsuccessful attempt to procure the passage of a "Declaratory Act" in relation to the half-mill tax.

Early in 1840 the trustees of the Catholic Free Schools made application to the Common Council to be allowed to participate in the school funds. The large and influential body of citizens whose views were represented in this application were much dissatisfied with many things in the internal condition and management of the schools of the Public School Society, "a gigantic and growing monopoly," as they considered it, under whose sole control were all the means of public instruction.

"It was alleged that, although the Society belonged to no particular religious denomination, and although it did not teach directly the creed of any particular sect, that still its schools were practically sectarian, and that its books and instruction had so strong a bias in favor of Protestantism, that Roman Catholics, who were by universal consent entitled to a perfect equality of rights, could not conscientiously send their children to the schools, although taxed for their support. The Society offered and endeavored to make their books acceptable to all, but an excitement of feeling had arisen which could not be thus allayed; the subject was brought before the

Common Council again in 1840, and discussed with extraordinary ability on all sides. It was thence transferred to the Legislature of the state in 1841, and became so important a question of state policy that at the opening of the session of 1842, the governor in his annual message, after stating that, under existing circumstances, twenty thousand children in the city were practically unprovided with instruction, proceded as follows:

"'Happily in this, as in other instances, the evil is discovered to have had its origin no deeper than a departure from the equality of general laws. In our general system of Common Schools, trustees, chosen by tax-paying citizens, levy taxes, build school-houses, pay teachers, and govern schools, which are subject to visitation by similarly-elected inspectors, who certify the qualification of teachers; and all schools thus constituted participate in just proportion in the public moneys, which are conveyed to them by commissioners also elected by the people.

* * * * * *

"'I submit, therefore, with entire willingness, to approve whatever adequate remedy you may propose, the expediency of vesting to the people of the city of New York what I am sure the people of no other part of the state would, upon any consideration, relinquish—the education of their children. For this purpose it is only necessary to vest the control of the Common Schools in a Board, to be composed of commissioners elected by the people, which Board shall apportion the school moneys among all the schools, including those now existing, which shall be organized and conducted in conformity to its general regulations and the laws of the state in proportion to the number of pupils instructed. It is not left doubtful that the restoration to the Common Schools of the city of this simple and equal feature of the Common Schools of the state would remove every complaint.

"'This proposition has sometimes been treated as a device to appropriate the school funds to the endowment of seminaries for teaching languages and faiths, thus to perpetuate the prejudices it seeks to remove—sometimes as a scheme for dividing that precious fund among a hundred jarring sects, and thus increasing the religious animosities it strives to heal—sometimes as a plan to subvert the prevailing religion and introduce one repugnant to the consciences of our fellow-citizens, while, in truth, it simply proposes, by enlightening equally the minds of all, to enable them to detect error wherever it may exist, and to reduce uncongenial masses into an intelligent, virtuous, harmonious, and happy people.'

"This recommendation of the governor was extremely unacceptable to a large portion of the people of this city; and had it not proposed to preserve the schools of the Public School Society, which had, deservedly, the confidence and affection of so large a number of the citizens, it is doubtful whether the popular will would have allowed the recommendation of the governor to go into useful effect. . As it was, however, the Legislature adopted the views of the executive, and extended by law into this city the Common School system, which had prevailed for thirty years in the residue of the state, placing the management of the schools in the hands of inspectors, trustees, and commissioners elected by the people, still allowing the Public School Society and other corporations to continue their existing schools, and participate in the public funds according to the number of their scholars, but prohibiting such participation to any school in which any religious sectarian doctrine or tenet shall be taught, inculcated, or practiced."[1]

Under that act, passed April 11, 1842, the first Board of Education was organized; and it now remains briefly to trace the progress of the two organizations, with their mutual reactions, during the ten subsequent years, until their final and harmonious consolidation into one great system.

[1] Report of Board of Education for 1853.

XII.

BOARD OF EDUCATION AND PUBLIC SCHOOL SOCIETY.

1842–1853.

Difficulties of the New System.—Great Opposition.—Prejudice.—Contrasts of the two Organizations.—Their radical Difference in Principle.—Direct Appeal to the People.—Gradual Development of the Ward Schools.—Teachers.—Amendment to the Act.—Progress of the Public Schools.—High School.—Beneficial Reaction of Ward Schools on Public Schools.—Leads to rapid Changes.—Financial Difficulties of the Society.—They can establish no new Schools.—Free Academy opened.—Its Effects on the System.—New Style of School-houses.—Further Embarrassments of the Society.—Interest on Mortgages.—Premonitions of the final Result.—M'Keon's Report.—Mutual Good-will of the two Bodies.—Successive Steps leading to Consolidation.—Act of June 4, 1853.—Final Meeting, and Dissolution of the Society.—Summary.

THE new guardians and guides of public instruction had no easy task before them. The outgrowth of intense excitement and bitter controversy, the subject of misconception and misrepresentation, with the prejudices, animosities, and fears of a large and influential portion of the citizens arrayed against it, the new system had to contend with difficulties that seemed well-nigh insuperable. A powerful and compact organization, strong in the character and influence of its individual members and the justly-earned approbation and sympathy of hundreds of thousands, already occupied a large portion of the field. The one thoroughly centralized, from its origin, and disciplined by long experience, both as an organization and from the continuance of its individual members, with subordinate committees and local sections, all of its own erection, and responsible to the central power; the other, discrete, apparently incoherent, with as many independent boards as there were wards in the city—a complex machinery of trustees, inspectors, and commissioners from all classes of society, and with powers and duties not so sharply defined as to prevent injurious disputes—with the central Board of Education virtually dependent upon the dictum of the local ones, with officers of every grade without experience, it would seem a wonder that the new system had not died at its very birth. But it contained a vital element more than sufficient to overcome all these difficulties, more than enough to overbalance the advantages possessed by its powerful rival. *It was based upon a* DIRECT and IMMEDIATE APPEAL *to the* PEOPLE. No body of men, no matter what their character or social standing, were placed, without or against the *will* of the people, between them and their children. If they have one interest which, in this land of *self-government*, they should jealously guard, and keep as closely as possible under their own control, surely it is the selection of those into whose hands is committed that most sacred and responsible trust, the education of their offspring.

It is interesting to observe the working of this principle in its gradual unfolding, as the citizens came to look more dispassionately and understandingly on school affairs. If there were mistakes, this would remedy them; if the wrong men were chosen, those most deeply interested would supply their places with better; if modifications of any sort were found necessary, the supreme will of the people would order them. And thus, little by little, and against all obstacles, gross misconceptions, and bitter prejudices, and after many errors, the system was developed by this, its innate force, till it should at last become, by universal consent, the chief ornament and pride of our city; at the least unsurpassed by any other on the globe.

The law as originally passed was very deficient. No school was organized under it during the whole of the first year. The amendments of the next year, however, enabled the local officers to build and open seven schools, besides three in hired premises; in 1844 three others were built; in 1845, two; in 1846, one. The locations selected by the ward officers had little or no reference to ward lines. By the provisions of the law, any pupil residing in the county was entitled, as in the case of the Public Schools, to attend any school. Availing themselves of this, officers often chose sites close to the ward lines, sometimes not far from the junction of several wards, so as to draw pupils from other wards, while secure that no other school could be built in their own. Some of the Public Schools suffered greatly from having new schools erected within a very short distance. The buildings were mostly small, and injudiciously constructed. In all matters involving expenditure, the trustees and the Board of Education were practically held in check by the rigid economy of the Public School Society, now more rigid than ever, it being highly important to either party that there should be no unfavorable comparative statement as to cost.

In the internal administration of schools, each ward being a "district," was virtually supreme. They selected their own teachers, subject to the approval of their inspectors, chose their own course of study, and decided upon the method of organization. The plan of three departments, as in the Public Schools, was generally adopted. By common consent, however, the unpopular monitorial system was abandoned, a larger number of teachers were employed, and a sufficient number of class-rooms constructed. The troublesome question of religion, by which the whole subject of the establishment and control of schools had been opened, was peaceably settled by allowing each local board to select their own books, and determine which version of the Scriptures should be used, subject only to the general regulation of the act that "no religious sectarian doctrines should be taught, inculcated, or practiced." Each ward purchased its own supplies at its own price, and sent in the bills to the Board of Education. Teachers were obtained from various sources, some of them of a high order of ability, but many others, appointed by individual influence, could never have passed the rigid examination of the Public School Trustees. The Public Schools themselves, however, were the chief source of supply, many of the best teachers in the employ of the Society passing over to the Ward Schools.[1]

Before the beginning of 1848, twenty-four schools had been organized in the various wards, some of them, however, not essentially different in grade from the public primaries. Time and experience pointed out improvements in the original act establishing the system, and various amendatory laws were from time to time passed, the whole tending to increased efficiency, activity, and harmony.

Meanwhile the Public Schools and their trustees were undergoing a new experience. While the new system was yet struggling with its initial difficulties, and before Ward School No. 1 had been opened, with even more than their usual energy No. 17, and then No. 18, had been established, and an unsuccessful effort made to repeal the new law. As the Acts of 1842 and 1843 left their authority to expend the public money in erecting buildings somewhat doubtful—indeed it was utterly denied by the Board of Education—both parties again resorted to Albany, and the Act of 1844, while legalizing the steps already taken and the expenses incurred, prohibited the establishing of any new schools without the consent of the Board of Education. The same act also provided that the Society should increase the number of elected trustees from fifty to seventy-five, who should have power to add to their numbers fifty additional members. The selections were judiciously made, and added many valuable members with new ideas to the old Board.

A committee was appointed, a memorial to the Legisla-

[1] There were many reasons for this: the pay was in most cases better; experienced subordinates were offered principalships; the direction of the studies, the selection of subordinates, and nearly every other point in the internal management was either put into the principal's hands, or greatly influenced by his advice; and there was in every way greater freedom of action and development of individuality, while formal and offensive official stiffness and distance in the governing power were replaced by cordial and manifest sympathy and consideration. To many a sensitive and noble spirit, escape from the cold, unsympathetic, almost military rule of the Society, was equivalent to an emancipation.

ture was prepared, and a vigorous effort made to obtain "authority and means to establish a High School for instruction in the higher branches of an English education, and in Latin and Greek." This measure, it will be remembered, had been discussed and approved by the Board of Trustees even as early as 1826, but action had been delayed as premature and, from financial embarrassments, inexpedient. Although their assistance was sought by a committee of conference, the influence of the Board of Education was cast against the effort as being yet premature, and some years passed before the plan of the proposed institution was realized in the Free Academy.

The steady progress and many excellences of the Ward Schools, which had now become more popular as the true scope and purpose of their fundamental principle was better understood, produced important internal changes in the Public Schools. Besides the effects of the loss of so many valuable teachers, to some of whom each additional building offered positions, the rejection of the monitorial plan, and the evident popularity of so doing, soon led to the final abandonment of the last remnants of this, their original system. Many additional teachers were of course found necessary, and added largely to the strain upon the straightening means of the Society. It involved also extensive alterations and repairs for the furnishing and fitting up of additional class-rooms. One phase of this increase of the corps of instructors marks another important departure from the traditional policy and views of the trustees. The new appointees in the boys' departments were females; and the effects of this step, as had already been found in the Ward Schools, were in the highest degree beneficial, not only to the discipline but to the character of the instruction. Another step, small perhaps in itself, yet unmistakably indicating the power of the great tide of innovating improvement which had set in from the newer system, was the introduction of *vocal music*, at least in the female departments, and its toleration in the boys' schools; the little ones of the Infant School in No. 10 had won a victory for themselves and all other "Primaries" in 1830.[1]

Still another change, which from its relation to the annual average attendance and the finances, indicates the growing pressure which the new system was steadily exerting upon the old, was the extension of the annual vacation by adding another week, the closing of the schools also between Christmas and New Year's day, and limitation of the daily sessions between the hours of nine A.M. and three P.M. during the whole year, instead of closing as heretofore, except in the winter, at five P.M. While the efficacy of their management was shown by the slowly-increasing numbers in average attendance notwithstanding their many difficulties and the rapid growth of the Ward Schools, the expenses of the Society were also increasing, and faster than their income. A large portion of the general fund was almost a fixed sum, and the great

[1] No feature of the schools of the Society seems more singular than this. Those first established were purely Lancasterian, modeled as closely as possible upon that of Lancaster himself, who it will be remembered was a member of the Society of Friends. The Public School Society, as well as the Female Association, originated in the ever-active benevolence of the same religious body, one of whose peculiarities has ever been an opposition to this form of æsthetic culture. To the last of its existence, the "Quaker" element was very influential, almost controlling, in the Public School Society; and one can hardly avoid the conclusion that their peculiar religious ideas as to music had much influence in strengthening other reasons assigned for its long exclusion. When La Fayette visited No. 3 in 1824, a class of girls *recited* a poetic address in concert, and he heard another poetic address in the Park. The minutes of the examination of No. 6 in 1827 state with evident approval that "*a hymn was spoken by the class.*" A strong effort for the introduction of vocal music was made by certain members of the Board of Trustees in 1836. A committee was appointed to consider the matter, and brought in a very decided report in its favor. "It had been *tried* in No. 10; the teachers were unanimous in its favor; the time required would be mostly out of school-hours; it had been introduced into large private and corporate schools here and in other cities; it would cost nothing whatever; and would not encroach upon the school-time." The report was promptly "tabled." After nine more years, on the 6th of March, 1845, Section No. 16 forwarded to the Executive Committee a copy of a significant resolution—"that the time has arrived when vocal music should be taught in the Public Schools." After being referred and reported upon, the measure prevailed.

increase of pupils taught reduced the *pro rata* to less than two-thirds of its previous amount, the pupils taught at the various classes of common schools having nearly trebled in the ten years previous to 1852.[1] They were driven to the most watchful economy in the expenditure, though the condition of most of their buildings, some of them in constant use for more than thirty years, was such as to call for large outlays for necessary repairs. Their funds ran short, and, as by law provided, they called upon the Board of Education for assistance. An examination of the statute showed that, while school buildings owned by the city might undoubtedly be repaired or improved by an expenditure of the public money, the case was far from certain when the buildings were the property of a private corporation, and might possibly be directed to other uses. As the law forbade them to *build* any more houses, the trustees had extended yet further their primary system by *hiring* premises and opening five additional schools. This was considered by the Board of Education as an evasion of the statute, the five schools were pronounced illegal, and the support asked for their maintenance was refused. Both parties again sought the Legislature, and a compromise was effected by an act, passed in 1848, admitting the five primaries to participation, but distinctly forbidding the opening or establishing of any kind of new school in any way whatsoever without consent of the Board of Education.

Meanwhile this latter body made still further advances in the development and improvement of the general system.

[1] See the following table, which also exhibits the rapid advance of the Ward Schools after the first four or five years:

AVERAGE ATTENDANCE.					
Year.	Ward Schools.	Public Schools.	Year.	Ward Schools.	Public Schools.
1842	0	15,420	1848	14,652	18,587
1843	2,079	15,938	1849	15,805	18,153
1844	6,806	15,978	1850	18,717	19,292
1845	7,522	16,602	1851	21,212	19,717
1846	8,793	17,698	1852	23,273	19,315
1847	11,538	18,646			

In 1847 four new school-houses of three departments each, and of better construction, had been built, and rapidly filled. Early in the same year a committee was appointed to inquire into the expediency of applying to the Legislature "for the passage of a law authorizing the establishment of a High School or College for the benefit of pupils who have been educated in the public schools of the city and county." On the 20th of January of the same year a report was presented "recommending that the Board should take the necessary steps to establish a Free College or Academy, and provide for the appointment of a committee to draft a memorial to the Legislature in accordance therewith. This report was adopted, and the committee thereupon appointed presented a memorial, which was approved by the Board, and forwarded in its name to the Legislature. This memorial states that 'one object of the proposed free institution is to create an additional interest in, and more completely popularize the Common Schools. It is believed that they will be regarded with additional favor, and attended with increased satisfaction when the pupils and their parents feel that the children who have received their primary education in these schools can be admitted to all the benefits and advantages furnished by the best endowed college in the state without any expense whatever.' The Legislature responded by the passage of a law authorizing the Free Academy, giving the Board of Education absolute power 'to direct the course of studies therein,' and providing that the question of establishing the same should be submitted to the vote of the people. The question was so submitted, and the result was 19,404 in favor of the Free Academy to 3409 against it."[1]

The anticipated influence of the new institution was fully realized. Thousands who had heretofore held aloof from all public schools now sent their children, and, in consequence, took direct and active interest in school affairs, and in the selection of proper parties for their management. It was soon seen that much more school accommodation would be necessa-

[1] Reports of the Board of Education, 1847, 1848, 1856.

ry. Accordingly, in 1849, three additional school buildings were opened, and at the same time introduced a new order of school structures. They were of much greater size, so that nearly two thousand children could be accommodated in a single building,[1] while their attractive and conspicuous appearance at once arrested the attention of the passer-by. They were the first of that magnificent series of buildings for the people's children which now tower aloft in so many parts of our city; plain and substantial, yet significant exponents of the appreciation in which the people hold the educational system which they subserve. The attractions of the interior have already been indicated in the sweeping changes which they forced upon the schools of the Public School Society.

The difficulties of the Society still continued to accumulate, notwithstanding the consummate skill, economy, and prudence with which its affairs were managed. The table already given eloquently testifies to the ability that, in old and now unsightly and dilapidated buildings, yet held fast their total average attendance, and even added largely to it, although some of their schools were depleted by their near and more magnificent neighbors. The furniture was old and worn-out, or had been only partly replaced by the more expensive and now indispensable styles with which their rivals were fitted. One of their largest and best school-houses had been burned to the ground, and, with the other extra appropriations required, the Board of Education could not assist them to a greater extent than $8000 in its reconstruction. A committee was appointed to make inquiry, and to report as to "which of their schools did not pay the cost of their maintenance." First one and then another of these were sold in order to assist in carrying forward the others. Large mortgages had also from time to time been effected upon their real estate, and the annual interest upon these, with the rents required for many of their primaries, together formed a heavy and increasing burden. The annual

[1] There are now some buildings in which from twelve to fifteen hundred children may be seen each morning in the Primary Department alone.

deficiencies became more and more discouraging, and the necessary appeals to the Board of Education more frequent and importunate. Assistance was rendered as far as seemed consonant to the laws and to the interests of the subject of their common efforts, and in accordance with the great trust committed to the charge of the Board. A question soon arose as to the legal right of the Board of Education to provide for the large annual interest required by the mortgages. A brief investigation was sufficient to establish the fact that they had neither legal nor moral right to carry the chronic encumbrances of a private corporation whose property, whatever the character of its present members, might at some time be diverted to other uses not in accordance with the purposes for which it was designed, and to which it had so long been honorably and faithfully devoted.

The inevitable and final result was already foreshadowed. As early as 1848, in the able report of Superintendent M'Keon, whose sound judgment, and long connection with both systems, entitled his views to consideration, may be found the thought toward which all minds were steadily gravitating. After referring to the fact that in the earlier years, and while the new system was struggling against the difficulties and prejudices which beset it, "recommendations had several times emanated from previous city superintendents to put *all schools* into the charge of the Public School Society, '*subject* to the Board of Education, through the hands of which alone its funds could be received,'" he says, "This suggestion was not heeded, and *never will be*. * * * * I venture to suggest a modification of the laws by a *compromise*, so as to *merge* the two systems. * * * * The wisdom and experience of that venerable body will be needed in the reorganization, both for guidance and for co-operation."[1]

[1] In his report for 1851, Mr. M'Keon speaks of the Public School Society as follows: "The men who founded that society were men who loved their species and country. Their schools have done much for a numerous class of persons who are now among us to speak their eulogium. But it is not in consonance with the voice of an intelligent community that a voluntary and corporate body should assume or perform the functions of the citizens at large, ex-

There was nothing in the official relations and intercourse of the two bodies to forbid so desirable a combination. Although themselves limited by the laws under which they were organized, the Board of Education from time to time, to the extent of their ability, and as far as was consistent with those great interests which were more especially committed to their care, had advanced the required funds, and assisted to meet the ever-recurring deficiencies. The Public School Society had again and again generously reciprocated in whatever could be made to advance the common interests of the schools. They had granted the use of their buildings to the Board for evening schools, and had thrown open the doors of their Saturday Normal Schools to all of the teachers of the Ward Schools who might choose to enter. In their report for 1850 they rejoice at the spirit of liberality shown in the new style of school-houses, and say that they would themselves have done the same if they had the means. They frankly state that in their opinion "the existing competition, if it may be called such, has already been an advantage to the public." In an earlier report they compliment certain of the Ward Schools for their efficiency, and "look upon the Board of Education and its teachers as coadjutors rather than competitors, and have therefore given the use of a room in the trustees' hall for the Ward School Teachers' Association." With these and many other indications of a spirit of mutual good feeling, it was not a difficult matter for them to take into serious consideration the expediency of a closer union of their efforts.

The first move came, as it should have done, from the

cept in cases of extreme dereliction on the part of the public. However beneficient their purposes, and however wise, from experience, the members of a society may become, there are many equally good and honest men who will doubt the policy of committing so great a matter as the education of the majority of the children of the whole community to an incorporated society over whose doings they have no direct control. It has been fortunate for the people of this city that men of pure intention have continued to control the councils of this great Society until other municipal and state provisions are made for the education of a large portion of the children of this community."

younger body, which at this time contained several members who were or had been members of the Public School Society, and were familiar with its history and position.

"At a special meeting of the Board of Trustees of the Public School Society, convened January 26, 1852, the following communication from a Committee of the Board of Education was read, and, on motion, ordered on record.

"To GEORGE T. TRIMBLE, *President of the Public School Society.*

"SIR—At a meeting of the Board of Education, held on Wednesday evening last, the following resolution was adopted, viz., '*Resolved*, that a committee of three members of this Board be appointed to confer with a Committee of the Public School Society for the purpose of effecting a union of the two systems of education.'

"Whereupon William H. Hibbard, Samuel A. Crapo, and Edward L. Beadle were appointed as said committee.

"Will you, sir, be pleased to lay this subject before the body over whom you preside, and signify to them the hope on our part that a similar committee will be appointed on their part, and advise us of the result at your earliest convenience?

"Very respectfully, your obedient servant,

"WILLIAM H. HIBBARD, Chairman.

"Saturday, January 24, 1852."

The subject was discussed at length, and President Trimble, together with Messrs. Peter Cooper and Joseph B. Collins, were appointed a committee to confer with the Committee of the Board of Education.[1]

At the same meeting the Executive Committee were authorized to invite the Board of Education, which hitherto had no suitable meeting-place, to make use of the Trustees,

[1] Minutes of the Board of Trustees. The committees were soon after enlarged by the appointment of Messrs. Cary, Carter, and Waterbury on the part of the Board of Education, and Messrs. Depeyster and Pierson by the Public School Trustees.

Room for that purpose. It is unnecessary to trace other than in outline the steps following one taken in such a spirit.

At an adjourned meeting, called soon after to consider the present position of the Society, the Secretary stated that the deficiency would be $32,000 more than the appropriation. After much discussion and another meeting, it was resolved to raise $40,000 by new mortgages.

At a special meeting, September 17, 1852, called to consider the financial condition of the Society, and to receive the report of the Committee of Conference, the Treasurer's Report was read, and then that of the Committee. Several motions were made without definite action. A very prolonged debate ensued, and a motion to lay the whole subject on the table failed. It was finally "*Resolved*, that in view of their present circumstances, the Board of Trustees of the Public School Society are in favor of a union with the Ward School system, *provided* they can be equitably represented in the management of all of the Common Schools of the city."

On the 15th of October, the following propositions, which had been unanimously agreed upon in the combined committee, were presented to the Board of Trustees, and were substantially those which were finally the conditions of union.

1st. The Public School Society to transfer to the city all the real and personal estate now held by said Society, subject to all debts, liens, and encumbrances thereon, the payment of which shall be assumed by the city; the property so conveyed to be forever devoted to the purposes of public education.

2d. Said Society to surrender and discontinue its organization and existence.

3d. Previous to the dissolution of said Society, it may select and appoint fifteen of its trustees to be Commissioners at large of the Common Schools, who shall serve as such during the continuance in office of the members of the present Board of Education.

4th. The said Society shall in the same manner appoint

three of its members in each ward, who shall be Trustees of Common Schools for the wards, and shall serve till January 1, 1855, 1856, and 1857, respectively.

If these propositions pass both Boards, the draft of a law shall be presented to the Legislature for consummating the union on the basis of this programme.[1]

The propositions were accepted, and the law drafted; and on the 19th of January, the whole body of the Society itself being assembled—the previous actions having been those of its trustees—the proposed act was read, and a resolution, with a very full preamble, adopted, conferring upon the trustees full power to effect the proposed transfer.[2]

The act was passed June 4, 1853, and the necessary steps rapidly followed. After raising the salaries of some of their teachers whose interests justly required this while the matter was yet in the control of the trustees, the fifteen commissioners and the trustees for the various wards were elected, and "this Board now adjourns *sine die* and *forever*."[3]

The members present, in accordance with due notice given, at once reorganized as a meeting of the Society itself, the deeds conveying the property were produced and examined, and a resolution passed to adjourn to a final meeting on Friday the 29th at 4 P.M. At this last, an eloquent address, suitable to so memorable an occasion, was delivered by Hiram Ketchum, Esq., and the votes of thanks to the President and Secretary

[1] Minutes of the Trustees: the corresponding minutes of the Board of Education are essentially identical.

[2] The long and full minutes of this meeting are very interesting, and show, as might well be anticipated, that a powerful corporation of nearly a half-century's activity was not ready to resign its existence, and its noble functions and trust, without evidences that the sacrifice was a very painful one. The preamble, after setting forth the legal history of the Society from its foundation, declares that they yield to necessity, and not to the conviction of their best judgment; and therefore authorize their committee to effect the necessary steps, and "hereby confirm all that they may do as if it were done by themselves."

[3] One can hardly read these words, written in large hand in the minutes of the last meeting of this useful body of veterans, without a feeling of regret at the necessary dissolution of so noble an organization.

F

were responded to by brief and appropriate replies. On motion, President George T. Trimble, and the agent of the Society, Mr. Samuel W. Seton, were authorized to place at the disposal of a competent writer such documents in possession of the Society as may serve to illustrate its rise, progress, and history.

A resolution was then passed, "that the Books of Minutes of the Society, the Board of Trustees, and the Executive and other Committees, together with all documents, etc., etc., be deposited with the New York Historical Society."[1]

And the resolution came at last, "that this Society do now adjourn."

Thus, by a voluntary surrender, terminated the separate corporate existence of a society without parallel in the annals of education. In the sketch that has been given, at least two important departments of its labors have been but briefly and inadequately referred to—the education of neglected children, and the relations of religious to popular and secular instruction. These will be considered in separate articles, and can not be omitted in forming a just estimate of the services of this useful body of men.

When we reflect upon the amount of labor which nearly half a century of vigilance and activity involved, the skill and prudence with which they conducted an enterprise involving questions of such magnitude, responsibility, and deli-

[1] The History of the Society, written by the party selected, is understood to have been long in manuscript, but, for some reason, has never come to light. The valuable Records ordered to be deposited with the Historical Society did not reach this their selected and appropriate resting-place until late in the spring of the present year, 1868, and the effort to obtain access to them has long delayed this report. Intensely occupied with other and exhausting labor, the compiler of the foregoing sketch had no opportunity to consult them till the heats of June and July had come. The enormous amount of manuscript to be gone over at such a time, comprising very full minutes, accumulating during the half of a century, and the brief time which could be given to the work will, it is hoped, be a sufficient excuse for such errors as have no doubt been made in the sketch. There was little time, there was no guide such as the promised "History" could have afforded, and only those who have performed similar labor under like difficulties can realize its vast amount.

cacy—the valuable time given through so long a series of years by men whose business relations made time precious, with no recompense other than the consciousness of duty performed, and the gratifying evidences that their labor was not in vain — when we remember that millions of the public money passed through their hands, and not one dollar had ever been diverted from its legitimate service, and that at the close of their long service, and notwithstanding their embarrassments, they transferred to the control of the Board of Education property valued at over $600,000, and which, when every liability was discharged, still amounted to nearly half a million—when we consider that through their instrumentality not less than 600,000 youth had been instructed, and over one thousand two hundred teachers educated and trained to service, we can not but feel that every friend of popular instruction and every lover of his race must hold this remarkable Society in grateful remembrance.

Their shortcomings, such as they were, were comparatively trifling, "and e'en their failings leaned to virtue's side." Beginning with a generous effort to give the simplest rudiments of an education to the poor and the outcast, ever the chief objects of their solicitude, many of the members were to the last practically unable to recognize the real wants or to sympathize with the advancing demands of the general public. The progressive element of the Society was too much held in check by these conscientious, well-intentioned, conservatives. Chiefly consisting of that valuable class, successful business men, who know how to unite private personal generosity with careful business thrift and economic expenditure, their sense of responsibility in spending the people's money, and their anxiety to make a comparatively small sum benefit the largest possible number, led to a policy toward their employés which plainly indicated their opinion that they had no right to be generous. Yet no one could charge them with favoritism; and as the appointing power controlled the whole field of the city, decided talent met a ready recognition in rapid promotion. As has been justly said by high authority, "They have imposed upon this city a debt of gratitude that can never be fitly estimated, much less repaid. Their inventories, vouchers, documents, and reports have been properly deposited with the New York Historical Society, but history can never tell how much these unostentatious details have contributed to the safety, prosperity, and glory of this great metropolitan city."[1]

[1] Speculations as to the possible history of education in the city of New York, had the Public School Society never been organized, would of course be out of place in a report, and could not detract from the value of their services. As a specimen of their work, the compiler would state from his own personal knowledge, that in 1835, in a ninth class of thirty-two boys, there were two future judges of the Supreme Court, at least one member of the Legislature, a City Register, several principals and assistants, and one Assistant City Superintendent of Schools, one clergyman, and three or four highly successful merchants. These were nearly all sons of men who earned their bread by daily toil. Many similar examples might no doubt be cited.

XIII.

BOARD OF EDUCATION.

1853–1868.

Beneficial Results of the Consolidation.—Measures of the Board.—Influence of the Representatives of the Society.—Depository System.—Extension of Normal School System.— Superintendent's Powers increased.— Rebuilding of old School-houses.—General Introduction of Music.—Effects of the recent War on Teachers' Salaries.—Other Expenses of the Board. —Patriotic Spirit of the Schools, and of the Community they represent.— Amendments of the Law.—Increased Powers of the Board.—Present Constitution of the Board of Education, and of the various local Bodies.

THE history of the Board of Education during the years subsequent to the combination of the two systems of schools is not marked by any striking events, or by any bitter religious controversy. Though a period of even greater activity than any preceding, its vast operations have been quietly carried on, and all parts of the system have manifested a steadily increasing efficiency.

The beneficial results of the union soon justified the anticipations of a new era in the history of the schools of the city. The gentlemen selected by the Society as its representatives both in the local boards and in the central one, were trained veterans in school matters, and thoroughly understood the importance of prompt action, and of ingrafting the results of their experience ere yet the brief three years of their legal connection with the schools should terminate. Respected and prominent members of the community at large, strong not only in their character but in their numbers, and in an essential unity of views and purposes, their unquestioned ability and long experience at once secured to them a leading influence in directing the legislation of the Board. There were now under its control, besides the ten corporate schools entitled to participate, the Free Academy, three Normal Schools, forty-six large schools, nearly all having three departments each, fifty-six Primaries, and nine Colored Schools; making, in all, two hundred and twenty-four schools, with an aggregate annual attendance of nearly forty-four thousand. As one of the first measures, the schools were all renumbered, the schools of the Public School Society retaining, in most cases, their old numbers, but changing their title to Ward Schools, the schools established by the Board taking the numbers following. This preserved a certain historic identity and continuity, and is one of many indications that the Board of Education, the legal successors of the Society, was to identify its history with their history, and to recognize its origin as in one sense the primal form of their own organization. The term Ward School was soon after exchanged for Grammar School.

Up to this period the several wards had purchased their own supplies, all books and other necessary school material being furnished to the pupils, as in the Public Schools, free of all expense. But the Society had great advantages in the economy of supplies, as all were purchased by a special committee, and upon requisition made at the general Depository, distributed at stated times, and under stringent regulations, to the several departments. The same system was now made general. The old Depository in the Trustees' Hall, now the Hall of the Board, was enlarged and stocked, pass-books for the monthly requisitions furnished, each order to be signed by the principal of the department, and approved by the proper ward officers, and an exact account kept of the supplies furnished, and the cost thereof to each school—the amount to be limited by a "tariff of supplies" annually furnished as a part of the by-laws, and based upon the annual average attendance and the general experience as to the quantity of each of the several articles required. The order being sent to the Depository-clerk, the supplies were delivered at the several schools on a day fixed in the by-laws, the city being divided into convenient districts for the purpose. This valuable and indispensable system, applied to every school from the Free College to the smallest Primary, remains essentially as it was introduced, with such improvements as time and experience have indicated.

This reform was one of the first of a series of measures acknowledged necessary by general consent, and leading to a farther and farther departure from the original Ward School system, in which each ward was in nearly every respect independent of all others, and by which, though all drew from the common purse, there was no uniformity in the proportionate amount expended.

Another important measure was the enlargement of the Normal School accommodations and the passage of by-laws establishing a Normal School Committee, and enforcing the attendance of teachers under conditions analogous, as far as the difference of circumstances would admit, to those which had previously applied to the Public Schools only. Provision was also made for an annual graduation of qualified pupils, based upon an examination of the school, conducted by the City Superintendent and under the supervision of the committee. The attendance soon rose in the Female Saturday Normal School from about two hundred to nearly six hundred, the Male Normal School and the School for Colored Teachers receiving proportionate accessions. The term normal, which early attached to these institutions, was not well chosen, as no normal instruction was given. They were really supplementary schools for teachers who did not hold the highest grade of certificates as to scholarship. In their way, they did a good work and continued in existence for several years, till their gradually declining numbers, the result, in part, of the large graduating classes, and the unpopularity of the coercive element, led to their abolition. A year or two's experience, however, pointed out the necessity of their restoration; and, in a greatly modified form, with a true and growing normal element, and the coercive principle applied only to a very limited class, they have been reopened with a larger and voluntary attendance, and are doing far more service than ever before. They will be again briefly alluded to in this report.

A third measure of yet greater importance in its permanent results was the remodeling of the system of general supervision by the Superintendent's Department. There had hitherto been only one such officer with very limited powers, and the peculiar relations of the Board of Education to the Public School Society had deprived his duties of the full measure of their usefulness. A chief Superintendent, with more extended powers, was now appointed, with a proper corps of assistants, and provision made for a frequent and stated examination into all the minutiæ of every school and department by the examination of classes of every grade, the inspection of the records, the discipline and the sanitary condition of the schools, and inquiry as to compliance with the by-laws and regulations of the Board. The examinations, licensing, and grading of teachers were also placed in the hands of this important officer. The systematic and minute inspection thus provided for has contributed, at least, as much as any other agency in advancing and securing the high standard of efficiency which now characterizes our city schools.

In consequence of the dilapidated condition of most of the school-houses transferred by the Public School Society, and of their general unfitness by size and construction for the purposes of a system of education so different from that for which they were originally erected, the Board were obliged, through a series of years, to expend large sums of money in rebuilding or remodeling such houses, and thus equalizing as far as possible the advantages offered to the citizens in all sections. Besides this, the general growth of the city demanded more and more school accommodations; a demand greatly enhanced by the gratifying fact that the growth of school attendance was vastly in advance of that of the city itself. While, in the ten years preceding the union of the two systems, the population of the city had increased sixty per cent., the attendance at the common school had increased about one hundred and twenty per cent. The houses now constructed, whether on the old or on new sites, were of substantial and superior character, and possessed of every advantage of arrangement and furniture.

In 1855 piano-fortes were introduced into the Boys' and Primary Departments and Primary Schools, having heretofore been provided in part only for the female departments. This step has greatly influenced the discipline of the schools, and rendered them pleasant, cheerful, and attractive, besides introducing a beneficial vocal training.

It is not necessary to follow in detail the various measures of the Board during the fifteen years following the consolidation. The era of improvement at that time begun, by no means ceased with the years in which it was initiated. On the contrary, each succeeding year has witnessed more or less of improvement in some one or more departments of the service, in no case more decided and general than in the one or two years immediately preceding the date of this report.

Two very important series of changes, however, demand a share of attention—the first of these resulting from the general rise of the prices of labor and all commodities, and the second from modifications of the organic law of the schools.

At the commencement of the recent war, the highest salary paid to any male principal was fifteen hundred, and to the female principal eight hundred dollars; to the various grades of assistants, from one thousand down to one hundred and fifty dollars. These rates of compensation were less than those allowed for corresponding positions in several other cities of inferior financial ability, and for services of no higher order in schools and classes averaging only from one-half to two-thirds the number in attendance. Besides this, even at that time the expenses of living in this city were largely in advance of those in any other, so that the actual compensation was practically much below its seeming proportionate amount. The effects of the war upon the remuneration of the teachers were greatly detrimental. It was not till nearly or quite every other form of labor was receiving double its former pay that the Board was enabled to increase the compensation of these its faithful servants. The city had continued to increase in population, and the demand for more school accommodation was imperative. Limited for its entire multiform expenses to a certain sum, it was not at once in the power of the Board to do full justice to its employés. An increase of about twenty, and finally about fifty per cent., was effected during the war, followed quite recently, and for similar and pressing reasons, by further advances. The salaries of the teachers and janitors of the Grammar and Primary Schools, exclusive of the Free Academy, the Evening and the Normal Schools, had risen from $703,962 in 1860 to $1,344,865 in 1865, and to $1,603,018 in 1867, or nearly 128 per cent. A part of this increase was due to the increase of the number of teachers from 1548 in 1860 to 2514 in 1867; but the chief cause was the generally and justly advanced compensation of all grades of instructors, whose individual salaries even yet, vast as they are in the aggregate, are by no means beyond a reasonable rate, as an inspection of the table will show.[1]

The same general cause has affected in an equal, and in some cases in even a greater degree, the other necessary expenses of the Board. The greater number of schools and of pupils taught accounts, in part, for the advance, but the general rise of prices is its chief element. The whole number taught in 1860 was 153,582; in 1867, 208,620—an increase of over 36 per cent.; while the sworn average attendance for 1860 was 58,505, that for 1867 was 90,183—an increase of over 54 per cent. It may be remarked incidentally, that a comparison of these figures, and especially the very much greater proportionate increase in the attendance, is testimony of the highest order as to that steady and quiet advance in the efficiency of the system which has already been referred to as characterizing this period in the history of the Board.

The total cost of books and other supplies furnished has in like manner been enhanced, even after making all due allowance for the increased number of pupils. The supplies

[1] See By-law on Teachers' Salaries.

are obtained, as by law provided, "by contract, proposals for which shall be advertised for the period of at least two weeks." The supplies for 1860 for all the various schools cost $73,845, while in 1867 they amounted to $184,370, being an increase of $110,525, or nearly 150 per cent.

This is not the place for a complete exhibit such as could readily be made of the application of the same law and cause of increase to every other department of the expenditures. The enhanced prices of the real estate from time to time needed for school sites; the great advances brought about by so many causes in the price of labor and materials employed in construction of new school buildings, and in the extensive repairs, additions, and alterations found necessary in furnishing more and more room in the old ones; the supply of fuel, and the many incidental expenses of the Board—each and all of these has felt the effects of the general financial condition of the country, and has unavoidably and greatly increased the aggregate expenditure; so that while the sum raised for school purposes in 1860 amounted to $1,278,781, it had risen in 1867 to $2,892,393.

Should we add to the expenditures of 1860 as much as 54 per cent., the proportion of increased attendance, the cost of the schools in 1867 at the rates of 1860 would have amounted to $1,969,323. Subtracting this from the actual expenditure for 1867, and we have $923,070 as the increase due to advanced prices and compensation, an estimate which is evidently too low, as the difference in teachers' and janitors' wages alone in the years 1862 and 1868 amounts to no less than $902,620—the total expense for 1868 not materially differing from the amount raised in 1867. Should we, however, add only 36 per cent., the rate of increase in the whole number taught, there would remain $1,153,251 increase due to the advance of the prices and compensation of 1867 over 1860—of which, as we have seen, about $900,000 is due to the increase of salaries of teachers and janitors' alone.

This subject has here been briefly considered on account of its prominence and importance among matters of educational interest, as exhibiting the financial effects of the war upon our Public School system.

In the multiplied duties which during the war devolved upon the various classes of citizens of the republic, we are proud to know that our schools and their teachers were not less zealous than those of any other community in our land. Many of our teachers and older pupils, in every military rank from private to general, hazarded or lost life or limb to maintain the integrity of their country. Long, indeed, is the sad yet glorious roll of names rendered forever sacred by the seal of their blood. The cannon-shot of Sumter awoke no louder echoes throughout our land than those that reverberated through the streets of the metropolis. No one who witnessed the enthusiasm of the memorable three days which succeeded, could ever doubt the loyalty and patriotism of the masses of our citizens. Each volunteer regiment had its full proportion of young men recently from our common schools, and fired with the spirit of patriotic devotion which they have ever inculcated.[1] And when the time came, as come full soon it did, that little hearts and little fingers had sad and loving work to do for the brave men who had been stricken down by the iron storm, or by the exposures of camp and field life, the grand army of school-boys and school-girls of the city of New York, under their teachers' guidance and example, did their full share in a spirit of love and gratitude, and of tender sympathy and self-denying and patriotic devotion, that gave sure indication of the soundness of their training in the schools of the people, and which will yet bear precious fruit in the long years to come. In sanitary fairs, in hospital contributions and services, in comforts and conveniences for the camp and the march, and in all their obligations and duties to the defenders of their country, our

[1] In the first regiment that started from the city the compiler recognized over thirty young men who were personally known to him as once pupils in the city schools, and afterward saw quite as large a proportion in other regiments. Many other old teachers saw in the same regiments equal or greater numbers who had once been under their instruction.

schools bore their full part and were a ready and ever-willing organization for generous collections of money and materials from every class in the community. No one could see the nation's flag waving over every school edifice, and their rooms dressed with the same sacred emblem, all at their own expense and at their own demand—no one could visit the morning assemblages in their large halls, and hear hundreds of young voices singing, with no feigned lips, hymns and songs of patriotic devotion—no one could become familiar with the earnest spirit manifested by these institutions, without being convinced that, in the grand lessons of love of country, they abundantly repaid all their cost, and that by these more than by any other agency was the future continuance of the republic to be secured.

The second of the series of changes already referred to are those arising from modifications of the organic law of the school system of the city. The Act of 1842, and the various subsequent amendments, left the powers of the several orders of school officers somewhat indefinite or conflicting. An application of the general state law established each ward as an independent district; and while it conferred on the Board of Education power to make general rules and regulations, it did not so sharply define its prerogatives as to enable it to compel compliance. Though many improvements were made and general regulations enacted especially after the combination of the two systems of schools, yet whatever of compliance there was arose chiefly from an experience of their necessity, and from the marked good sense manifested by most of the local boards.

The power of appointment and dismissal of teachers, of procuring supplies, of assigning salaries, of granting holidays, of controlling expenditures for repairs, cleaning, building, fuel, and nearly every other form of outlay, all these were claimed both by the Ward Boards and by the Board of Education, and led to much confusion and irregularity, and to great inequalities in the distribution of advantages to different sections of the city, though all were sustained by the common treasury. Some boards were nearly or quite indifferent as to the interests committed to their charge, while others, by various means, obtained undue advantages. The members of the Board of Education itself being *ex officio* members of the boards in their several wards, naturally looked more to the local interests which they specially represented than to those more general ones for which they were nominally chosen. The powers confided to the inspectors, though seemingly very extensive and searching, were really nullified by the fact that they were powerless to effect any reforms or to exert any check upon the expenditures of the local boards, had they seen fit to attempt it. In some few sections members of the local boards treated their teachers with great injustice, or were guilty of gross irregularities, the exposure of which not only brought the just indignation of the community upon the few who deserved it, but also involved in unmerited obloquy or unjust suspicion men of a far different stamp, whose duties had ever been uprightly and wisely performed, and who were entitled, by their uncompensated labors, to the respect and gratitude of all good citizens. Of course, the enemies of the system and a class of reckless writers for the public journals made the most of these scandals, and contrived to leave in a great number of minds an impression that evils, which were really exceptional and local, were more or less general. Yet the system under which such irregularities could arise was evidently in fault, and, in consequence, various successive amendments were made to the school law, conferring upon the Board of Education more definite power to remedy such abuses by the prompt dismission of the offenders—a power which they have not hesitated promptly to use in all cases where their interference was needed.

On the 25th of April, 1864, the Legislature passed an act which has already done very much to bring the entire system into full harmony and unity, and to remove nearly all, and certainly the chief sources of difficulty. The lower business wards, having a few small schools, with a limited number of pupils, had heretofore been equally represented in the Board of Education with wards that educated several thousands of children. This inequality, as well as the injurious identification of the members of the Board with the several boards of trustees, was removed by dividing the city into seven school districts of nearly equal school population, each of which sends three commissioners to the Board of Education. These commissioners hold office for three years, one going out of office, and his successor being elected each year. The Board, therefore, consists of twenty-one members, instead of the previous number of forty-four, or two from each ward. This smaller number is a decided gain, in the efficiency of its working, while at the same time the members being no longer *ex officio* members of the local boards, are not so closely identified with narrow local interests. The extension of the term of office from two years to three, and the loss of only one-third of the Board at the end of each year, insures an experienced majority in all its deliberations.

The local boards of trustees were in the same manner improved by being reduced from eight members—ten, with the two commissioners—to five, one elected each year, and holding office for five years.

The inspectors, clothed with new and enlarged powers and made equal in number to the commissioners, hold office for the same time, and represent corresponding districts; but in place of being elected by the people, are nominated by the mayor, and elected by the Board of Education.

An abstract of the law will be found in this report, and to this reference is made for the details of the organization and powers both of the central and local boards.

XIV.

THE RELIGIOUS QUESTION.

Religious teaching in the Dutch Period.—Purposes of the Free School Society at its Foundation.—Influence of the Friends.—Voluntary Association of fifty Ladies.—Religious Census of Schools.—Special moral Instruction ordered in 1819.—Visit of Moffit and Sommerfield in 1820.—Address of Moffit.— Non-sectarian Catechism and Scripture Lessons.— Bethel Baptist Church, and the Controversy of 1822.—Controversy of 1832, and Admission of Orphan Asylums to Participation. — Controversy of 1840–'42.— Remarkable Excitement.— Expurgation of School-books.— Law of 1842 establishes the Board of Education.—The present Condition of the Question.

THE Dutch colonists, as we have already seen, made religious sectarian teaching an essential part of the work of their public school. "The Heidelberg Catechism, the Articles of Religion, and instruction in the Holy Scriptures," claimed equal attention with reading and writing. The school of the Reformed Dutch Church has of course continued to teach its distinctive faith; and in the latter half of the nineteenth century follows, as the "good old way," the custom established early in the seventeenth.

The subject of special religious instruction to children on the ordinary school-days of the week first became a matter of importance, so far as the design of this report is concerned, upon the establishment of the Free School Society in 1805. The historic and legal position of this society, as the predecessor, the associate, and finally, though briefly, as an organic part of the Board of Education, the long period during which it represented all there was of instruction at the public expense, and more especially the successive struggles in which it was forced to engage in defending or enforcing its views on this subject as well as the influence which partly, through the force of traditional usage, it continued to exert upon many of our city schools long after its own legal existence had terminated, all these and yet other considerations, give this society great prominence in a review of the development of the principles underlying the question of religious instruction in the Common Schools.

It has already been noticed that the original title of the society implied the importance of religious and moral instruction—"for the education of such poor children as do not belong to any religious society." The well known character of the founders is itself enough to assure us that such instruction was an essential part of their scheme. In the first address to the public, dated May 18, 1805, and nearly a year before the opening of their first school, they say, "It is proposed, also, to establish on the first day of the week a school, called a Sunday School, more particularly for such children as, from peculiar circumstances, are unable to attend on other days of the week. In this, as in the common (week-day) school, it will be a primary object, without observing the peculiar forms of any religious society, to inculcate the sublime truths of religion and morality contained in the Holy Scriptures."[1] The adoption of the Lancasterian system seems to have led to the abandonment of the Sabbath School enterprise as originally projected; but under the limitations set forth in their prospectus, the religious element was introduced into the schools actually established, and ever remained a "primary object" in the labors of the Society. The variety of religious sentiment represented by its members, and perhaps, to some extent, the preponderating influence of the Friends, reduced the religious devotional exercises to the simple reading of a portion of the Bible to the whole school at the opening of the morning session, the use of the sacred volume or of the New Testament by the pupils as a reading-book being also introduced as a part of the regular work of each day.

It was no doubt felt by many pious persons who contributed to the support of the Society that this was far from sufficient for the great purposes of positive religious training.

[1] Signed by De Witt Clinton and the entire Board of Trustees.

Accordingly, "on the suggestion, and to meet the wishes of numerous well-meaning individuals," an arrangement was made by which a voluntary association of fifty or more ladies from the various religious denominations met in the school-room on Tuesday afternoon of each week and gave instruction from the catechisms of their various churches, the pupils being grouped according to the ascertained preferences of their parents. For this purpose a census of the pupils according to their religious connections seems to have been taken in each of the years during which this arrangement continued, until the wide extension of Sabbath Schools in the year 1816 led to the abandonment of the whole plan.[1] During its continuance the children were required to meet at the school-room on Sunday morning, and upon being divided into the proper groups, marched, under care of monitors selected from among them for that purpose, to such places of worship as had been designated by their parents or guardians.[2]

In 1819, in pursuance of their design of assisting to form proper habits, and of preventing the adoption of injurious or immoral ones, the trustees, by resolution, ordered "that the children be taught once a week to repeat some suitable passages out of tracts on the subject of the destructive use of ardent spirits; and in order that this may not be omitted, it is directed to be inserted in the by-laws." This was followed by a widely-circulated address to parents and guardians abounding with moral and religious advice both for them-

[1] The number of children educated in the peculiar tenets of each religious community is, at the present time, as follows:

Presbyterians	271	Baptists	119
Episcopalians	186	Dutch Church	41
Methodists	172	Roman Catholic	9

From the Ninth Annual Report, 1814.

The report for 1815 gives:

Presbyterians	365	Baptists	144
Methodists	175	Roman Catholics	57
Episcopalians	159	Dutch Church	33

[2] "In cases where an attendance at school previous to going to church is particularly inconvenient, liberty has been given for the children to attend public worship in company with their parents or guardians."—*Report of* 1815.

selves and their children, particularly urging the duties of cleanliness and temperance, and setting forth the importance of the Scriptures as the rule of life, of the observance of the Sabbath, and the attendance of the children upon the Sabbath Schools.

In 1820, the Rev. Messrs. Moffit and Sommerfield, of England, being in this country on a religious tour, visited, attended by a special committee, the several schools of the Society; and soon after the pupils of all their schools, with their teachers and monitors, being assembled to the number of 2300 in the large Baptist Church in Mulberry Street, were again addressed by Mr. Moffit as seemed to him suitable to the occasion. Their experience in this instance seems to have convinced the Society that they had overstepped the bounds of prudence; for an application for like privileges to those that had been granted to Mr. Moffit having been made by one Thaddeus Osgood, a travelling missionary, and probably a Quaker, it was promptly refused, and no further similar occurrence appears in all the subsequent minutes of the Society. Their own efforts to confer moral and religious benefits upon their pupils, however, by no means ceased; two thousand copies of the Universal Non-sectarian Catechism being purchased for use in the schools, and at the same time a book entitled the Scripture Lessons, a compilation for the schools of Russia, and which had also been used in England, was adopted as a reading-book for some of the advanced classes. This plan of using a catechism was soon abandoned, and never resumed.

The first serious controversy in which the Society became involved arose in the year 1822 on a question as to the participation of certain denominational schools in the distribution of the interest of the Common School Fund, and is so important, from the principles evolved in the wide discussion to which it gave rise, that it is desirable to trace it to its origin.

On the 2d of April, 1805, the same year in which the Free School Society was founded, the Legislature passed an act providing that the net proceeds of 500,000 acres of the vacant and unappropriated lands of the people of this state, which should be first thereafter sold by the surveyor-general, should be appropriated as a permanent fund for the support of Common Schools; the avails to be safely invested until the interest should amount to $50,000, when an annual distribution of that amount should be made to the several school districts. This act laid the foundation of the present fund for the support of Common Schools.[1] This fund was further added to by the proceeds of certain bank stocks, and of the lotteries authorized by the Act of 1803.

On the 19th of June, 1812, an act was passed establishing Common Schools in the state, and provision made in accordance with the Act of 1805 for the distribution of the interest of the fund. There were at this time, as we have already seen, several societies engaged in educating the poor; and on the 12th of March, 1813, a law was passed "directing that the portion of the School Fund received by the city and county of New York shall be apportioned and paid to the trustees of the Free School Society, the trustees or treasurers of the Orphan Asylum Society, the Society of the Economical School,[2] the African Free School, *and of such incorporated religious societies in said city as supported or should establish charity schools* who might apply for the same."[3] The distribution was to be in the proportion of the number of pupils on register. Under the provisions of this law, which was confined in its operation to the city of New York, and had no parallel in any other portion of the state, several religious bodies drew a certain share of the School Fund, either for new schools or for those previously established. In 1820 the Bethel Baptist Church, in Delancy Street, opened a school which, like the others, was admitted to participation.

Meanwhile the schools of the Free School Society had in-

[1] Common School System of the State of New York, by S. S. Randall.

[2] The Economical School was a school for the children of refugees from the West Indies. In 1822 it reported ninety-seven pupils on register.

[3] The first distribution of the School Fund was in 1815.

creased from the two which were in existence at the date of the Law of 1813 to four—the school No. 4 having been opened in May, 1819. The rigid economy practiced by the Society, and the comparative smallness of the expense per scholar in large schools on the Lancasterian plan, had, as early as 1816, the second year in which a distribution was made, left them an unexpended surplus, a special provision of the law of distribution being that it should be expended *for teachers' wages only*. Justly anticipating a wide extension of their sphere of usefulness, the trustees in 1817 applied for and obtained the passage of a special law in their favor, permitting the expenditure of their surplus in new buildings, or in the education of masters on the Lancasterian plan. This exclusive privilege was then understood to be granted them, because the Society, having been organized for the *sole* purposes of education, it was believed would ever hold its buildings and property sacred to that object, and consequently no perversion of the state fund could ever be apprehended in the use of an appropriation designed to extend the education of the poor in the metropolis of the state. As has been stated, No. 3 was opened in 1818, No. 4 in 1819, and arrangements were made for No. 5 in 1822.

Early in this year, the Bethel Baptist Church, through their energetic pastor, the Rev. Jonathan Chase, again sought the Legislature, and obtained powers for that organization similar to those already granted to the Free School Society; that is, power to expend any surplus in erecting new buildings and opening them for schools.[1] A second, and soon after a third school were opened by the Baptist Society, and other religious bodies prepared to follow their example.

The Free School Society soon gave expression to the alarm felt by them in common with a large portion of the citizens, while many others, and more especially of the Dutch and the Episcopal churches, made common cause with the Baptists. A warm controversy arose, and soon involved the whole question as to the propriety of the participation of any

[1] See Table on following page.

religious sectarian school. On the one hand it was claimed that the Free School Society had come to be a monopoly in the absorption of the public funds, and in all that related to the education of the poor; that by the law of the state, as by common right, each religious body was entitled to its proportionate share in the School Fund for the education of the children of the several congregations, and that buildings erected by them for school purposes were no more liable or likely to be turned to other and non-legitimate uses than in the case of the Free School Society itself. On the other hand it was contended that if the Society was in any such sense a monopoly, it was one of which every citizen had a legal right to become a member, and that such general participation in its rights, duties, and government was earnestly solicited; that the distribution of the limited amount of the School Funds among many societies deprived it of very much of its usefulness by rendering a thorough economy impossible, the result being a large number of poor schools, under poorly paid, and therefore inefficient teachers; and that a true regard for the public interests required the most careful confinement of expenditure to as few channels as were consistent with the rights of all concerned; and that as to the possibility of the perver-

The following table exhibits the distribution of the School Fund in the city of New York in 1822:

	PUPILS.	AMOUNT.
New York Free Schools	3412	$6687 52
African " "	862	1689 52
Female Association	776	1520 96
Bethel Baptist Church	755	1479 80
St. Patrick's	345	679 20
St. Peter's	316	619 36
Methodist Churches	315	617 40
Orphan Asylum	136	266 36
Episcopal Churches	124	243 04
Reformed Dutch Church	100	196 00
Economical School	97	190 12
Hamilton Free School	81	158 76
Mechanics' Society	52	101 92
St. Michael's Church	36	70 56
Roman Catholic Benevolent Society	32	62 72
German Lutheran	24	47 04
Scotch Presbyterian	23	45 08
First Baptist Church	18	35 28
Christ Church	15	29 40
First Presbyterian Church	15	29 40

sion of the property acquired by religious bodies through their unexpended balances of the school money, the facts in the special case justified all their fears in this particular. It was also declared that the Board of Trustees were ready, on behalf of the Society, to assist in procuring the passage of a law that should render their property inalienably and sacredly pledged for the avowed object of their institution, while the schools themselves should be placed under the general supervision of the Common Council as the direct representatives of the people, and that the Society would gladly unite with their fellow-citizens in any general plan for the efficient extension of the monitorial system.

A memorial was therefore presented to the Legislature of 1823, asking for a repeal of the law granting privileges to the Baptist Church, so far at least as related to the expenditure of surplus moneys, and for an amendment of the law relative to the distribution of the School Fund, so as to prevent any religious society entitled to a participation in the fund from drawing for any other than the poor children of their respective congregations. Owing to the lateness of the session, and a want of knowledge as to the facts of the case, no further progress was made than the passage of a resolution requiring the Superintendent of Common Schools to report in detail the expenditure of the school money, and the manner of its appropriation by the various societies receiving it.

The general results of this investigation are given in the 19th Annual Report of the Society, and would seem fully to justify the alarm felt, and the measures taken in regard to the alleged evils.

It is stated in this report that some 300 children had been induced by various means to leave Free School No. 3 in Hudson Street and attend Bethel School No. 3 in Vandam Street; that since by the law each society participated in proportion, not to the average attendance, but to the number on register, the Bethel Society had taken undue advantages—their reported register being 1547, while the whole number present at inspection was only 886; that one school drew money for a register of 450, yet could possibly accommodate only 300; that being allowed to expend the surplus, after paying teachers, in building more school-houses, the cheapest sort of teachers had been provided, although nominally at salaries equal to those paid by the Free School Society, both sets of schools being conducted on the monitorial system; that teacher Buyce of No. 1 testified that he signed an agreement for a salary of $900 with the understanding that he was to pay $450 of it over to Mr. Chase; that the teacher of No. 2 got $600, and agreed to return $200 as a "donation;" that by such means Mr. Chase and the Bethel Baptist Church received some $2500 per annum, and at the same time brought the Lancasterian system into ill-deserved repute by the shocking inefficiency of its management; that by funds so accumulated a building was being erected, the basement of which, dark and ill-ventilated, was to be the school provided by law, while the upper and better portion was to be devoted to church purposes; and that, owing to the success of the Baptists, other religious societies were preparing to follow their example.

They also state with great force that, having for years urged their pupils to attend Sabbath Schools for religious instruction, they are pained to find those schools now made the means and opportunity of urging children to abandon the Free Schools altogether; thus leading off large numbers of pupils, who, in their turn, naturally persuaded away others of their school-mates, and that in this manner these sectarian schools, supported by the public money, are made a most convenient means of proselyting. As a conclusive test of the results of the moral training given by the Free Schools, they assert that, although in eighteen years they had instructed 20,000 poor children, only *one* of these had been traced to a criminal court. The primary object of denominational schools being not a literary but a religious sectarian education, the consequences of such training are the inevitable sharpening of the lines dividing sects, the systematic sowing in the young mind of those germs of conscientious antagonism which had so often ripened into a harvest of blood, and the destruction of Common Schools the only common ground in which the future citizens of the republic could from their childhood learn to know and respect each other. To do this at all was a grievous evil; to do it at the expense of the public, whose future harmony was thus, however remotely, imperiled, was an offense against the fundamental principles of the republic itself.

These considerations induced the Free School Society again to apply to the Legislature in 1824 "that the religious societies might be restricted to what was justly deemed the obvious intention of the act providing for their participation in the School Fund. To a bill prepared for that purpose, they obtained the sanction of the city Corporation, who, after a full examination of the subject and mature deliberation, unanimously adopted it, and memorialized for its enactment." Several religious societies also indorsed the memorial of the Free School Society. The final action of the Legislature seems to have taken all parties by surprise. Instead of themselves deciding any of the questions involved, they passed an act transferring the whole subject of the local distribution of the School Fund to the Common Council of the city of New York, with full powers to make such assignment as they might deem just and expedient.[1]

This transfer of the duty of the decision to the Common Council led, as may well be supposed, to a most important and exciting series of debates in that body, and before the special committee which took charge of the subject. The best talent the city afforded was represented on both sides; the discussion took a far wider range than was originally proposed, and the respective parties were fully and patiently heard before this final tribunal. "The grounds on which the restriction was now advocated were, that the intention of the Law of 1813, grant-

[1] The minutes and committee reports of the Society make mention in several places of the strength and activity of the opposing "lobby," and particularly name the Rev. Messrs. Chase, Wainwright, Matthews, Milnor, Onderdonk, and some others, representing the Dutch, Baptist, and Episcopal churches, as opposed to the efforts of Rutgers, Jay, C. D. Colden, and S. Allen.

ing the church schools a portion of the funds, was solely for the education of *their own poor*, never contemplating an extension of their schools that would at all interfere with those of the Free School Society, the design of which was solely the extension of common schools, and especially for the poor. It was considered further that the principles that had heretofore guided all legislation on this subject were infringed, and a fund designed for civil purposes diverted to the support of religious institutions, contrary to the spirit of the acknowledged principles of our Government, which has ever left religion to be sustained by voluntary contributions, and the individual effort and patronage of its own votaries." The committee, "deeming that the School Fund of the state was purely of a civil character, designed for civil purposes, and that the intrusting of it to religious or ecclesiastical bodies was a violation of an elementary principle in the politics of the state and country," reported "against distributing *any portion* of the School Fund to the schools of religious societies," and in 1825 introduced an ordinance, which was *unanimously* adopted, directing the distribution to be made to the "Free School Society, Mechanics' Society, the Orphan Asylum Society, and the trustees of the African Schools."[1]

No further agitation of the question of the participation of religious denominational schools in the distribution of the School Fund occurred for about ten years. The period from 1822 to 1832 witnessed, as we have seen, extensive changes in the organization, management, discipline, general object, and even the name of the schools as well as that of the Society itself. The Free Schools had become pay schools, and then "Public Schools," and the Society was now the "Public School Society." Its income had greatly increased, while its field of labor had even outrun its means of support. The four schools of 1822 had now become twelve, in nearly every one of which was a large and flourishing Primary Department; and two other buildings equally commodious were

[1] The schools and societies cut off by this ordinance may be seen by consulting the list of participators in 1822 already given.

in contemplation, having been demanded by citizens of certain parts of the rapidly-expanding community.

It will also be remembered that in 1829 the Legislature, in response to a remarkable petition from a large portion of the tax-paying citizens, had granted for the support of the schools an annual levy of one-eightieth of one per cent. on the assessed value of city property, which was only one-fourth of the amount asked for, the remaining three-fourths having been omitted through the agency of the Common Council. In 1831 an effort was again made to obtain the full amount originally asked for by the five thousand memoralists. The Common Council, by the legislation growing out of the Baptist controversy, and through the Commissioners of the Common School Fund, were now the agents in its distribution. In compliance with the request of the Society, they presented a memorial to the Legislature in 1831, but inserted a clause providing that the proceeds of the additional three-eightieths of one per cent. "shall be and remain under the *immediate* and *sole control* of the Common Council."[1] The Society, alarmed at this new phase of affairs, made earnest efforts to have this provisional clause stricken out, in the belief that it was certain to lead to a diversion of the funds from their legitimate purposes. While the matter was still unsettled, formal application was made to the Common Council by the Roman Catholic Benevolent Society for their Orphan Asylum, and by the Methodist Episcopal Church in behalf of their charity schools for renewed admission to a participation in the school moneys. The petition in relation to the Orphan Asylum was favorably entertained by the Corporation, and referred to a committee before whom the Trustees of the Public School Society appeared as remonstrants, at the same time, through an address which was published in nearly all the newspapers, appealing to the general public.

They alleged that the Roman Catholic Benevolent Society was a close corporation, all of its members being necessarily Catholics; that the education they gave was strictly sectarian,

[1] See page 57.

and that if they were admitted to participate in the School Fund persons who had conscientious scruples against such a measure would be *forced* to contribute; and that such taxes were in fact, and to all intents and purposes, *tithes;* that the decision of 1825 had been thought to be final, and proceeded from the conviction that the school moneys ought not to be diverted, in whole or in part, to purposes of sectarian instruction, but should be kept sacred to the great object emphatically called "Common Education," and that for these reasons not only the Roman Catholic Society, but other equally benevolent societies, among them the highly meritorious Female Association, had been excluded from any share in the funds; that it was not in their special favor that they were willing to receive all orphans of every sect, similar willingness being manifested by all church schools, and, however well-intentioned, would be only a means of proselyting at the public expense, and that the sympathy naturally felt by every humane mind for their state of orphanage did not change the principle in regard to a school confessedly sectarian; that the high character, interest, and manifest usefulness of the Roman Catholic Asylum call upon the benevolent for its generous support, but only by *voluntary contributions*, and not by *compulsory levies.*

By the friends of the Asylum it was argued that the right of their orphans to the advantages of the school moneys was in every way equal to that of the inmates of the New York Orphan Asylum, who had for years enjoyed the benefits which the state thus provided for her needy and helpless little ones, and whose claim no one had thought of disputing; that if it were true that the institution whose rights they sought was in any sense a sectarian school, the same was practically and really true of the other asylum which was indeed popularly known and designated as the Protestant Orphan Asylum. Its school-books and its religious exercises were, in several important particulars, distinctively Protestant, as was also its management, although the membership of the Society was ostensibly open to all; that the petitioners did not seek to take from these friendless ones the bounty which the state had so wisely and in such Christian spirit provided, but only to have another and equally necessitous gathering of homeless children admitted to the same privileges.

They also urged that these little ones, and all such as they, though orphans, had equal rights with other children in the benefits provided for all, and that, if any distinction was to be made, the loss of their parents and their generally destitute condition really gave them greater claims than any other class upon the means provided for fitting them for a self-sustaining citizenship; that their orphanage could not cause a loss of their rights; that having now no other home, and no natural protectors to claim these rights for them, the Society was their only remaining means of so doing; that it was not asked that the chief burden, the cost of their maintenance, should be furnished from the public coffers, for they were already housed, clothed, fed, attended in sickness, and had every bodily want supplied by those "*voluntary contributions*" of the benevolent, which, as had been alleged by their opponents, were necessary for their general support, but that in the matter of education the pecuniary means were already provided for them, as for all others, by the whole community, and that they now looked to the Common Council as their civil guardians, to see that these benefits were no longer withheld.

The claims of the Asylum prevailed; the Committee of the Common Council, while directly acknowledging the soundness of the cardinal principles of the ordinance of 1825, could not but feel that the peculiar character of an orphan asylum rendered a departure from the stringent and literal application of these principles a moral and obvious necessity. Such institutions were therefore to be considered as exceptions to the general rule; and the committee having reported accordingly, their report was adopted, and the Society admitted to participation in the school moneys. At the same time the Common Council compromised with the Public School Society and its friends by striking out of the pending enactment the clause relative to the sole control of the large additional tax of three-eightieths of one per cent., and the act passed the

Legislature, directing these new funds into the old channels of distribution.

The Methodists now renewed their claim in behalf of such orphan children as were attending their church schools, and were again opposed by the Public School Society; but the Common Council, by a *unanimous vote*, decided that exceptions to the fundamental rule could only be made in the case of those who had no other home than an asylum, and the claim was accordingly rejected.

Meanwhile the trustees continued their efforts to induce their pupils to attend the various Sabbath Schools, a census of the schools having frequently been taken to determine the proportion so attending.[1] Persuaded also that there was a great middle ground upon which all believers in a divine revelation could harmoniously stand, they again endeavored to introduce some degree of systematic religious training in their own schools free—in their opinion—from all offensive sectarian bias. Toward the close of 1838 a committee was appointed "to report upon the expediency of introducing into all the schools suitable books setting forth in concise terms the fundamental truths of the Christian religion free from sectarian bias; also special articles upon the moral code upon which the good order and welfare of society are based, the substance of which shall be committed to memory by the pupils." The committee reported favorably as to the general measure, but again urged that "special care must be taken to avoid any instruction of a sectarian character; but the teachers shall embrace every favorable opportunity of inculcating the general truths of Christianity, and the primary importance of practical religious and moral duty, as founded on the precepts of the Holy Scriptures."

No practical application seems to have been found feasible of that part of the resolution which refers to the introduction of suitable books, probably from a difficulty of finding or originating such as would meet the requirements.

[1] Of an average attendance of nearly 16,000 in the year 1838, only 3337 are reported as not attending Sabbath School.

Early in 1840 the Trustees of the Catholic Free Schools made application to the Common Council, in whose hands the law still vested the distribution of the school moneys, for a proportionate share in the distribution. The earnestness, respectability, and powerful influence of the applicants, the large number of these schools, the certainty of their rapid extension with the growth of the city, and equal certainty that the success of this application involved that of all other sectarian schools, and the consequent overthrow of the "Common" School system, gave to the new controversy, which immediately arose, an importance superior to any that had preceded it. The remarkable talent engaged on both sides, the interesting and exciting debates which took place before and in the several deliberative bodies to which the subject was in turn referred, and the many and important social, political, and religious interests involved in the discussion, render it impossible within the limits of this report to do more than make brief reference to the subject, the most essential points having been already stated in the eleventh chapter in reciting the origin of the Board of Education. The intensity and extent of the excitement produced in the public mind, as indicated by the utterances of the public prints, of the pulpits, and of the many meetings of citizens called to consider and act upon what was generally felt to be a question of the first order of importance, have been already alluded to in a previous portion of this communication.

The application for participation was followed by a remonstrance from the Public School Society, copies of this and all other important documents throughout the controversy being widely circulated. Objections having been made to certain books used in the schools as containing sectarian passages and depreciating remarks and attacks upon the Roman Catholic religion, a committee of revision and expurgation was appointed by the Society in order to remove all matter to which reasonable objection could be made.

Careful examination showed that the charge was well-founded, and that the trustees had inadvertently permitted a serious evil. When patient and thorough investigation had determined its full extent, a remedy was applied promptly and completely. The expurgation was at once ordered, and the work was thoroughly done. The calm judgment of all who have since studied the circumstances of the case with the objectionable passages before them, has justified and commended this action of the trustees; while the fact that from that time to this book publishers and school trustees have been careful to exclude all such passages from school-books, so as not to expose themselves to similar difficulty, is significant and sufficient testimony both as to its justice and its policy.

A full hearing of all parties was given by the Common Council and its committees, and by a unanimous vote of the Assistant Aldermen, followed by a similar one in the Board of Aldermen, with the exception of a single dissenting voice, the remonstrance of the Public School Society was sustained, the principles of the decision and ordinance of 1825 emphatically reiterated, and the application denied.

An appeal was made to the Legislature. It is not necessary to the purpose of this report to follow further the outlines of the controversy; scarcely any important point was raised which had not been fully discussed in previous controversies. The attention which had been drawn to the subject, the interest generally taken, and the important and delicate nature of the principles involved, made the task of the Legislature no easy one. A decision could not be reached in 1841, and its transfer to the session of 1842 gave time and opportunity for the further increase of the public excitement. The proposition of the governor to extend the state system to the wards of the city, so as to allow each to manage and control its own school affairs, was felt to be the nearest approach to a settlement which could probably be made, and cut the knot that none could untie. Of course, both the contestants were disappointed. The friends of the Public School Society considered that the cause of public education had received irreparable injury, and probably its death-blow. After sufficient time had elapsed under the new system to allow the full working of its vital principle, the groundlessness of this fear was abundantly manifest, and none were more ready to acknowledge it than those members of the Society who in 1853 took their seats as members of the Board of Education.

During the first years of its existence the Board itself was by no means entirely free from trouble arising from the same subject. From the very nature of its constitution, it contained representatives of all sides of the recent controversy, and its proceedings were not altogether harmonious. But time gradually closed all important differences; changes bearing upon the religious question, and which had been proved neccessary, were made in the organic law by the Legislature; and with the acquisition of the wisdom and experience of the Public School Society to the councils of the Board, all irritation ceased, and the vexed question no longer agitates the community.

Bearing in mind the fundamental principle upon which the system was established in 1842, and that, under such limitations and checks as experience has proved to be necessary for the general interest, the several boards of trustees "have power to conduct and manage the schools," the following extract from a report of S. S. Randall, City Superintendent of Schools, will sufficiently exhibit the present condition and harmonious operation of the system as now existing. It must also be remembered that every school is open, as has been already stated, to the children of all citizens, without distinction of ward lines; so that if there be any thing in the local management unsatisfactory to any parent, there are always schools within a very short distance where no such objection will be found; and that as a result of this, all may feel safe in regard to the matter of religious influence.

"In all our public schools and departments, at frequent and appropriate intervals during the day, songs imbued with the purest principles of Christian morality form a portion of the course of instruction, and are participated in by all the pupils. In all of them, without a solitary exception, lessons and precepts of virtue and Christian conduct are daily inculcated by the teachers, school-officers, superintendents, or visitors, the fundamental principles of religion recognized and enforced, and the importance and necessity of strict honesty and integrity, undeviating truthfulness, frankness, sincerity, mutual affection and regard, obedience and respect to parents, and the conscientious and uniform observance of all the requisitions of a pure Christian morality taught by precept and example. In all of them the daily routine and discipline of the school are directly and powerfully adapted to the formation and perpetuation of habits of order, quietude, neatness, punctuality, fidelity, industry, obedience, honor, truth, uprightness, deference to the wants, the rights, and conveniences of others, and to the assiduous culture of the highest and noblest principles of action and conduct in all the varied relations of life. This is the character of the teachings of our public schools, these are the agencies and instrumentalities in daily operation within their walls; and no influences at variance with these are permitted, under any pretense, to find access or gain a footing among them. Neither the mind nor the heart of the child most religiously and scrupulously trained and disciplined in the domestic circle or the sanctuary of the Church, is exposed to the slightest contamination by the instruction or discipline of the school; while, on the other hand, every lesson of pure Christian morality or ethics, communicated in either of the former, is strengthened and confirmed by the pervading instruction and influence of the latter."[1]

In concluding this part of the report, it seems indispensable that some reference should again be made to a subject which has already received incidental mention—the expansion of the systems of Sunday School instruction. Every form of distinctive religious organization, Christian or Hebrew, is engaged, with greater or less earnestness and success, in this

[1] Report of City Superintendent of Schools.

important field of effort. In these useful institutions are gathered by far the larger part of all the children, attending, during five other days of the week, the various secular schools, public and private. Divided into little classified groups of from four or five to a dozen pupils of every age, from lisping infancy to early manhood or womanhood, they are committed to a vast array of devoted teachers, selected from the best and purest of the self-denying elements of the various religious bodies, each filled with love and sympathy for the little band of immortal spirits, and prayerfully endeavoring to instill those religious principles, distinctive or general, which they conscientiously believe necessary for present guidance and for future happiness. Each religious body, in conformity to its peculiar organization, is thus enabled to bring its choicest talent, its concentrated efforts, and its most approved supervision and direction, to the moulding of the religious character of those who are rightly considered its most precious trust. Year by year, the many powerful associations and societies, with their varying degrees of organic compactness, are developing a greater and greater skill and zeal in the special work to which they are devoted. Practically each denomination is coming more and more distinctly to realize that the true protection of the young from adverse proselyting influences is to be found, not in withdrawing them from the common ground of the future citizens, the Common School, but in thus fortifying their minds and hearts, through the teaching of parents and the systematic weekly training of special religious instructors.

XV.

THE VAGRANT QUESTION.

Original Purpose of Free School Society.—Special Efforts in 1819 and 1821.—Society for the Prevention of Pauperism.—House of Refuge for Juvenile Delinquents.—Renewed Efforts of 1828.—Appointment of Mr. Seton as Visitor.—His Reports.—Efforts of 1832.—Coercive Measures of the Common Council.—Their Failure.—Extra Meeting of 1838.—Its Report.—Results.—Five Visitors appointed.—Plan abandoned in 1841.—Relation of the Board of Education to the Question.—Industrial Schools.—Truant Laws.—Difficulties of the Subject.—Census.

THE original purpose of the Free School Society, as set forth in its first charter and title, was "for the Establishment of a Free School for the Education of Poor Children who do not belong to or are not provided for by any Religious Society." A like school, but for the benefit of female children only, had been opened a few years before by the Female Association, while both of these were preceded as early as 1787 by an essentially similar institution for the children of manumitted slaves. Both of these schools, with some others of an analogous character, were, as we have already seen, finally merged into the Free School or Public School Society, either by formal transfer or silent absorption.

In the rapid expansion which the excellence of its management, the efficiency of its system, and the high social position and devoted attention of its members secured to this vigorous society, their original function and purpose unavoidably came to be more and more subordinate to the new and wider duties which circumstances devolved upon them. Yet they never lost sight of this their first field of labor. During the whole period of their corporate existence the subject claimed and received much of their systematic and benevolent attention, and for the first ten or fifteen years gave shape, in a greater or less degree, to their entire policy. So thoroughly did they set forth their claims as conducting the schools of the poor, that to this day it is by no means rare to find persons still imbued with the idea that all public schools are, and necessarily must be, charity schools; even going so far as to censure such of the wealthier portion of the community as send their children to participate in their advantages for occupying places to the exclusion of those to whom they rightfully belong. This ingrained and antique misconception of the function of the Common Schools was a serious obstacle to their progress until after the act of 1842, by which the schools were placed more immediately under the control of the people. So complete has since been the change in the views of the more intelligent portion of the community, that such persons are more and more looked upon as curious fossil intellects, and must soon come to be an altogether extinct race.

Yet the number of poor, neglected, and untaught children is far greater than ever, increasing with the growth of the city, and calling upon the philanthropic for their most earnest efforts in their behalf. From various causes, and notwithstanding the most vigorous exertions to secure their attendance, they constitute but a comparatively small proportionate part of the vast army of children in our Public Schools. The position of the Board of Education in relation to this mass of mental and moral destitution will be considered in the sequel.

Early in 1819 a special effort was made to bring a larger number of neglected boys into the Free Schools. The Society at this time had three schools: Nos. 1 and 2 had long been established; No. 3 had just been opened in temporary quarters in the village of Greenwich, and the new building, No. 4, in Rivington Street, near the extreme northeastern limit of the city, was nearly ready for occupancy. In No. 2, a portion of the pupils being girls, it was resolved to transfer these to the schools of the Female Association, in order to make room for such poor boys as could be induced to attend. Accordingly hand-bills were circulated throughout the eastern part of the city inviting their attendance, soliciting the co-operation of the benevolent to this end, and stating that on this account no more girls would be admitted.

The subject of such poor children was again claiming the serious attention of all thoughtful citizens. It was, as we have seen, the chief purpose of the Society at its establishment in 1805. It was now again so prominent a theme among the benevolent that a society known as the "Society for the Prevention of Pauperism" had been organized,[1] its

[1] The formation of this Society was chiefly due to the efforts of a remarkable and useful man, Professor John Griscom. A portion of its labors has so direct a bearing upon the subject under consideration as to require more than a passing notice of the Society itself. It was publicly organized on the 16th of December, 1817, at the New York Hospital, at a meeting of which General Clarkson was chairman, and Divie Bethune secretary. A committee was appointed "to prepare a constitution, and a statement of the prevailing causes of pauperism, with suggestions relative to the most suitable and efficient remedies." Mr. Griscom was chairman of the committee, which also comprised seven other leading citizens. Their report was written by the chairman, and was one of the earliest, if not the first of the essays on pauperism and its preventives which have appeared in the city of New York. It is a very able document, and drew much attention both in this country and in Europe. The constitution defined the objects of the Society to be as follows: "To investigate the circumstances and habits of the poor; to devise means for improving their situation both in a physical and moral point of view; to suggest plans for calling into exercise their own endeavors, and to afford the means of giving them increased effect; to hold out inducements to economy and saving from the fruits of their own industry in seasons of greater abundance; to discountenance, and, as far as possible, prevent mendicity and street-begging; and, in fine, to do every thing which may tend to meliorate their condition by stimulating their industry and exciting their own energies." The report was an analysis of the causes of and remedies for pauperism. These causes were stated to be, 1st. Ignorance; 2d. Idleness; 3d. Intemperance; 4th. Want of Economy; 5th. Imprudent and Hasty Marriages; 6th. Lotteries; 7th. Pawnbrokers; 8th. Houses of Ill-fame; 9th. The numerous Charitable Institutions of the City; 10th. War. These were severally discussed at length, and in such a manner as to show that the writer had studied both their theory and application.

Many valuable results followed the efforts of this noble society; among them, the establishment of the first Savings' Bank, the Apprentices' Library, and the House of Refuge for Juvenile Delinquents.

The substance of this note is from a Memoir of John Griscom, N. Y., 1859, by his son, John H. Griscom, M.D.

individual members being, to a great extent, identical with those of the Free School Society. It was already practically realized that in this wide field at least two distinct departments of labor were necessary, although these might have intimate relations to each other; that the details of the adequate support and efficient management and inspection of an increasing system of schools made larger and larger demands upon the disposable time of those who had them in charge; while the growth of the city, and particularly from the character of a part of the large immigration, the great increase in this class of the juvenile population furnished abundant room for the efforts of those who would make this their sole care.

The new Society reported in 1820 that there were probably some 7000 or more children of proper age who attended no school. The entire population of the city at this time was about 130,000. A memorial on the subject was presented to the Legislature by the Free School Society in 1821, and aid asked to provide more extended accommodation, their schools being then already full. In 1824, through the agency of the Society for the Prevention of Pauperism, the House of Refuge for Juvenile Delinquents was incorporated, the institution being opened on the 1st of January, 1825.[1] It was the first of its kind in the United States, and still remains one of the most important of our reformatory agencies. Its estab-

[1] The committee whose report in 1823 led to the establishment of this valuable institution consisted of *Professor Griscom*, Isaac Collins, Cornelius Dubois, Hiram Ketchum, Daniel Lord, Jr., William M. Carter, and *James W. Gerard;* all of them gentlemen who have done much for the defense or advancement of the interests of public education, more particularly the last named, whose cheerful face, gratuitous instructive lectures, and encouraging and active sympathy, have endeared him to every pupil and every teacher in our city Grammar Schools. His interest is as marked as ever, and he is still a respected member of the Board of Inspectors of our city schools. He has the high honor of having been the actual originator of the House of Refuge, his address to the citizens of New York delivered in 1823, and now about to be republished in a special history of that institution, being the first step toward its establishment. It is a remarkable instance of wise forecast and broad and generous philanthropy. To his persistent efforts New York also owes its *uniformed* police.

lishment marks also the first of the compulsory measures which have in various sections of the country been deemed expedient to secure the education of the "dangerous or perishing classes." It was pronounced by De Witt Clinton "the best penitentiary institution ever devised by the wit or established by the beneficence of man."

In 1825 the total population under the age of 16 years was estimated at 53,000. About 27,000 were between the age of five and fifteen years, and of these 20,000 were taught, to a greater or less extent, in the various public and private schools, and about 7000 were not taught at all.[1] The direct and indirect personal efforts of the members of the Free School Society, together with those of their families and friends, had heretofore been chiefly relied upon as a means of bringing into the schools this class of neglected children.

In 1828 the evil had grown to such magnitude that the Society felt compelled to appoint a special agent to visit the families of the poor and urge the attendance of their children. They were remarkably fortunate in the selection of this officer. Among the most earnest and efficient members of the Board of Trustees was a gentleman whose cultivated mind, ready speech, affable manners, and unselfish devotion to the interests of the poor, rendered him in every way qualified for so difficult and delicate a mission. For many years he had labored in this wide field during such brief intervals as a business life affords. Now, at what he felt to be the call of duty, he abandoned his business life with all its hopes, and for a salary of $800 a year devoted all his time and all his energies to his new office of Visitor. All honor to SAMUEL W. SETON. Such men are far too few. For nearly half a century, and in various capacities, he has continued faithfully to labor for the children of our city, and still, as assistant and associate of the City Superintendent of Schools, affords us the benefit of his councils and of his long experience.

His first report, dated only a few months after entering upon his official duties, shows that with characteristic energy

[1] Approximate estimates in the 17th Report of the Free School Society.

he had already visited about 1700 families, representing about 10,000 individuals, of whom over 3700 were children. Many were induced to go to school, but much difficulty was experienced in getting them to become regular attendants.

Notwithstanding all their efforts, in 1829 and 1830 the Society was the subject of many and repeated attacks in the newspapers because of the great number of vagrant children in the streets. A careful analysis of the reports of the visitor, as well as the individual experience of other members, showed that the chief causes were the poverty and apathy of ignorant parents. In 1831 the visitor's report advises some form of coercive law, and the withholding of municipal and other assistance from all families that neglect to send their children to some school. In 1832, the Society, with growing concern at the increasing magnitude of the evil and their own comparative want of success notwithstanding their urgent efforts, appointed a special committee to investigate the condition of the same question in other communities, and to report such measures as they might deem adequate. The school system of Boston being at that time by general consent considered the most developed, the committee visited that city, to benefit as far as might be by the experience of another community. Two special queries were to receive their attention: the proportion of children of school age actually attending school, and the means found most efficient in securing attendance. In regard to the first, an immense difference was found in the relative attendance in the schools of the two cities, being largely in favor of Boston. This was chiefly attributed to the many Dame Schools for the younger children scattered throughout the city, securing the attendance of the pupils while yet very young, and thus forming habits of regular attendance not so easily established after long education in the streets alone. As we have already seen, the same policy was now adopted by the Society, and the great system of Primary Schools was established, with a success that fully established the wisdom of the measure. This was in part an answer to the second query. It was also found that in Boston there were far more stringent truant and other coercive laws, and that these were more rigidly enforced. Habitual truants were almost certain to find themselves, sooner or later, members of the School of Reformation, the local equivalent for our House of Refuge. There were also a far less proportion of the undesirable elements of immigration, and a more general and longer established popular habit of obedience to coercive laws when found necessary for the good of the general public. Efforts were accordingly made by the Public School Society for analogous restrictions. In the report in which these views are advocated, and which was printed in many of the city journals, they argued that "Every political compact implies the surrender of some individual rights for the public good. In our government, universal education is indispensable to permanency; and therefore, if parents are so ignorant or so careless as to neglect it, authority should compel. We must have safe and consistent members of society."

The subject was brought before the proper authorities, and steps were taken to carry out the suggestions of the Society. In April, 1832, the following resolutions passed the several branches of the city government:

"*Resolved*, that the Trustees of the Public School Society and the Commissioners of the Almshouse be requested to make it known to parents and all persons, whether immigrants or otherwise, having children in charge, that unless said parents and persons do and shall send such children to some public or other daily school for such time in each year as the Trustees of the Public School Society may from time to time, designate, that all such persons must consider themselves out of the pale of the public charities, and not entitled, in case of misfortune, to receive public favor.

"*Resolved*, that the Trustees of the Public School Society and the Commissioners of the Almshouse are hereby authorized to take such steps as they may deem expedient from time to time to give publicity to these resolutions, and the commissioners are hereby requested to use such means as may be in their power and discretion to carry the same into effect."

Large printed copies of these resolutions, duly authenticated, were posted throughout the city, and 20,000 other copies in the form of handbills, with a suitable caption, were circulated by Mr. Seton.

For a short time a limited beneficial effect followed these strong measures; but for several reasons it was found impossible to secure their general enforcement, and the whole plan was soon abandoned as impracticable. There were so many cases of extreme and utter poverty that a rigid application of these regulations would have been unpardonable cruelty.

The Society, however, was far from abandoning the subject as hopeless. Various efforts were from time to time made, and, in 1838, the subject again assumed such importance that on the 19th of December of that year an extra meeting of the Board of Trustees was called "to devise measures to increase the attendance, especially of vagrant children." A full report was presented by a special committee.

The chief obstacles were of two classes. The first were *moral*, and among these were enumerated the indifference and viciousness of both parents and children—the results of ignorance, intemperance, and indolence—the dislike of such children to all proper control, and their love of the excitements and amusements of the streets. The second class of obstacles were *physical*, and were only phases and accompaniments of extreme poverty—want of clothing, and the need of some help by the children themselves.

The committee had again sought the accumulated experiences of neighboring states and cities in dealing with the formidable evil. Connecticut had statutory provisions which, probably from their stringency, were rarely enforced;[1] and the opinion is expressed that "the morbidly excitable sensi-

[1] Parents and guardians were required by statute to have their children taught to read and write, and to cipher as far as through the "four rules." The selectmen were instructed to inspect the conduct of the heads of families, and, in case of neglect, "shall take charge of and bind out the children of such parents." * * * "When children or minors are stubborn and refuse to obey their parents, they may be committed to the county jail for thirty days."

tiveness of our laboring classes would not permit a scrutiny of so inquisitorial a character." An interesting communication had also been received from Boston, but seems to have embraced no new points. The various measures hitherto employed at various times by the Society were then passed in review; printed addresses, tracts, cards, circulars, visits of trustees, of teachers, and of the special agent; the last having uniformly produced the best results.

The report concludes with several recommendations: the appointment of three visitors, a modified form of compulsory law, and the establishment of a Farm Reform School in an insular position.

A memorial to the Corporation was also presented and adopted. This recites the flourishing condition of the schools, but laments "that so small a number of those for whom they were originally intended" were found in them. It asks that measures be taken to enlighten public opinion upon the subject, and that authority may intervene to prevent the stolid ignorance and indifference of parents from robbing their children of an education, and thus injuring society. It further refers to the delicate and difficult problem of "how to reconcile the principles of free government with the necessary enforcement of such laws as must supersede in such cases the parental authority," and concludes by urging the establishment of a Farm School, a renewal of the handbills of 1832, and a memorial to the Legislature for a law for the control of refractory minors.

The results of all these efforts were not encouraging. The Corporation refused all compulsory measures. Four visitors were employed by the trustees, and many children were thus brought in, but comparatively few could be induced to stay. In one report it is stated that out of 1177 vagrant children admitted, only 356 remained. The plan was faithfully tried under the vigilant attention of a select committee of five for three or four years, but with less and less beneficial results to justify the necessary expenditure, and in 1841 it was reluctantly abandoned.

In the interval between the establishment of the Board of Education in 1842 and its absorption of the Public School Society in 1853, neither of the two bodies was enabled to pay marked attention to this important subject. The time, means, and energies of the first were fully occupied, through the local boards, in establishing the various schools which were called for by the people of their respective wards. The latter body, as we have seen, had more than enough to do in continuing the schools already in their charge.

But the attention of the benevolent had by no means relaxed in relation to the interests of this class of our population. Various societies had sprung up in rapid succession, many of them occupying wide fields of labor, and most of them making the amelioration of the condition of children an important, if not the principal department of their efforts. Among these we may mention as yet in full and useful operation, the Home of the Friendless, established in 1848,[1] with its dependent schools, now seven in number and providing last year for some 3700 little ones; the Five Points' House of Industry and the Five Points' Mission in 1850; the Juvenile Asylum, the Orphan Home of the Protestant Episcopal Church, and the New York House and School of Industry in 1851; and the Children's Aid Society in 1853, now numbering, among its many-sided operations, sixteen schools, with nearly 2500 on their rolls, and providing more or less during the past year for the education, food, and clothing of at least 4000 children. Conspicuous among the various agencies in this unspeakably important work, directly or indirectly originating many of the above-named institutions, and assisting many thousands of suffering families so as to enable them to keep their children at the Public Schools, was that yet active society, the "New York Association for Improving the Condition of the Poor."

The efforts of the Roman Catholic Church have also been largely directed to the same field, and many noble institutions both on this island and its immediate neighborhood

[1] The American Female Guardian Society itself was founded in 1834.

bear eloquent witness to the comprehensive and practical benevolence of this ancient organization.

Most of these schools and asylums, together with others previously or since established, have been admitted to participate in the school moneys, subject to the inspection of the Board of Education; a list of those so participating will be found in the statistical portion of this report.

In 1853, under pressure of the influence of large numbers of benevolent persons, the Legislature passed a stringent truant law, applicable to cities and incorporated villages throughout the state. "It authorized the arrest of all such children between five and fourteen years of age, and their examination before a magistrate. If their parents or guardians did not give bonds to send them to school or keep them employed, then the magistrate could issue his warrant to commit them to some place of detention—the almshouse, jail, or penitentiary, until they could be bound out to service. It was made the duty of the cities and villages to provide some suitable place for the reception of such children, their employment, and their education in the elementary branches of knowledge, and for their proper support and clothing."[1]

About this period the subject became a prominent topic of interest in the deliberations of the Board of Education. Scarcely a year has since passed in which it has not been felt to be a matter of extreme concern, and in some years has been the chief subject of anxiety. There are two principal considerations which have constituted the basis of this anxiety: first, and most important, the urgent necessities of this particular class of children themselves; and, secondly, the fact that the necessity to the whole community that education should be *universal* is a main, and even the chief argument for its public support; in other words, that the increase of this necessitous and dangerous class of our juvenile population places in jeopardy the very foundations of public instruction. The question has been attacked with greater or less vigor. Its consideration by successive Boards, constitutes a very large share

[1] As given in abstract in Superintendent Rice's Report.

of the documentary history, but it still remains an unsolved problem. The difficulties are manifold, and complex in their character. The Board of Education very properly has no form of police power. The authority to arrest vagrants, and the authority to dispose of them, are committed to other and not always harmonious branches of the city government. There is also a deep-seated feeling that the masses of our city population, and especially the classes more directly interested, would not peaceably allow the general enforcement of such laws as we now have. It is also apprehended that the cry of "religious proselytism" might easily be raised upon the slightest basis, popular resentment of official interference be aroused upon the occurrence of some unavoidable mistake, and the peace of the community be thus put in danger. These fears are probably more or less unfounded, yet, in connection with some other considerations, they have heretofore assisted to prevent any continued and general effort to carry out the provision of the law. Already overburdened with so many other duties and responsibilities, our justices naturally shrink from a department of action so difficult, troublesome, and delicate. While the openly vicious and criminal may be promptly disposed of, police officers would naturally hesitate to arrest children whose only crime is to have parents so poor as to be unable to furnish them sufficient clothing to go to school, who possess no home but the crowded, ill-ventilated room in some dirty tenement-house, and whose only place of exercise is the public street. The number of those who may be classed as suffering extreme poverty is beyond conception, except to those whose self-imposed philanthopic labors have made them familiar with the homes of the poor. The experience of the Public School Society has been again and again confirmed by that of the Ward Schools. Where the lowest orders of such pupils are brought in, it seems almost impossible to induce them to continue, and the causes of this must be obvious to every experienced student of human nature. In the majority of instances, both they and their parents are extremely sensitive concerning their personal appearance when brought into contrast with those who are better provided for, and avoid this added suffering by their absence. Both children and parents need material aid—food and clothing, and the opportunities and inducements to personal cleanliness. These are indispensable in securing their attendance, but their supply is beyond the province of the Board of Education. It has again and again been demonstrated that the efforts of public officials must ever be inadequate to master the giant evil. The demoralizing effect of training this class of the community to rely upon public support instead of their own exertions is but too well known.

It is these considerations that give such importance and value to the labors of the benevolent societies that have made this the chief or entire department of their philanthropic efforts. A host of unofficial visitors and other agents actuated by the noblest motives, and learning by continued experience a proper discrimination in granting relief, reduce the evils both of destitution and of injudicious charity to their lowest practicable limits, and endeavor to assist the poor to the opportunities and habits of self-reliance. The individual history of these excellent institutions does not lie within the province of this report.

In regard to the number of children between five and fifteen who do not attend any school in the course of the year, the most vague estimates have been made, ranging from 20,000 to 60,000. No thorough school census of the city has ever yet been taken; the nearest approach to it being that already referred to in 1829, and the more full one embodied in the statistical tables of this report.

There is great difficulty in making any correct estimate of the number of children in our city who never attend any school. It has been set as high as fifty or even sixty thousand. That any such estimate is merely an extravagant guess, will be apparent from a few considerations. The present total population is probably not far from one million. The many lines of travel by boat and rail radiating from the city as a centre have removed from us to suburban homes a large proportion of a class of families which furnish the most regular attendants upon schools both public and private. In consequence of this, there is an increased proportion of poor families in every grade of poverty whose children's services are indispensable to their parents, either from the wages directly earned, or by their staying at home in charge of those yet younger while both parents are away at employment. This causes a very irregular attendance. The wide prevalence of this state of things is in part indicated by the fact as shown by the special census after making all allowances that there are 15,000 less girls who can attend school during the year than there are boys. Most of these have been several years at school, though more or less irregularly, but were withdrawn, as the school registers show, at as early an age as ten or eleven years, or even younger. They can not, in any just estimate, be classed as vagrants. So great is the demand for the services of children, both boys and girls, that only 29 per cent. of school children, regular and irregular, are twelve years of age or over.

The numerous parochial schools include great numbers of the same class, those supported by the Catholic Church alone reporting their whole number taught during the year at over sixteen thousand. A large part of the newspaper boys and bootblacks attend school during a part of the day, and follow their out-door occupation before and after school-hours. Of the rest, most have reached or are beyond the years at which the greater number of pupils leave school permanently. Very many of these attend evening school. As already stated, our total population is not far from a million. The proportion of clerks and other resident adults from country districts is very large, and greatly reduces the proportionate number of school children. The whole number reported as taught in all the various grades of public and private schools is about 270,000. Deducting from this 25,000 for adults in the various advanced institutions and in the evening schools, and 27,000 attending private schools, besides the large number taught at home, and making every allowance for pupils counted twice by reason of readmission or removal of residence, and for those who attend first the public and then the parochial schools, it will be apparent that of unemployed children of school age who attend school during no part of the year, the number, though far too great, must be much less than is usually estimated, probably not exceeding ten or fifteen thousand, if indeed it is so many. For a more exact estimate, we need yet to know the actual population of the city, the real number within the school age, and the number of readmissions annually made in all schools, private, public, and parochial.

To this end it is highly desirable that the Board of Education should cause a special census of the city to be taken, to ascertain with the utmost possible accuracy all the necessary data—not only the actual numbers of such children, but the special condition of each locality in all important details. Such a measure will furnish the essential basis for a systematic and intelligent practical treatment of the evil. The necessary expense of such census would be well repaid in the beneficial results sure to follow.

XVI.

ORGANIZATION AND PRESENT CONDITION OF SCHOOLS.

Number and Classification of Schools.—Primary Schools.—Grammar Schools. —Evening Schools.—Normal Schools.—Colored Schools.—Condition and Course of Study of each.—College of the City of New York.—Teachers.—Their Examination, License, Appointment, Removal, Salaries.—General Control and Supervision.—Departments of the Clerk and Superintendent.

THE schools under the full control of the Board of Education and the local boards are designated as Primary, Grammar, Evening, and Normal Schools. Each of these classes is divided into schools for whites and schools for colored pupils, the latter being known as Colored Schools. The institution recently known as the Free Academy, which was under the direct and sole control of the Board of Education, has been erected into the College of the City of New York, with all the ordinary powers and privileges of such institutions, the members of the Board of Education being *ex officio* its trustees. It is therefore a separate and distinct organization, and not under the control of the Board.

Besides these, are forty-one schools, under a variety of benevolent associations, subject to the jurisdiction of the Board of Education, and participating in the apportionment of school moneys.

The corporate schools are variously distributed, more than half of them being Industrial Schools, under the control of the American Female Guardian Society and the Children's Aid Society, the latter organization having sixteen schools.

The condition of the different classes of schools will be briefly considered. The course of study in each is also submitted.

The following list exhibits the classification and whole number of schools:

	WHITE.	COLORED.	TOTAL.
Normal Schools	1	1	2
Grammar Schools for boys only	40	2	42
Grammar Schools for girls only	42	2	44
Grammar Schools for mixed	9	2	11
Primary Schools for mixed	87	5	92
Evening Schools for males	13	0	13
Evening Schools for females	11	0	11
Evening Schools for mixed	0	3	3
Evening High School	1	0	1
Corporate Schools	37	4	41
Total	241	19	260

PRIMARY SCHOOLS.

The City Superintendent of Schools has provided for a thorough supervision of the various schools and departments, by assigning to two of his assistants the special charge of the Primary Schools. Every effort is being made, with the co-operation of the local officers, to advance these schools to their highest possible efficiency. The most improved methods of instruction are introduced, incompetent or unfaithful teachers are carefully weeded out, and the sure progress of the system in general provided for in the better training of these little ones, who will soon, in their turn, constitute the more advanced departments.

On the importance of this class of schools it is not necessary to dwell. Their pupils are a majority of the whole number under instruction. The large foreign element in our city, and its peculiar character and condition, with the great number of those who, from various causes, are only able to keep their children at school for a limited period, render these Primaries, in some respects, the most valuable and essential part of our whole system. A large part of the pupils are not able to continue their attendance through the Grammar Departments. Many reach only the higher classes in these introductory schools. It is therefore the more essential that the training in these shall be of the highest order suitable for their grade, and that the course of study be arranged so as to meet as fully as possible the necessities of the case.

The efficiency and popularity of these departments are unmistakably manifested in their universally crowded condition. From every part of our city the cry comes to us for more room. Greatly increased accommodation in this respect is urgently needed. Many of these schools have several hundreds more in attendance than they can in any proper sense accommodate. Should all be provided with room, with proper reference to the laws of health and the best opportunities for instruction, should the space allotted to each pupil be equal to that which is given in some other cities, it is evident that we should have many more school edifices, and that this would only supply the present demand, without any reference to the increased attendance from year to year.

The high rents and the great number of tenement houses, exert a marked influence upon school accommodation. With the advancing rates, a greater and greater number of families come to occupy a given number of houses, and the number of children attending school in the district steadily increases. The character of their homes renders it all the more essential that the school-room should present the opposite condition of things, and supply the maximum of light, and air, and room consistent with a true economy.

When this crowded state of these departments is taken into consideration, the excellent condition of these schools, as regards both discipline and scholarship, is a remarkable evidence of the skill, patience, and energy of the teachers, and of the efficiency of the general management which has made these traits the rule and not the exception. Never, in their entire history, have they been in so decided a condition of usefulness; never have the results of the instruction given been of so high an order; yet, with proper accommodation, even these results must be exceeded.

The following is the

COURSE OF STUDIES IN PRIMARY SCHOOLS:

FIFTH GRADE.—ALPHABET CLASS.—*Reading*—Alphabet and familiar words from blackboard or chart; exercises in enunciating simple elementary sounds of letters.

Numeral Frame—Counting and adding on numeral frame by ones and by twos.

Arabic Figures—Reading at sight any number from 1 to 99.

Object Lessons—Teaching the children, by means of common objects, to observe simple forms, colors, positions, and parts of objects, of the human body, and of familiar animals; each lesson to be conducted with a view to cultivate *habits of attention and observation.*

PRIMER CLASS.—*Reading and Spelling* from charts, blackboard, and primer, with illustrations of the meaning of the words used; exercises in enumerating elementary sounds of letters.

Numeral Frame—Adding on numeral frame by twos, threes, fours, and fives; also taking away ones, twos, and threes, from greater numbers.

Arabic Figures—Reading at sight numbers through three figures (999), and writing numbers on slates as far as 100.

Roman Numbers—I, V, and X, with their combinations.

Object Lessons—The subjects of the alphabet class continued, with new objects and illustrations.

Tables—Adding with and without the numeral frame, by fours, fives, sixes, sevens, eights, nines, and tens; also taking threes, fours, and fives from greater numbers.

Mental Arithmetic.—Simple questions in addition, chiefly with concrete numbers.

Object Lessons—On form, color, place, size, and parts of objects, for leading the pupils to make observations on common things not in the school-room. Let the teacher give simple descriptions of familiar objects, and the pupils give their names from the descriptions.

Lessons in Morals and Manners—Continued by means of school incidents, reading lessons, etc.

THIRD GRADE.—*Reading*—In the last half of a First, or the first half of a Second Reader.

Spelling—With simple *definitions;* also spelling by the elementary sounds, as far as necessary, to correct faults in pronunciation.

Punctuation—With the uses of the common marks in the sentences read.

Roman Numbers—Through C, D, and M.

Written Arithmetic—Numeration through 100,000,000; additions through examples of six or seven short columns.

Mental Arithmetic—Simple questions in addition and subtraction.

Multiplication Table—Through 6 times 12.

Object Lessons—Continued on form, color, place, size, and human body, with lessons on animals, plants, common minerals, and qualities and uses of objects, directing the children's attention to such qualities only as may be readily perceived. Place forms, familiar objects, and pictures, before the pupils, and request them to give simple descriptions.

Lessons in Morals and Manners.—Continued.

SECOND GRADE.—*Reading*—In a Second Reader.

Spelling and Definitions—The meaning of words illustrated by their use in short oral sentences; also exercises in elementary sounds, continued as above.

Punctuation—Continued with applications.

Roman Numbers—Reviewed.

Written Arithmetic—Through subtraction, and in multiplication by one figure.

Mental Arithmetic—In subtraction and multiplication.

Multiplication Table—Through 12 times 12.

Drawing and Writing on Slates—From copies on blackboard or charts.

Object Lessons—Extend the subjects of the preceding grade.

Lessons in Morals and Manners—Continued.

FIRST GRADE.—*Reading*—Lessons of the grade of those in the last half of Second Reader.

Spelling and Definitions—The pupils to illustrate the meaning of words by using them in short sentences, oral or written.

Written Arithmetic—Through multiplication and division by two figures, with simple practical applications.

Mental Arithmetic—In multiplication and division.

Tables—Division, time, weights, measures, and Federal money, taught by illustrations as far as practicable.

Geography—From outline maps—the hemispheres, and North and South America; also the definition and description of continents, mountains, islands, bays, rivers, etc.

Writing and Drawing on Slates—From copies, also writing from dictation words and short sentences.

Object Lessons—Select objects that require descriptions which will embrace form, color, size, parts, uses, materials, etc. Extend place so as to include the chief objects in the local geography of the city and the prominent locations in this vicinity; adding descriptions necessary to prepare the pupil for an intelligent use of text-books on geography.

Lessons in Morals and Manners—Continued.

Vocal Music—Practiced throughout the school.

Home Lessons—No lessons shall be given to be studied after school-hours, nor shall any text-book be taken from the schools except by pupils in the two higher classes.

GRAMMAR SCHOOLS.

A corresponding arrangement is made in the case of the Grammar Departments. Two of the assistant superintendents are especially assigned to this class of schools, thus insuring, as in the case of the Primary Departments, a minuteness of supervision and a consequent thoroughness and efficiency that, in the result, may safely challenge a parallel in any school system in the world.

The course of study for Grammar Schools presents six regular grades and several supplementary. These last are intended to meet the wants of a large number of pupils whose parents desire to have them instructed in certain subjects beyond the ordinary Grammar School Course. A glance at the list will show the high character of the instruction demanded. Many of these pupils remain with the design of becoming teachers, and the largest part of the appointments made by the various local boards are of graduates from these supplementary classes.

In all the Grammar School grades much attention is given to arithmetic, both for its directly utilitarian and for its disciplinary character. While securing a thorough knowledge of business arithmetic, beginning, as will be seen from the following course of study, at an elementary stage, at every step of the process the subject is made the means of disciplining the reasoning powers—of doing for the lower part of the course of study that which geometry does for the higher.

Mere rules are never relied upon, are not learned till a pupil has been taught to give clearly, and in his own language, a connected statement of the course of reasoning involved in the solution of the problem. Servile dependence upon a text-book is never allowed. The teacher is required to teach the subject, and not the book, which, when used at all, is to be only an accessory.[1] It is this vigorous process

[1] The following extract from a recent special report upon the schools of the city of New York very clearly indicates the plan pursued, and its importance as an element in the system.

"But the most important feature in the New York Schools is that the course of instruction is indicated by the *subject of study*, and *not by text-books*. There is no uniformity of text-books. The local committee, the trustees in each ward, order the use of such as they may select from the list permitted by the Board of Education, and they are sometimes similar and sometimes different in different schools. But the Board of Education determine the *subjects*

of training, applied not only to arithmetic, but, with the proper modifications, to all other subjects of study that, steadily accumulating its results as the successive grades are reached, and fixing the proper mental habits, is the chief agent in that constant advance of the system to which reference has been made, and which becomes more and more operative as the teachers throughout the city enter into its spirit.

Much attention is given to geography, as being important in a commercial city, as an assistant to a proper knowledge of history, as indispensable in preparing for that great teacher of the citizen, the daily newspaper, and as a means of disciplining the mind while increasing the general intelligence, and developing the ability of the pupil to give a clear, connected, oral statement. As will be seen, the other subjects receive due share of attention.

COURSE OF INSTRUCTION IN GRAMMAR SCHOOLS.

SIXTH GRADE.—Reading, of the grade of a Third Reader, with a review of punctuation and Roman numbers, and exercises on the subject-matter of the lessons; spelling and definitions, from the reading lessons, with exercises on

---

that shall be pursued by the different grades, and these are uniform in all the grades, and in all the schools; and as the programme of instruction and study is thus indicated by subjects, the examination is by subjects, and not by text-books, and is conducted by experts—by the Superintendent and his assistants—that is, by persons who are *masters of the subject*, and care nothing about particular text-books. * * * * The New York teacher, on the other hand, knowing that his pupils are to be examined not by or in any particular text-book which he uses, but in the general subject of that text-book, and that they will be expected to know all about it up to the point which the pupils of that grade should reach at the time of the examination, has no inducement to confine himself too closely to the text-book, or to make its particular forms the mode and limit of his instruction. On the contrary, the text-book becomes only a help, hardly a guide, and nothing of a restraint or boundary; but through that, and a large amount of oral instruction and conversation, the teachers aim to give the pupils a broad, general comprehension of the subject, so that they may understand and be able to answer questions on that subject in whatever form they are put. * * * * The two features which have just been considered—the programme of instruction indicated by *subjects*, and *not by text-books*, and the consequent examination by the Superintendent in subjects, and not in text-books, seem to be giving to the New York Schools a remarkable degree of uniformity, and a steady progress in each school."—*Boston Report*, 1866.

the formation, spelling, and definition of compound and derivative words; the meaning of words also to be illustrated by requiring the pupils to use them in sentences; written arithmetic, through the simple rules and Federal money, with practical applications; mental arithmetic, as far as in written arithmetic, to include exercises in the analysis of operations and examples, and in rapid calculation without analysis; tables of weights, measures, etc., reviewed, with practical illustrations; geography, primary geography reviewed, and outlines of North America, including the United States, with definitions, and illustrations by means of the globe, of the form, magnitude, and motions of the earth, latitude and longitude, etc.

FIFTH GRADE.—Reading, of the grade of a Third Reader (latter half), with exercises as in the Sixth Grade; spelling and definitions, from the reading lessons, with the exercises of the preceding grade, continued; written arithmetic, through common fractions, with their simple practical applications; mental arithmetic, to the same extent as in written arithmetic, with exercises in analysis and calculation; geography—to include a full knowledge of the United States, and the other divisions of North America, including descriptive geography.

FOURTH GRADE.—Reading, of the grade of a Fourth Reader, with exercises as in the preceding grades; spelling and definitions, as in the preceding grades; with instruction in the meaning of the prefixes of derivative words; written arithmetic, through decimal fractions, and their practical applications, with a review of common fractions; mental arithmetic—analysis of common and decimal fractions, with exercises in calculation; geography, local and descriptive, through South America, with a review of North America; English grammar commenced—the analysis and parsing of sentences, containing principal parts and simple word adjuncts, with definitions of the terms used.

THIRD GRADE.—Reading, of the grade of a Fourth Reader (latter half), with particular attention to emphasis, intonations, and variety of expression, and with exercises on the subject-matter continued; spelling and definitions from the reading lessons, with exercises in writing miscellaneous words from dictation, and instruction in the prefixes and suffixes of derivatives; written arithmetic, through the compound rules and reduction, with denominate fractions, both common and decimal; mental arithmetic—a review of preceding grades, with exercises in calculation and analysis applied to compound numbers and denominate fractions; geography, both local and descriptive, through Europe and its divisions; English grammar, the analysis and parsing of sentences, with simple phrase or clause adjuncts; history of the United States—early discoveries, and the outlines of colonial history.

SECOND GRADE.—Reading, of the grade of a Fifth Reader, with exercises as in the Third Grade; spelling from the reading lessons, with exercises in writing miscellaneous words, and in the analysis and construction of words according to the rules for spelling; definitions, from the reading lessons, with instructions in etymology, including the prefixes and suffixes, and easy Latin roots; written and mental arithmetic, through percentage, and its application to commission, insurance, stocks, and interest, both simple and compound; geography, both local and descriptive, through Asia, Africa, and Oceanica; English grammar—the analysis and parsing of easy complex and compound sentences, with exercises in the correction of false syntax and in composition; history of the United States through the War of the Revolution; algebra (for boys only), through fractions.

First Grade.—Reading, spelling, and definitions, as in the Second Grade; etymology continued, with the analysis of words and their formation from given roots; written and mental arithmetic, for girls, through the problems of interest, discount, profit and loss, and proportion; for boys, through evolution; exercises as in preceding grades; geography, local and descriptive, reviewed, with outlines of physical geography, and exercises in map drawing; English grammar—the analysis and parsing of sentences of ordinary construction, with the correction of false syntax, and exercises in composition; history of the United States—outlines completed and reviewed; astronomy—the solar system, with a description of the sun and planets, and definition of terms; Constitution of the United States and book-keeping (for boys exclusively); algebra (for boys), through simple equations.

Penmanship shall be taught in each grade of the above course. Instruction in sewing may be given in the Female Schools.

Every pupil passing a thorough examination in the studies prescribed for the Grammar School Course shall receive a certificate of graduation for that course which shall entitle to promotion to the Supplementary Course.

SUPPLEMENTARY COURSE OF STUDIES FOR FEMALE GRAMMAR SCHOOLS.

In addition to the regular course of studies above prescribed, the following Supplementary Course may be pursued in the Female Grammar Schools:

Second Grade.—For a period not less than one year; arithmetic and English grammar reviewed; physiology; astronomy; algebra, through simple equations; natural philosophy, including mechanics, hydrostatics, and pneumatics; ancient history; geometry, through the first book of Legendre, or an equivalent; composition; elocution.

First Grade.—For a period not less than one year; review of English grammar and arithmetic; algebra, through quadratic equations; higher astronomy; natural philosophy, completed; rhetoric and composition; modern history; geometry, through the fourth book of Legendre, or an equivalent; elocution.

SUPPLEMENTARY COURSE FOR MALE GRAMMAR SCHOOLS.

The following course of studies may be pursued in the Male Grammar Schools, to occupy one year or more, as may be necessary; arithmetic and English grammar, continued and reviewed; algebra, through quadratic equations; geometry, first four books of Legendre, or an equivalent; mensuration; elements of natural philosophy, chemistry, and astronomy, science of government, including a knowledge of the government of the United States, and the general provisions of the State Constitutions, with a brief outline of municipal and international law; book-keeping; mechanical and architectural drawing; declamation and composition.

STUDENTS FOR SUPPLEMENTARY COURSE, HOW SELECTED.

The City Superintendent of Schools, or one of the assistant superintendents, shall select at every examination of a Grammar School such of the pupils as may be found qualified to pursue the Supplementary Course, and additional pupils, who have not attended any Grammar School during the year next previous, may also be admitted to the Supplementary Course by the principal of the school; but no class shall be formed in the Supplementary Course with less than fifteen pupils, nor shall any such class be continued, if the actual average attendance of pupils for a period of three months be less than fifteen.

MUSIC, DRAWING, LATIN, GERMAN, ETC.

Exercises in vocal music shall be given in each Primary and Grammar School, and instruction in musical notation and reading shall be given to the pupils of the First, Second, and Third Grades, and of the Supplementary Course in Grammar Schools; drawing, with exercises in perspective, and the delineation of objects, shall be taught in the same grades. The Board of Trustees may also authorize the Latin language to be taught in any Grammar School in the ward in which the Supplementary Course is pursued; but the same shall be taught only by teachers employed in the schools to give instruction in other branches of study. The French or German language may be pursued in connection with the studies of the first and second grades, and the Supplementary Course of studies.

A WEEKLY REVIEW IN EACH CLASS.

Once in each week there shall be in every class of each course a review of the studies of the previous week, at which review all text-books shall be laid aside by teachers and pupils.

PUPILS PASSING EXAMINATION IN STUDIES OF SUPPLEMENTARY COURSE ENTITLED TO GRADUATION.

Every pupil passing a thorough examination in the studies prescribed for the Supplementary Course shall be entitled to a full certificate of graduation.

REGULATION OF STUDIES OUT OF SCHOOL.

No lesson shall be given to a pupil to be learned out of school, until it shall have been sufficiently explained and illustrated by the teacher to the class; nor shall the lessons assigned for such preparation be such as to acquire a period of study each day, in the case of a child of average capacity, longer than two hours. Exercises in grammatical analysis and parsing, and written and mental arithmetic, shall not be assigned for home study except to pupils in the First Grade or the Supplementary Course.

LIMITATION OF STUDIES TO THE PRESCRIBED GRADE.

The studies of each grade shall be pursued in the order herein prescribed, and without the addition of any study or studies belonging to a higher grade or to the Supplementary Course.

REVIEW TO PRECEDE EXAMINATION FOR PROMOTION.

Every examination for promotion to a higher grade, shall be preceded by a thorough review of all the studies pursued in the previous one.

CITY SUPERINTENDENT TO REPORT VIOLATION OF COURSE OF STUDIES.

It shall be the duty of the City Superintendent and his assistants, at each visitation of a school or department, to inquire specially whether the provisions relating to the course of study have been strictly followed; and the City Superintendent shall, without delay, report the case of any violation of the same to the Board, stating the name of the principal of the school and the teacher of the class concerned in such violation.

EVENING SCHOOLS.

The Evening School system constitutes an important part of the educational institutions of the city. The tendency in our day to diminish the number of hours given to physical labor is giving time and opportunity for mental improvement to thousands who have hitherto been cut off from such advantages.

The advanced age of the pupils, as compared with those of the Day Schools, brings with it greater maturity of judgment, and a more just estimate of the value of the opportunities which the school offers. After making all allowances for the exhausting effects of previous physical labor upon the nervous system, there still remains a capacity for improvement which, whenever the will of the pupil is fully aroused, leads, under judicious training, to the most valuable results.

For the present season, these schools are twenty-five in number—thirteen for males and twelve for females. Each school is held in a separate building. The term commences on the first Monday in October, and, exclusive of the usual holiday vacation, continues for eighteen weeks. The sessions are held five evenings in each week, from 7 to 9½ P.M. for the males, and from 6½ to 9 P.M. for the females. No pupils are admitted excepting those whose ages or avocations are such as to prevent their attending the Day Schools. At the application for admission, they must be accompanied by some responsible person, or present to the principal some satisfactory evidence as to their identity and respectability. No male pupil is admitted who has not reached the age of fourteen years, and no female who has not attained the age of twelve. This restriction as to age has been found necessary in certain cases, in order to restrain parents from taking their children from the Day School at too early an age for physical labor, and relying upon the Evening School as a means of their obtaining the rudiments of an education.

Reading, spelling, definitions, and penmanship are taught in all the classes. When the other attainments will justify it, geography is taught by means of the outline map and oral instruction. No female teacher can be employed in any Evening School for males who has not had at least two years experience as a teacher in a male Grammar School, and no teacher can hold a position of any grade in any Evening School who has not been specially licensed for such position by the City Superintendent of Schools.

Corporal punishment is not allowed, the penalty for persistent disobedience or immoral conduct being dismission, and pupils thus dismissed can not be admitted to any Evening School in the city without the consent of the City Superintendent of Schools, into whose hands the general supervision is committed, with essentially the same powers and duties as in the case of the Day Schools.

The principals of these schools are required to report every two weeks to the Clerk of the Board the average attendance of pupils and the number of teachers employed. In case the average per teacher falls below thirty, the number of teachers is reduced, while, if increased attendance will warrant it, additional teachers are employed.

Adult classes are an interesting feature in these Evening Schools. Every effort is made to attract that large class of persons already spoken of whose hours of labor are such as to give time and opportunity to devote a part of their evenings to improving their education. In several localities, large numbers of foreigners attend for the purpose of learning the language. In one male school on the east side of the city, no less than four hundred Germans attended with this object, and were taught by three competent teachers.

EVENING HIGH SCHOOL FOR MALES.

The sessions of the school begin on the first Monday in October, and are held for a term of twenty-four weeks, exclusive of the holiday vacation. The restrictions in regard to admission are similar to those of the other Evening Schools, excepting in the higher grades of attainment necessary. Pupils are required to pass a good examination in reading, spelling, elementary geography, and grammar, and in arithmetic, through common and decimal fractions, and their applications to denominate numbers.

COURSE OF STUDY.

The course of study embraces the following branches: English grammar and composition; reading and declamation; penmanship, book-keeping, and arithmetic; algebra, geometry, and trigonometry; natural philosophy, chemistry, and astronomy; American history and political science, the latter to include a knowledge of the Constitution of the United States, the State Constitution, with the outlines of municipal and international law; architectural and mechanical drawing; practical mechanics; navigation; and the French, Spanish, or German languages may also be taught, provided the number applying for instruction in the same or any one of them shall be at least fifteen. No class thus formed shall be continued in case the average attendance for the period of one month shall be less than ten.

Pupils may be admitted to receive instruction in any part of the course, or in any single branch of study under the direction of the principal, and it shall be the duty of the latter to arrange an order of exercises for each evening, and give public notice of the same.

In addition to the principal, there shall be a teacher of English grammar, reading, and declamation; a teacher of penmanship, arithmetic, and book-keeping; a teacher of algebra, geometry, and trigonometry; a teacher of natural philosophy, chemistry, and astronomy; and a teacher of history and political science, with such other assistants and special teachers as may be required.

The classes and special subjects are taught by a full corps of teachers of high ability, among them several experienced principals of Grammar Schools, under a competent general management.

NORMAL SCHOOLS.

There are two Normal Schools, one for white and the other for colored teachers. The sessions are held on the Saturday of each week, from 9 A.M. to 1 P.M. The pupils are themselves teachers, engaged in the several schools during the week, or graduates from the supplementary classes of the Grammar Schools who desire to become teachers.

Every teacher employed in a Primary or Grammar School holds the Superintendent's certificate of qualification and license to teach, which is either of the first, second, or the third grade, and known as A, B, or C. Certificates of Grade C are no longer issued, although a limited number of the Primary teachers continue to hold them. Those holding the certificate of Grade A are excused from other than voluntary attendance upon the Normal Schools; those holding Grade B are excused if teaching in the Primary Schools; all others, unless excused by the Committee on Normal Schools, are required to attend until they obtain at the Normal School examinations a higher grade certificate. The teachers thus attending as pupils are formed into classes having a course of study in many respects similar to that of the supplementary classes of the Grammar Schools. Their number is steadily diminishing, few appointments being now made unless with certificate of Grade A.

But by far the largest and most interesting portion of the actual attendance is of a voluntary nature, and the number is steadily increasing. These pupils are formed into what are known as the post-graduate classes; they already hold the highest certificate required, yet attend the school for mutual benefit and instruction. It is therefore a perpetual "teachers' institute" of a high order. Among the most regular attendants are many of our experienced and successful principals of Primary and Grammar Schools, who week by week set the noble example of placing themselves as learners side by side with their junior assistants, many or most of whom have been their own pupils. The exercises are almost exclusively normal in character, and have special reference in the several post-graduate classes, to the wants of the teachers of the Primary, Grammar School, or supplementary portions of the general course. An earnest desire is manifested to learn, discuss, and adopt the best methods of instruction and discipline, and to assist in every way in advancing the general character of the system. The exercises being as far as possible conversational, or made the subject of discussion, it will be seen that the amount, variety, and character of the experience thus concentrated and contributed must make this school a central point of influence of our entire system.

When it is remembered that all this is voluntarily done, at the cost of a large part of the Saturday holiday, and at the close of a week of severe labor, it is not too much to say that such a spirit manifested by those holding such high positions is one of the strongest assurances that can be given that the system has the elements of a true and healthful growth, and that it will continue to hold and to deserve the confidence of the community.

Another element which distinctly marks the function of this interesting school is the fact that its classes are in the charge of veteran teachers, nearly all of whom are principals of Grammar Departments, and that included in the corps are three of the City Superintendents, one of whom is the principal of both the Normal Schools. The Saturday's instruction is thus made to tell with the utmost directness upon both Primary and Grammar Schools, contributing no small share to the excellence of the general result.

COLORED SCHOOLS.

These are graded in the same manner as those for white children, into Primary, Grammar, and Normal Schools. After being the charge of a special committee of the Public School Society, they passed in 1853 to the care of the school officers of the several wards in which they are situated. The change was not, upon the whole, beneficial. While, in some cases, they received proper attention, in others, from obvious causes, they were either wholly or in part neglected.

The recent act has placed them directly in charge of the Board of Education, who have appointed a special committee for the purpose, and systematic efforts are being made to advance as far as possible the general condition of this class of schools. Better houses are in process of erection. Every opportunity and convenience is afforded that is given any other class of schools. The teachers are of the same race as their pupils. They have many difficulties to contend with, chiefly those arising from the irregularity in the attendance of their pupils. The pupils themselves are gathered from wide areas, some of them coming from long distances. Yet in consequence of the new and encouraging measures adopted by the Board and its committee, an improvement has begun which, it is hoped, will continue to mark their future history.

COLLEGE OF THE CITY OF NEW YORK.

This institution continues to hold the same relation to the Common Schools of the city as under its former title and organization. Its students must have been pupils in the Public Schools, the conditions of admission being as follows:

CONDITIONS OF ADMISSION OF STUDENTS.

No student shall be admitted to the College unless at the commencement of the next term he shall be fourteen years of age, and have attended the Common Schools for twelve months, and shall have passed a good examination in reading, spelling, writing, English grammar, geography, arithmetic, elementary book-keeping, history of the United States, and algebra, through quadratic equations.

PRE-REQUISITES TO EXAMINATION FOR ADMISSION.

No candidate shall be examined for admission unless he shall present to the President of the College a certificate in the form prepared by the Executive

Committee, signed by the principal of the school or schools of which he has been a member, and specifying the age of the candidate, the Common Schools of this city which he has attended, the length of time in each, and when. If the number qualified for admission shall be more than can be admitted, the preference shall be given to those who have attended the Common Schools the greater period.

REQUISITES OF ADMISSION.

At either of the regular examinations students may be admitted to one or all the classes, to pursue the studies of any one or more Departments, provided they shall have attended the common schools the requisite period, shall be of the proper age, shall pass the proper examination in the requisites for admission, and an examination satisfactory to the faculty, in the previous studies of the class or Departments to which they are to be admitted.

TIME AND MANNER OF EXAMINATION.

The examination of candidates for admission shall take place immediately after the general examination in July, and at such other time or times as shall be fixed by the Executive Committee, and shall continue at the same hours until concluded. No person shall be present at the examination except the instructors of the College and members of the Board of Trustees, and other school officers. Neither the names of the candidates, nor the schools from which they come, shall be made known to the instructors conducting the examinations, but each candidate shall be designated during the examination by a number given him on a card by the President.

RETURNS OF EXAMINATION TO BE MADE TO FACULTY.

The instructors conducting the examination shall make full returns of the same on a scale of ten to the faculty, who, from such returns, shall certify the names of the candidates who have passed the requisite good examination, and also the result of the examination of each candidate, which shall in all cases be recorded in a book kept for that purpose. The examination papers of each student shall be preserved and filed.

EXAMINATION AND LICENSING OF TEACHERS.

For the examination and licensing of teachers, the following rules and regulations have been adopted by the City Superintendent.

Candidates for examination must, in all cases, have attained the age of seventeen years, and must have made, or be about to make, application for a situation actually vacant, or expected soon to be vacant. The fact of such vacancy must be attested by a certificate from one of the trustees of the ward, or the commissioners of the district within which said vacancy exists or is expected to occur. Satisfactory evidence of good moral character will also be uniformly required; and in the case of pupils of any of the Grammar Schools, the recommendation of the principal, and his or her certificate of character or deportment.

The qualifications for the several grades are as follows:

GRADE B.—[For teachers of Primary Schools.] Reading, spelling, definitions, English grammar, geography, mental and written arithmetic, through percentage and proportion, penmanship, and outline drawing. Also a knowledge of the methods of teaching proper for Primary Schools, including object teaching in its application to number, form, color, size, etc., as well as lessons on animals, plants, common minerals, and the qualities and uses of familiar objects.

GRADE B.—[For teachers of Grammar Schools not above first assistant.] Reading, spelling, definitions, etymology, English grammar, with parsing and analysis, elementary astronomy, history of the United States, geography, mental and written arithmetic, through evolution, penmanship, algebra, through simple equations, and geometry, through the first book of Davis's Legendre, or an equivalent.

GRADE A.—[For Females.] Same as above, with higher astronomy, arithmetic complete, algebra, through equations; second, third, and fourth books of geometry, with the applications to problems and mensuration; ancient and modern history, natural philosophy, physiology, and rhetoric.

[For Males.] Geometry, through spherical; trigonometry; and outlines of chemistry, in addition to the preceding.

A certificate for a limited period only will be conferred, except to such candidates as have shown by actual experience in the schools of this city or elsewhere ability to impart instruction, and success in discipline.

The examinations are held in the presence of the inspectors designated by the Board of Education on Friday of each week, commencing at nine o'clock A.M. Candidates are requested to present their credentials previous to the day of examination. No candidate after rejection will be re-examined until after the expiration of three months.

In the case of limited certificates, they are usually given for six months or a year; and if, at the end of that period, the holder has given satisfactory evidence of a proper ability to teach and to govern, a full certificate in the usual form is granted. If no such ability has been manifested, the license expires by limitation, and is not renewed.

APPOINTMENT AND REMOVAL OF TEACHERS.

It is provided by law that

The schools in the several wards shall be classified as Grammar, Primary, and Evening schools, and teachers for the said schools shall be appointed as follows: Principals and vice-principals by the Board of Education, upon the written nomination of a majority of the trustees of the ward, stating that the nomination was agreed to at a meeting of the Board of Trustees at which a majority of the whole number in office were present. Other teachers shall be appointed by a majority of the trustees for the ward at a meeting of the Board of Trustees. Any teacher may be removed by the Board of Education upon the recommendation of the City Superintendent, or of a majority of the trustees for the ward, or a majority of the inspectors for the district. The Board of Trustees for the ward, by a vote of a majority of the whole number of trustees in office, may also remove teachers employed therein other than principals and vice-principals, provided the removal is approved in writing by a majority of the inspectors of the district, and provided further, that any teacher so removed shall have a right to appeal to the Board of Education, under such rules as it may prescribe; and the said Board shall have power, after hearing the answers of the trustees, to reinstate the teacher.

These regulations are the more important in that it has been the custom in the city of New York from the foundation of the Free School Society not to make annual appointments of teachers, as is believed to be the general practice elsewhere. Once appointed, no new appointment is required for the same position, and the teacher is secure, so long as he or she faithfully performs the duties assigned.

The Board by regulation also provides

That no teacher shall be appointed principal or vice-principal of a Grammar School except of Grade A, and no assistant teacher shall be employed therein without a certificate equal to Grade B. No teacher shall be appointed principal or vice-principal of a Primary School without a certificate equal to Grade B.

It has also been found necessary to provide

That the salary of any principal or vice-principal whom this Board, after the application of any Board of Trustees, shall have refused to remove from his or her position, and the salary of any teacher, whose appeal to this Board from the action of a Board of Trustees in removing him or her from the position he or she held, shall have been sustained; and the salary of any teacher whose removal, by request of a Board of Trustees, has not been approved by the inspectors of a school district, or a majority of them, shall not be reduced by any Board of Trustees below the amount he or she received at the time said Board took action to effect the removal of such principal, vice-principal, or teacher, without first obtaining the approval of this Board.

It will thus be seen that every care is taken in the licensing of teachers, that, when necessary, they may be promptly removed, and that competent and worthy teachers are protected from all hasty, injudicious, unjust, and oppressive measures, and made to feel that faithful performance of duty will furnish them that guaranty which justice demands.

No principal of any school is obliged to teach a particular class. His duties are chiefly those of general supervision and superintendence. By frequent visits to the several class-rooms, as well as by the general rules he may adopt, he may so influence the whole department as to make it throughout bear testimony to his faithfulness and skill. This regulation is believed to be peculiar to the schools of the city, and is a large element in their success.

SALARIES OF TEACHERS.

The following are the by-laws relating to the salaries of teachers.

1 *Male Department.*

The salaries paid to male principals of schools shall be based upon the average attendance of their respective Departments, for the year ending on the preceding 31st day of December, and shall be as follows, viz: For each school having not more than one hundred and fifty pupils average attendance, two thousand two hundred and fifty dollars. For each school having more than one hundred and fifty, and not more than three hundred average attendance, two thousand five hundred dollars. For each school having more than three hundred and not more than five hundred average attendance, two thousand seven hundred and fifty dollars. For each school having more than five hundred average attendance, three thousand dollars.

To vice-principals of schools having more than one hundred and fifty average attendance, two thousand dollars. To male assistants, where but one is employed in a school having more than one hundred and fifty average attendance, fourteen hundred and fifty dollars; when more than one is employed, an average not exceeding fourteen hundred dollars.

To female assistants, an average not exceeding seven hundred and twenty-five dollars.

2. *Female Departments.*

To principals of each school having one hundred pupils or less in average attendance, twelve hundred dollars. For each school having more than one hundred, and not more than one hundred and fifty pupils in average attendance, thirteen hundred dollars. For each school having more than one hundred and fifty, and not more than three hundred average attendance, fifteen hundred dollars. For each school having more than three hundred, and not more than five hundred average attendance, sixteen hundred dollars. For each school having more than five hundred average attendance, seventeen hundred dollars.

To vice-principals of schools having more than one hundred and fifty average attendance, eleven hundred dollars. To assistants, an average not exceeding six hundred and fifty dollars.

3. *Primary Departments and Schools.*

To principals for each school having two hundred pupils or less in average attendance, one thousand dollars. For each school having more than two hundred, and not more than four hundred pupils average attendance, eleven hundred dollars. For each school having more than four hundred, and not more than six hundred average attendance, thirteen hundred dollars. For each school having more than six hundred average attendance, fifteen hundred dollars.

To vice-principals of schools having more than three hundred, and not more than ten hundred pupils average attendance, nine hundred dollars. To vice-principals of schools having more than ten hundred pupils average attendance, one thousand dollars.

To assistants, an average not exceeding five hundred dollars. The minimum salary paid to any teacher employed in the schools under the control of this Board shall be four hundred dollars. The section shall not apply to teachers who have not a full or permanent certificate.

CLERK'S AND SUPERINTENDENT'S DEPARTMENTS.

The duties of these officers, and especially those of the Superintendent, are fully stated in the law, of which a copy is found in this report. Yet the practical working of their powers and duties is so clearly and succinctly set forth in a masterly report which has recently been published in a neighboring city, that liberty is taken to transcribe some of its statements, as apposite to this occasion.

"Under the administration of the system as carried out by the Board of Education, a degree of order, precision, and energy of action has been attained, which has carried, and, if persevered in, must continue to carry forward the great work of popular education in the city of New York with a steady and strong progress, both in the broadness of its diffusion and the excellence of its character. In the administration of the system, while it is important that all its officers should be competent and faithful, yet its practical efficiency is largely dependent upon the capacity and fidelity of two of these officers: First, the Clerk of the Board of Education, who has under him a deputy clerk, and as many assistant clerks as the Board may direct, all of whom are under the direction of the clerk. We can not undertake to enumerate all his powers and duties, but we can only say generally that his office is the centre around which the whole work revolves, the point from which essentially every thing emanates, and to which it returns; and the returns are required to be made so full and precise, and the record of them kept so perfect and so arranged, that it is possible to obtain at the clerk's office at any time all the essential facts in relation to every school, viz., the names, number, salaries, grades of its teachers, the number of its pupils, the average attendance, and the amount of supplies of all kinds, books, stationery, fuel, etc., with the cost of the same; also the cost of repairs, cleaning, rents, gas, printing, advertising, etc., and this for each District School, from the Free Academy down to the smallest Ward School. Second, the Superintendent of Public Schools and his assistants, who visit and examine the schools, as to their condition and progress, and the fidelity and efficiency of the teachers. As the clerk's office is the centre of the material administration of the New York system, so the superintendent's office is the centre of its intellectual and moral efficiency, of the character of the schools as instrumentalities of education, and of the character of the teachers as competent and efficient instructors, exemplars, and guides to the young. The trustees of the ward have the power to appoint the teachers of all grades in the schools of the ward, but the superintendent virtually determines from among whom the appointments shall be made, and the tenure of office depends mainly upon him, because no person can be appointed as teacher by the trustees unless holding a license or certificate, signed by the superintendent, stating the grade of teacher for which the holder is qualified; and if subsequently experience, reached through the visits and examinations of the superintendent or his assistants, shows that the holder is not qualified, wants tact, energy, efficiency, or is in any way incompetent or unfit for the work, the license or certificate is revoked, and the teacher removed. This plan of intrusting the visitations and examinations of the schools, the power to judge of the practical efficiency, competency, and fidelity of the teachers, etc., mainly and specially to experts, to persons appointed to the work because their culture, mental habits, and experience specially fit them for it, must tend to make the schools progressive, to secure the services of the best teachers and the adoption of the best methods.

"Of course there are other officers, such as the superintendent of school buildings, the engineer, the inspector of fuel, and the various sub-committees of the Board of Education, whose fidelity in the special work assigned them contributes largely to the successful working of the whole organization. Yet it seems to be mainly through these two channels—the Clerk of the Board of Education, with his assistants, and the Superintendent of Public Schools, with his assistants, that the New York system has reached its thorough and exact *external*, its spirited and progressive *internal* administration."

XVII.

SCHOOL-HOUSES.

School-houses of the Public School Society.—Successive and Recent Improvements.— Specimens of New Buildings.—Illustrations.—The general Policy of the Board as to School-houses.

In looking over the history of the Common Schools of the city of New York, some consideration must necessarily be given to an examination of the nature of the buildings erected for the use of these schools, both on account of the extent of the provision that has been made in the way of sites and buildings, and because the schools themselves must be helped or hindered—in all that pertains to their efficient usefulness—by the character and condition of the accommodations provided for them. While very much or most of the success of a school depends on the ability of the instructors engaged in its management, it is yet a matter of no little importance that the school-house and its appointments should be of the best character that it is possible, in the circumstances of the case, to give. There is a sort of inspiration almost about a well-arranged and properly-appointed building that affects both teachers and pupils, makes the work of the school-room seem easier, and gives that cheerful and hopeful spirit by which success is attained.

The construction and arrangement of school-houses in this city have undergone numerous changes within the last half-century, all of which have been made with a view of obtaining the best type—for the time—of a city school-house. And it is interesting to note through these gradual changes that the progress made has been almost uniformly on the same line, as though the various improvements that have been introduced from time to time were but an amplification and

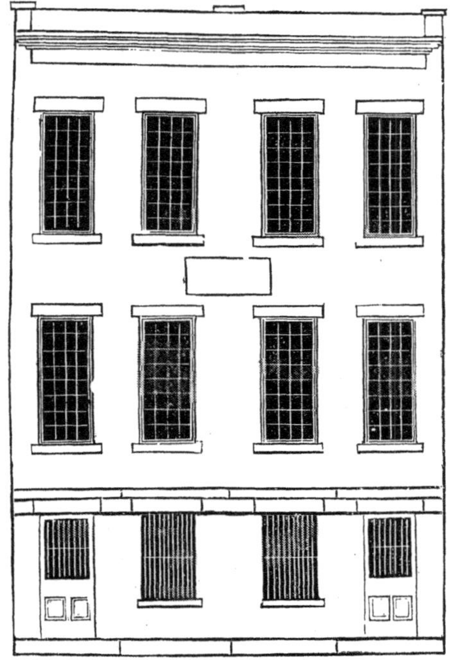

A PRIMARY SCHOOL.

FIGURE 1. (Front View.)

Elevation of a Primary School, built on a lot of ground 25 by 100 feet. The first story is used as a play-ground, which is more fully explained in Fig. 2. The main building is 25 feet front, by 62½ feet deep; the stair building is 27 feet by 11 feet 8 inches. The main building is placed 6 or 8 feet from the line of the street, according to the depth of the lot. The walls above the ground are built entirely of brick. The roof is of tin, and the gutters of copper. The lower doors and windows have iron bars inserted for safety and to admit a free circulation of air in summer, but are closed with sashes in the winter.

The sashes in all the Primary Schools are hung the same as those in the Public Schools, so as to be moved up and down at pleasure. The first story, or play-ground, is 7½ feet high in the clear; the second and third stories, each 12 feet high in the clear.

Figures 1 and 2 exhibit the plans and elevation of a Model Primary School House (for two departments) adopted by the Public School Society. That Society, after 1844, erected all their Primary Schools after this plan.

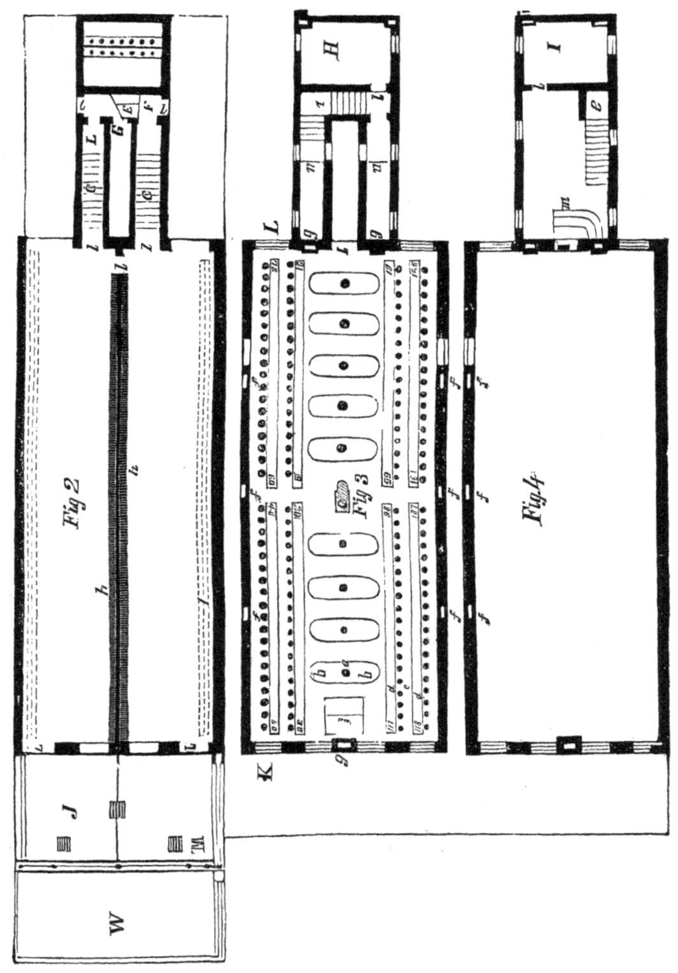

FIG. 2.—GROUND PLAN OF FIRST STORY, OR PLAY-GROUND, YARDS, PRIVIES, STAIR BUILDING, ETC.

N—Side-walk, blue-stone flagging.

J—Court-yards, blue-stone flagging; separated from the side-walk by iron railing.

C C—Stairways; the side on which Fig. 2 is marked leading to the Boys' Department, or third story.

F L—Places for pine (kindling) wood, under the stairs.

E—Sand-box for both departments.

h h—Piles of wood, about 4½ ft. high.

I I—Lines on which the scholars are marshalled previous to entering school.

natural outgrowth of the original idea brought about by the experience gained in the workings of the system.

The school buildings erected by the late Public School Society were all built upon the same general plan, and that plan—owing no doubt to the limited funds of the Society—was a very economical one. Their "Model Primary School-house" was built upon a single lot, covering the whole width—twenty-five feet—to a depth of sixty-two feet, and at that point was joined by a rear stairway wing some eleven feet wide by twenty-eight feet long. By this reduction in the width, some rear light was secured; but this was of service only on the brightest days, and when the fresh air and sunshine were not shut out by rear buildings on adjoining lots.

Plans of one of these buildings are herewith presented, which will show very clearly the arrangement of the several floors.

It will be seen that compactness and severe plainness are the main features of this plan. A building like the above accommodated about three hundred and fifty scholars. The arrangement of seats was very inconvenient, yet one of these buildings was considered, thirty years ago, as a great improvement on any thing that had preceded it.

The buildings for "Public Schools," as they were called, corresponded to the present Grammar School-houses, and contained rooms for three departments, which were designated as "Boys'," "Girls'," and "Primary." The last of these was located in the basement, the floor of which was generally about five feet below the sidewalk line, and the ceiling perhaps the same distance above it. The "Girls'" school was on the main floor, and the "Boys'" on the upper, or second floor. The Primary consisted of one large room, comprising the whole space enclosed within the walls, which was divided in the middle at times by sliding doors so as to separate the smaller children—the abecedarians—from those who were more advanced in their studies. For the accommodation of these little ones, a gallery of rising steps was provided at one end of the room; for the larger scholars, there were two rows of seats next the walls on the sides and opposite end of the room, and the teacher's desk being placed midway between the two sections, near the line of the sliding doors, necessitated "giving the cold shoulder" to one division when facing the other. By the arrangement of seats referred to, a large space was left in the central portion of the room for marshaling the scholars, and for the numerous drafts of the monitorial system.

The Boys' and Girls' Departments were usually similar in their plan, and were much better arranged for seating purposes than the Primary; yet even in these schools the facilities for instruction were very limited. Usually but two class-rooms were provided, and these would each seat about fifty pupils, the remainder of necessity received were taught in the large room, or alternated in the use of the two class-rooms. A visitors' entrance at the front led to two, and sometimes to all of the Departments, and pupils' entrances for each department were located at the rear of the building. This was in many cases a long, straight, narrow stairway, and external to the building.

The capacity of these buildings was for about ten or eleven hundred pupils. The accompanying diagrams, representing "Public School No. 17" (now Grammar School No. 16), on West Thirteenth Street, in the Ninth Ward, will give a general idea of the arrangements of the floors of such a building as has been described; but this being the last but one of the buildings erected by the late Public School Society, has embraced in it many improvements that were not to be found in the earlier buildings, not the least important of which is the abandonment of the under-ground basement, the providing of one or two more class-rooms, and the adoption of staircases having frequent landings. Such buildings, being of small size, were not as economical as they might at first seem. They required a large number of buildings for a moderate number of pupils; and were the same sort of economical views to prevail now, and school-houses to be built upon the plans just considered, it would require for the accommodation

GRAMMAR SCHOOL HOUSE NO. 16.

(Formerly Public School No. 17.)

THIRTEENTH STREET, NEAR THE SEVENTH AVENUE.

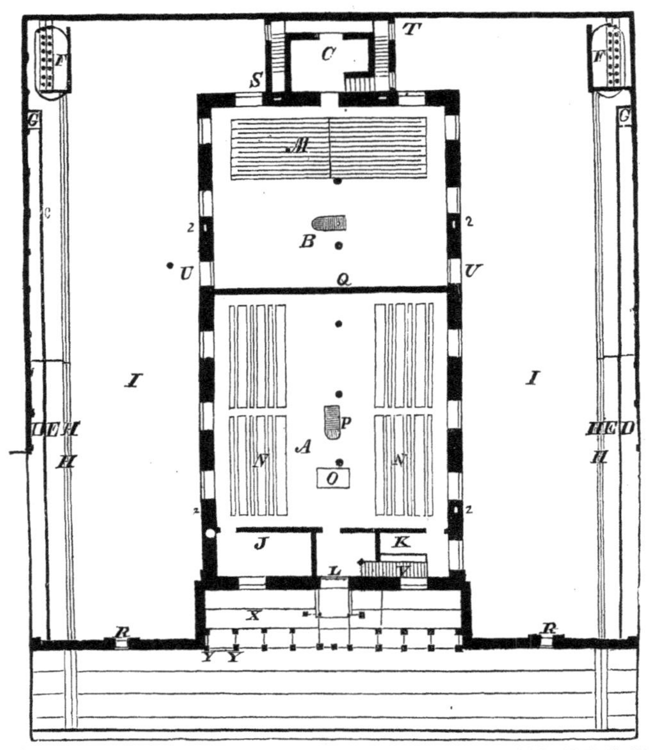

FIG. 1.—GROUND PLAN OF PRIMARY DEPARTMENT, YARDS, WOOD-HOUSES, ETC.

A—Primary School-room, 39 by 38 feet.

B—Infant School-room, 39 by 30 ft.

C—Room in stair building for brooms, brushes, pails, etc.

J—Boys' wardrobe, 16½ by 8 ft.

K—Girls' wardrobe, 12½ by 8 ft.

M—Gallery, 32 by 11 feet; seats for 200 children.

N N—Desks, each 16½ feet long—each 12 or 13 scholars.

O—Teachers' table.

L—Front door, or main entrance.

The stations for the classes, when reading, is in the centre passage, fronting the desks. All doors open outward.

R R—Gates, or scholar's entrance.

U U—Scholars' entrance to Primary Department.

S—Scholars' entrance, Boys' Department.

T—Scholars' entrance, Girls' Department.

Q—Sliding-doors, 28 by 9½ feet.

P P—Stoves.

Z Z—Flues, or chimneys.

I I—Play-ground, or yard, 102 by 26 feet; paved with brick.

D D—Wood-houses, 83 by 2½ feet, and 6 feet high; the front of which is made of hemlock strips, 4 by 2 inches, set perpendicularly 2 inches apart, to allow a free circulation of air.

E E—Roof of wood-houses, projecting 3½ feet beyond the front of the houses; forming a shelter for the scholars in stormy weather.

H H—Gutters of blue stone, to conduct the waste water from the wood-houses and yards to the street.

F F—Privies, 12 by 8 feet.

G G—Boxes for sand, 3 by 2½ feet.

W—Front walk, blue-stone flagging.

X—Court-yard, 8½ feet wide.

Y Y—Stone foundation blocks, to which iron railing in front is secured.

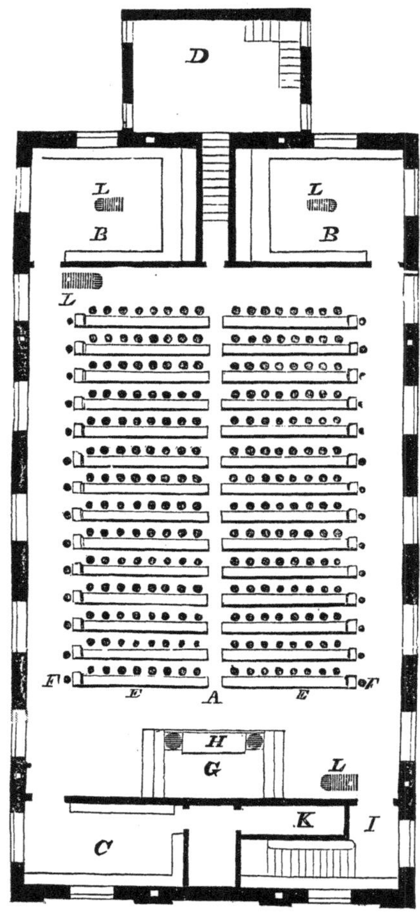

FIG. 2.—GROUND PLAN OF THE BOYS' DEPARTMENT, OR THIRD STORY; AND WILL ANSWER ALSO FOR THE SECOND STORY, OR GIRLS' DEPARTMENT, EXCEPT SOME SLIGHT DIFFERENCES IN THE STAIRS.

A—School-room.
B B—Recitation-rooms.
C—Recitation-rooms.
D—Receiving-room, and scholars' entrance; this room is furnished with a sufficient number of cloak and hat hooks, to accommodate all the scholars in each department.
I—Front entrance and stairway.
K—Book closet.
L L L L—Stoves.
G—Platform.
H—Teachers' desk, with a shelf at each end for globes.
E E—Scholars' desks; each 12 feet 8 inches long—19 inches for each scholar.
F F—A seat at the end of the desk, with a movable shelf for the purpose of a desk.

The front of the teachers' desk toward the scholars is formed by a blackboard 3 feet wide, and extending the whole length of the desk.

of the present number of children attending the public schools of this city, nearly two hundred buildings instead of the eighty or ninety that are now used for the purpose, and the cost of managing the school system would be greatly increased.

It is unnecessary at this late day to enter into any argument in favor of large buildings as being more economical—either in construction, repairs, or convenience, than an equivalent number of small ones for school purposes. The *fact* is too long and too well established to require any thing to be said to substantiate it.

It has already been stated that the "Model Primary School" on a single lot, as formerly erected, gave accommodations for some three hundred and fifty pupils. The modern Primary School on two or three lots gives much better accommodation for three or five times that number. It will be noted that the modern plans, both Grammar and Primary, furnish a large number of class-rooms; by which the schools can be thoroughly classified, and the ends of teaching be better subserved.

When, in 1853, the Public School Society was united with the Board of Education, that society transferred to the Board some thirty-four buildings which were owned and had been erected by them. Five of these have since been abandoned, being no longer wanted for school purposes, and, with the sites on which they stood, surrendered to the city authorities. All of the others have been extensively altered and improved, in obedience to modern requirements, and to furnish the additional accommodations that have been so urgently demanded. Nine of them have been entirely rebuilt, some even after having previously undergone enlargement.

In addition to such alteration and rebuilding of the *Public School* edifices, the Board of Education has, since the year 1853, enlarged or rebuilt thirty-two of the Ward School-houses (Grammar and Primary), and has erected twenty-nine new buildings.

There are now in this city twenty-nine Primary School-houses and fifty-five Grammar School-houses, in addition to the hired premises that are used by the schools under the control of the Board of Education; nine of the former and five of the latter are all that are left of the thirty-four buildings that were erected by the late Public School Society. Of the remaining Primaries, four are buildings that were purchased with the sites on which they stand, and have been altered and adapted to school purposes. The others have been erected by the Board for the special purpose for which they are used, and, in accordance with the best known principles of construction and arrangement, fitted with all conveniences for teachers and pupils, and supplied with the best styles of furniture, and the most approved heating and ventilating apparatus. The play-grounds are in all cases ample, and so arranged that the pupils at recess can enjoy their sports in the open air or under cover, as they may prefer, or circumstances may admit.

The school sites belonging to the Board comprise over three hundred lots, and, if placed together in blocks with the streets usually allowed, would include upward of twenty acres of ground; and the floors of the school buildings placed in the same manner, would comprise some sixty acres more—quite a little farm, upon which many laborers are busily engaged sowing the seed, from which abundant harvests of untold value are annually gathered to enrich the nation.

From the general statement preceding it will be seen that great improvements have been made within a few years past in the school buildings of this city; formerly the Primary Departments were located in basements that were seldom light and cheerful, and always subject to annoyances of various kinds — now all these schools are well provided for above ground, and free from disturbance; then a couple of class-rooms for an upper department were considered sufficient; now there are few buildings that have less than eight of these rooms for any department including the Primary. A building that accommodated one thousand pupils was considered a wonder. Modern buildings on the same sites accommodate in a better manner double that number. Once the school-houses of the city were remarkable for their extreme plainness, but now a wiser economy provides for the judicious adornment of these edifices, that they may present attractions to those for whose benefit they were erected.

The school-houses of to-day are solidly built, conveniently arranged, well supplied with apparatus, and yet probably cost less than any other public buildings of the same class constructed at the same time and under similar circumstances. Improvements are constantly sought after each new building is better in some point than its immediate predecessor. As an indication of the latest stages of advancement in this respect, the following views and diagrams, with descriptions, are given, of several buildings that have recently been commenced, or about being put under contract.

GRAMMAR SCHOOL-HOUSE NO. 56.

On West Eighteenth Street, between Eighth and Ninth avenues, a new building is in course of erection which is to be occupied by Grammar School No. 56. This is a school for females only, and will consist of two Departments—one Grammar and one Primary—each of which will have assigned to it several more class-rooms than could be allowed in a building arranged (as most of the Grammar School-houses are) for three departments. There are many advantages in this arrangement, the most prominent of which is the additional room that can be assigned to the scholars of the Primary grades, these forming about two-thirds of the whole number of pupils. Their proper accommodation is an important matter. Some idea may be formed of the character of the structure upon an examination of the exterior view, and the plans of the internal arrangement that are herewith presented. The whole front of the building, one hundred feet in length, and having a depth of about thirty feet, is occupied on each floor by the entrance-hall and stairways, with two large class-rooms on either hand; behind the central portion of this front is the main body of the building

—about fifty feet in width, and running back nearly sixty feet—which contains on the second floor the reception and gallery rooms of the Primary Department; the second floor is given entirely to class-rooms, and the whole of the upper floor of this portion of the building is occupied by the grammar reception-room; two additional class-rooms on each floor are contained in the wings on each side at the rear. On each of these floors two large wardrobes are provided for the use of the teachers of the school, in addition to those for the use of the pupils. Four stone stairways for the pupils' use connect with each of the floors from the ground to the upper department. On the ground floor are the enclosed play-rooms, apartments for the janitor, a meeting-room for the school trustees, etc. This building will accommodate from fifteen hundred to two thousand scholars.

The exterior of this school-house is very effective in its design; and while it can not well be mistaken for any thing else *than* a school-house, it is yet a pleasant departure from the set order of things that has hitherto marked this class of public buildings. The "squat" appearance that generally accompanies a building of the same breadth of front as this, is here avoided by the recessions in the front, which break the horizontal lines, and give instead so many vertical sections. And the bold bringing out of the central tower, making the main entrance a prominent feature, carries the eye upward with pleasant relief. While the building is one of the most solid and substantial character, there is yet no appearance of undue heaviness. The ornamentation is simple, and consists rather in the judicious use of material than in having it highly wrought. The windows and other openings exhibit in a variety of forms the strength and beauty of the arch line, yet variety is not introduced at the expense of the unity of the design. The first story of the front of the building is of brown stone, channeled with vermiculated blocks and voussoirs at the openings; the other stories are faced with Philadelphia pressed brick, and trimmed with polished brown stone.

The exterior sections of the front are ornamented with

GRAMMAR SCHOOL NO. 56.

(For Females.)

WEST EIGHTEENTH STREET, BETWEEN EIGHTH AND NINTH AVENUES.

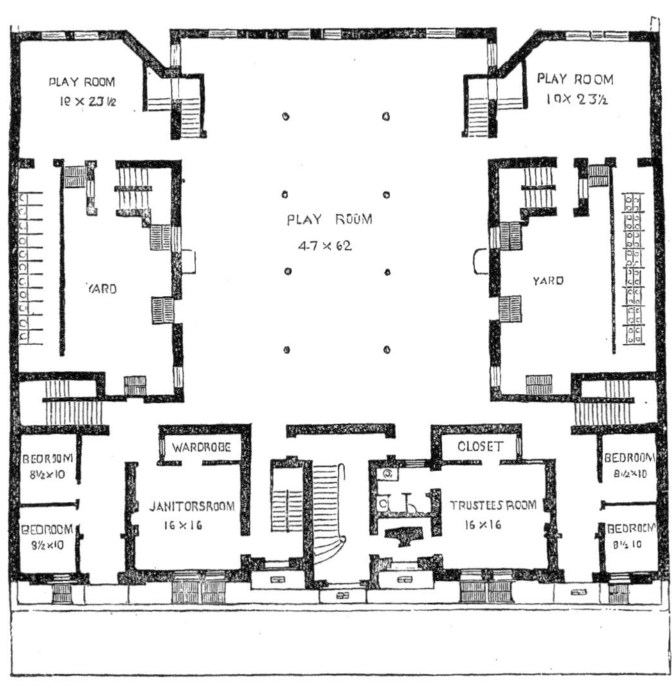

SIXTEENTH WARD SCHOOL NO. 56.

EIGHTEENTH STREET. (FIRST STORY.)

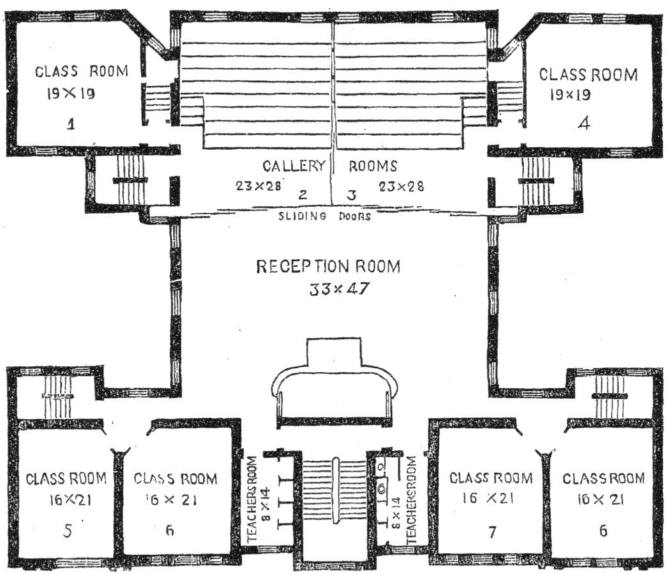

SIXTEENTH WARD SCHOOL NO. 56.

EIGHTEENTH STREET. (SECOND STORY.)

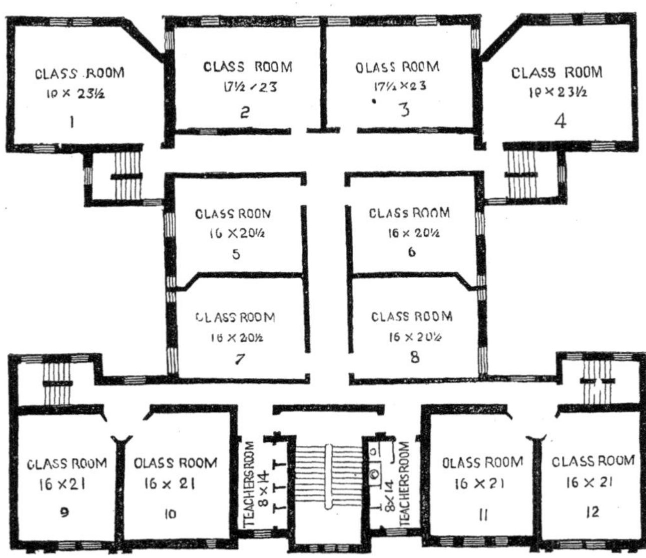

SIXTEENTH WARD GRAMMAR SCHOOL NO, 56.

EIGHTEENTH STREET. (THIRD STORY.)

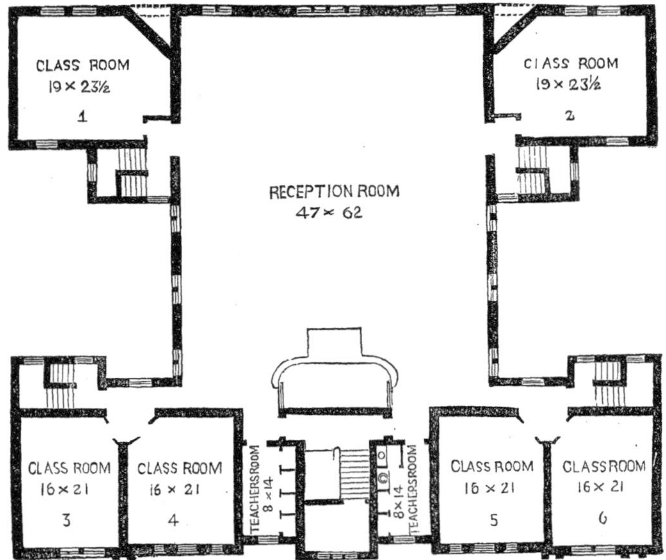

SIXTEENTH WARD GRAMMAR SCHOOL NO. 56.

EIGHTEENTH STREET. (FOURTH STORY.)

paneled pilasters of brick, and the corners of the tower are decorated with groins of brown stone. A heavily moulded cornice with coupled brackets and scroll modillions surmounts the building, above which is a curved roof slated in two colors and crowned by a handsome balustrade. The tower rises some feet above the main cornice, and has a light and airy lookout above the roof.

Built of the best materials, and with the most skilled labor, this school-house will be a source of pride, not only to those who are immediately engaged or interested in its construction, but also to every citizen who desires that the schools of New York should maintain the supremacy they have so long and so justly held.

PRIMARY SCHOOL-HOUSE NO. 16.

The rapid growth of the city constantly creates new demands for school accommodation, and the class of inhabitants in a given locality frequently determines the grade of accommodation required in that neighborhood. In one case Grammar pupils may constitute the majority requiring these facilities, while in another the Primary applicants may largely outnumber the Grammar. In the Twenty-first Ward there are two Grammar School buildings, the Primary Departments of which are always full to overflowing, their combined average attendance being upward of twenty-five hundred; yet so great has been the number seeking admission where not another could be taken, that it became necessary to establish in that section of the city a new Primary School. Lots were accordingly purchased on East Thirty-second Street midway between the two schools already established, and a building—of which the accompanying diagrams are a correct representation—is about to be erected thereon, to be known as Primary School-house No. 16.

In its general features the plan of this building does not differ materially from the Grammar School plan just considered; although the frontage of the lots is some twenty feet less, the arrangement of the rooms and stairways is very much the same; the purpose of the building, however, is different. The front of the first floor contains the janitor's apartments, very conveniently arranged; back of this are the play-grounds, both open and covered, for the pupils. A visitors' entrance at the centre of the front leads to all the Departments, and four fire-proof stairways, conveniently located, connect the play-grounds with the several floors above. The second and third floors are similar in arrangement, each having a large assembling-room, with gallery-rooms for the smallest scholars in the rear of this. There are two class-rooms at the sides of the gallery-rooms, and four more in front of the main room. In the stairway wings are found the rooms with wardrobes, etc., for the teachers' use. The accommodation afforded by this building will be for between twelve to fifteen hundred pupils, which will materially relieve the pressing wants of the neighborhood in which it is situated.

The exterior view shows again what may be done toward securing a really handsome building by a judicious use of simple material, without incurring the expense involved in elaborate ornamentation. The characteristics of this front are boldness and simplicity: the material used is principally Philadelphia pressed brick; the rustic-work of the first story, and the keys and spring-blocks of the windows, with the sills and sill courses, being of polished brown stone. The imposing entrance, with its tower, the wing projections, and the arches of the windows and doors, give an air of solidity to the structure that is at once pleasing to the eye and satisfactory to the sense. Above the cornice—which is a fine feature in itself—the roof of the front section is carried up in a convex Mansard curve, handsomely slated, and finished with a balustrade. The other portions of the building are covered with a tin roof.

This building possesses many improvements over any previously erected, and may be fairly considered a model Primary School-house.

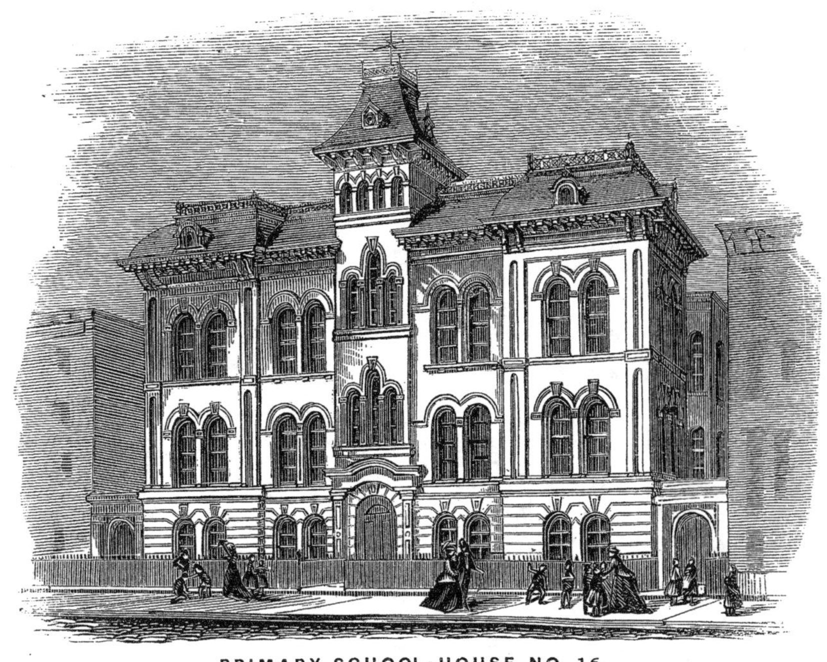

PRIMARY SCHOOL-HOUSE NO. 16.

EAST THIRTY-SECOND STREET, NEAR THIRD AVENUE (TWENTY-FIRST WARD).

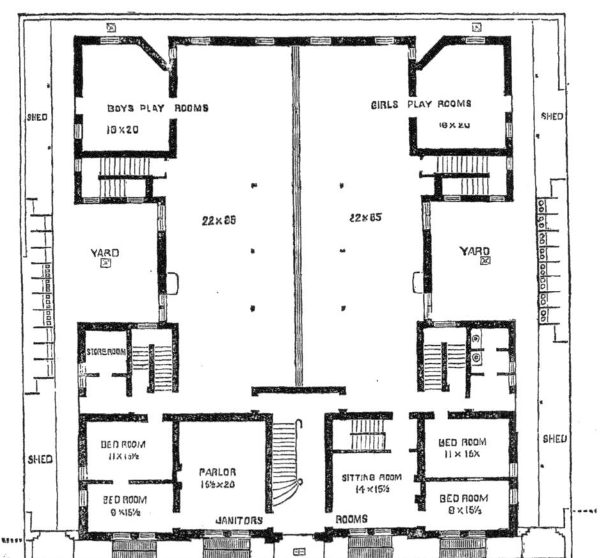

TWENTY-FIRST WARD PRIMARY SCHOOL NO. 16.

THIRTY-SECOND STREET. (FIRST STORY.)

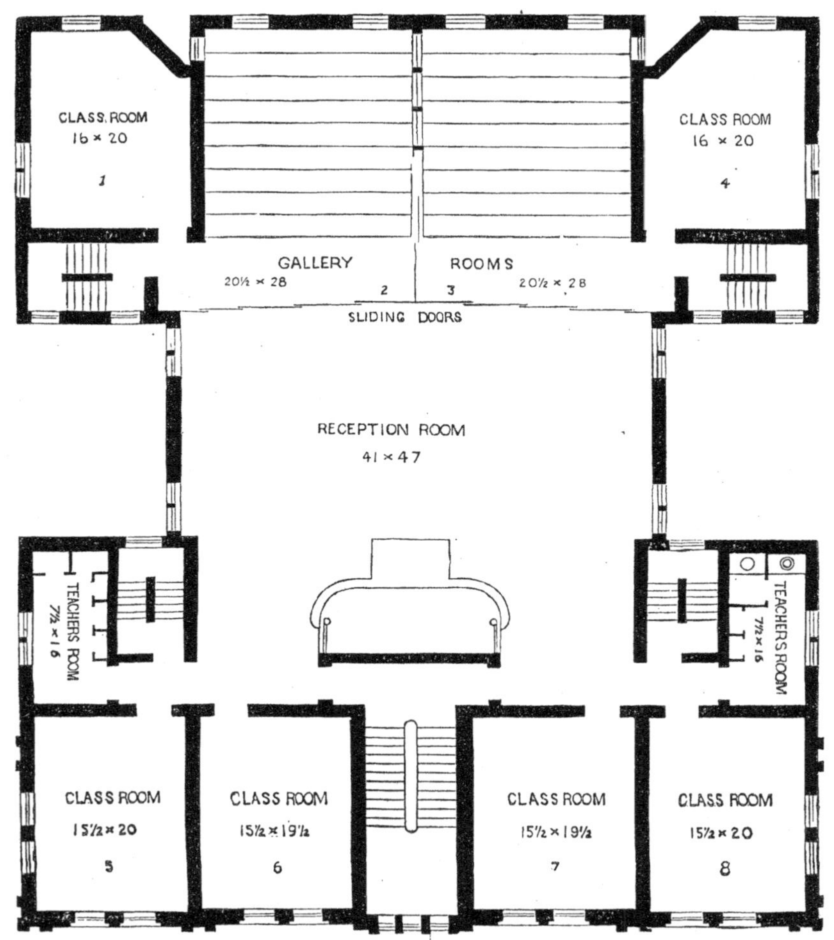

TWENTY-FIRST WARD PRIMARY SCHOOL NO. 16.

THIRTY-SECOND STREET. (SECOND AND THIRD STORIES.)

COLORED SCHOOL-HOUSE NO. 3.

For more than half a century the colored children of this city have been provided with the means of education in the same manner as the children of white parentage. The school buildings, the instructors, the supplies of books and apparatus have been of identically the same character in either case. The colored people are given to colonizing, and, in recognition of this fact, the schools for their use have been located in the immediate neighborhood, if not directly in the midst, of the communities thus formed.

The late Public School Society erected two buildings for Colored Schools, which at the time they were built were as good as any others in the city. One of these, No. 2, on Laurens Street, is still standing, and in good order, having recently been thoroughly overhauled and remodeled; and the other, No. 1, after having been used for many years, was demolished, and a new building erected in the year 1859, which was generally considered to be the finest colored school-house in the United States.

By the changes of population already alluded to, quite a large number of the colored people within a few years past have left the lower for the upper wards of the city, and for their benefit Colored School No. 6—now known, however, as No. 3—was established. Success attended this school; and the Board of Education, with a desire to furnish it as good accommodations as for any other, has recently purchased a fine school site on the northerly side of West Forty-first Street, between Seventh and Eighth Avenues, on which to erect a building for its use. The view, and plans accompanying, represent new Colored School-house No. 3.

The several floors of this building are very much alike. A commodious assembling—or reception-room—and five class rooms being furnished on each floor. The three class-rooms at the rear can be thrown into one large open room—

in connection with the assembly—by the use of the sliding doors; the usual visitors' entrance and pupils' stairways are shown on the plans. The ceilings are high, and the windows of good size, to secure proper light and ventilation. The building is calculated for three departments, if it shall be found necessary to organize them, and has accommodations for about one thousand children. The yards are very roomy, and have broad sheds at the sides for protection in stormy weather. Apartments for the janitor are provided in the basement, and in the story formed in the Mansard roof over the front portion of the building.

The front of this school-house presents a very neat and tasteful appearance that must excite admiration, and will be a credit to the neighborhood in which it is situated. Built of the same materials as the other buildings that have already been described, it is yet unlike them, and has a character all its own.

The foregoing examples are given simply to show what is being done by the Board to meet the demands of the ever-swelling throng of eager applicants who are knocking at the portals of already filled school-houses, and presenting their claims to a share in the benefits conferred by our system of free education. As readily and as fully as the means of the Board will permit, these claims are allowed, but they can not be entirely satisfied. The time is not yet, and probably will not soon be, when the demand for school accommodation shall cease; for liberal as is the fund contributed by our citizens for the maintenance of our Public Schools, yet it can not, in the natural course of things, equal the demands that will be made upon it by our rapidly-increasing population. These citizen tax-payers are urging the erection of additional school-houses, and it would undoubtedly be a matter of no little difficulty to obtain their consent to the erection of a poorer class of buildings than those hitherto erected; and each succeeding year will see arise in various sections of our city these stately edifices to be devoted to this good cause. They are emphatically the schools of the people, are extending their influence

COLORED SCHOOL-HOUSE NO. 3.

WEST FORTY-FIRST STREET, BETWEEN SEVENTH AND EIGHTH AVENUES.

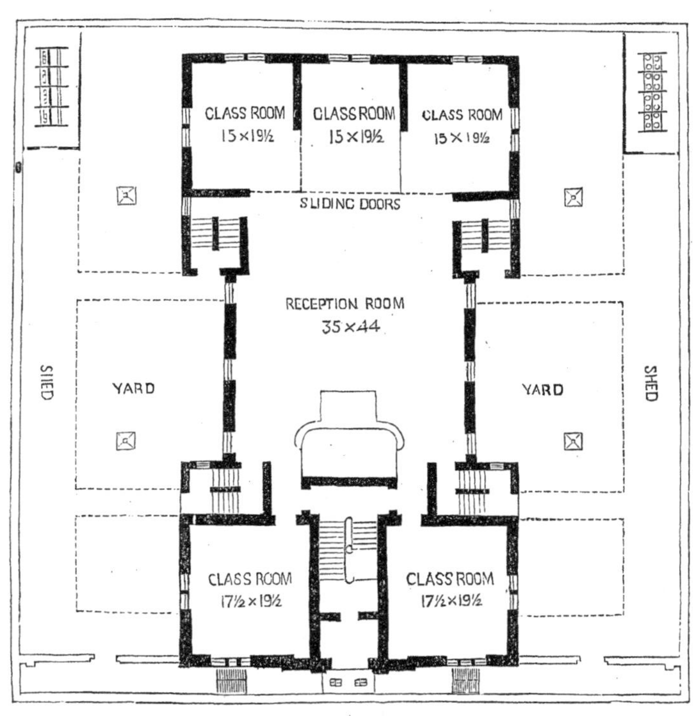

COLORED SCHOOL NO. 3.

FORTY-FIRST STREET. (FIRST STORY.)

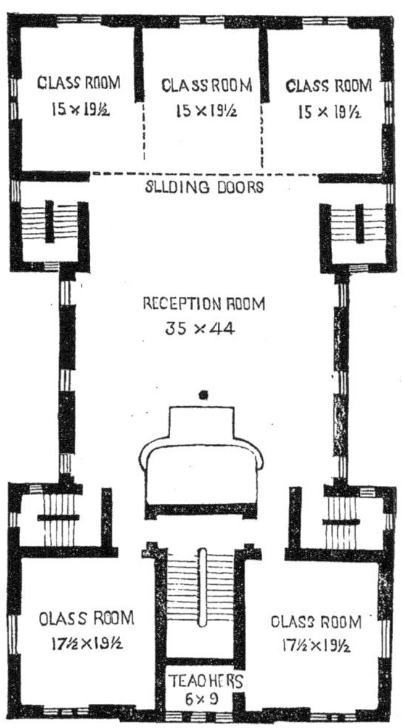

COLORED SCHOOL NO. 3.

FORTY-FIRST STREET. (SECOND AND THIRD STORIES.)

for good day by day, and the attractions they present are wholesome in their effects.

The buildings required will be erected as fast as circumstances permit. All parts of the city will receive favorable consideration whenever additional accommodations are necessary. In neighborhoods that have school-houses of the old methods of construction, they will be remodeled to meet this want; but in case this is not practicable, they will be removed, and new houses built. In building or altering, the Board has taken every precaution to guard against an extravagant use of the public funds under its control. All the work in this line is done by contracts based upon competitive estimates obtained through public advertisement, and made by numbers of the best mechanics in the city. The material used is always the best of its kind, and the labor is required to be of the first class. All the work undergoes a rigid superintendence, in order that the various provisions of these contracts may be fully carried out.

XVIII.

LAWS RELATIVE TO PUBLIC INSTRUCTION

IN THE CITY OF NEW YORK.

An Act to amend, consolidate, and reduce to one Act, the various Acts relative to the Common Schools of the City of New York.

Passed July 3, 1851.

As amended by the Acts severally entitled, "An Act relative to Common Schools in the City of New York."[1]

Passed June 4, 1853.
March 31, 1854.
April 15, 1854.

The People of the State of New York, represented in Senate and Assembly, do enact as follows:

OF SCHOOL OFFICERS AND THEIR ELECTION.

§ 1. There shall be two Commissioners, two Inspectors, and eight Trustees of Common Schools, in each of the wards of the city of New York, who shall be known as the School Officers of the ward.

At every general election, there shall be elected in each of the said wards, one Commissioner, one Inspector, and two Trustees of Common Schools, who shall take office on the first day of January next succeeding their election, and hold the same for the following terms: the Commissioner and Inspector for two years each, and the Trustees for four years each.

Every vacancy in the office of a Commissioner, Inspector, or Trustee of Common Schools, occurring more than twenty days previous to any general election, shall be filled at the

[1] For most recent and important changes, see Act of 25th of April, 1864, on page 192.

next general election; and every person chosen to fill a vacancy shall take office on the first day of January next succeeding the election, and hold the same for the residue of the term; and, in every such case, the person voted for to fill a vacancy shall be designated in the ballot by the words, "to fill vacancy," written or printed immediately over his name, and shall also be so designated in the returns of the election; and if there be more than one vacancy in the office of Trustee of any ward, to be filled at the same election, each person voted for to fill a vacancy shall be designated on the ballot and in the returns, by adding the number of years for which he is to serve to the words "to fill vacancy;" so that the designation will read, "to fill vacancy of — years."

In case in any ward the number of Trustees in office shall at any time be less than eight, the Board of Education shall have power, upon the nomination of the School Officers of the ward, to appoint as many Trustees as will make, including the Trustees previously in office, eight Trustees for the ward; but the Trustees so appointed shall cease to hold office on the first day of January next ensuing, and their successors shall be chosen at the next general election, to serve for such number of years, respectively, as the Board of Education may designate.

The Board of Education shall, at least fifteen days previous to every general election, cause to be filed in the office of the Clerk of the Common Council, a list of the school offices to be filled at the next general election, stating the names of the officers whose terms will expire; and also, in each case of an unexpired term in which a vacancy is to be filled, stating the number of years which the person elected to fill the same will be entitled to serve.

The elections held by virtue of this Act, shall be subject to the same laws and regulations, in all respects, as those which govern the general elections in said city. The ballots for School Officers shall be indorsed "Common Schools," and deposited in a separate box to be provided therefor.

Every School Officer shall, before entering on the duties of his office, and within fifteen days after the commencement of the term for which he is elected, or from the time of being notified of his appointment to fill a vacancy, take and subscribe before the Clerk of the Board of Education, the oath prescribed by the Constitution of this State. And any school office to which any person, who shall omit to take the said oath within the time and in the manner above prescribed, may have been elected or appointed in said city, shall be considered as vacant from and after the expiration of said fifteen days, and the vacancy shall thereupon be filled in the manner in which other vacancies in school offices are filled.

The Board of Education shall be judges of the election or appointment and qualification of its members.

Every School Officer shall, at the time of his election or appointment, be a resident of the ward for which he is elected or appointed; and the Board of School Officers of any ward shall have power to declare vacant the office of any Commissioner, Inspector, or Trustee elected by the people, or appointed by the Board of Education, who shall have removed from the ward; and it shall be the duty of such Board of School Officers to consider the subject, and determine whether or not the seat of the officer who shall have removed from the ward shall be declared vacant.

OF THE BOARD OF EDUCATION—ITS POWERS AND DUTIES.

§ 2. The Commissioners of Common Schools shall constitute a Board of Education for the city and county of New York. They shall meet on the second Wednesday of January, in each year, for the purpose of organization, and thereafter for the transaction of business as often as they may determine; they shall elect one of their number President, and shall appoint a Clerk, and as many Assistant Clerks, and other officers for the transaction of the business of the Board as may be necessary, who shall severally hold their offices during the pleasure of the Board, and whose respective duties, powers, and compensation shall be regulated and determined by the Board.

The Board of Education shall have power:

1. To take and hold property, both real and personal, devised or transferred to it for the purposes of Public Education, in the city of New York.

2. To appoint a City Superintendent of Schools, and one or more Assistant Superintendents, and also a Superintendent of School Buildings, whose respective duties, powers, salaries, and terms of office, except as herein otherwise provided, shall be regulated and determined by the Board of Education, and to employ, under the Superintendent of School Buildings, necessary workmen, and provide necessary materials for repairing, altering, and enlarging school or other buildings; but this provision shall not be construed to compel the Trustees of any ward to use or employ such workmen or materials for any purpose whatever.

3. On the nomination of the School Officers of any ward to fill vacancies in school offices which may occur in such ward between the general elections; and upon the presentation of a majority of the School Officers of any ward, to remove any Inspector of Common Schools for such ward, who shall be proven to the satisfaction of the Board of Education to have willfully, or without good cause, neglected to perform any duty imposed upon him by this act; and it shall be the duty of the said Board to remove from office any Commissioner, Inspector, or Trustee, who shall be, or become, directly or indirectly, interested, by way of commission or otherwise, in any contract or undertaking for the furnishing of any supplies of books or materials, or for the performing of any labor or work for any of the schools or buildings under his charge.

4. To establish new schools, as hereinafter provided.

5. To draw from the moneys which shall be raised for the purpose of Public Education, such sums as may be required for the purpose of defraying the necessary incidental expenses of the Board, and such further sums as may be required for the payment of the salaries of such clerks and other officers as may be appointed by virtue of the authority vested in the Board by this act, and of such other expenses as may be necessarily incurred by the Board in pursuance of the provisions of this act.

6. To visit and examine the schools subject to the provisions of this act.

7. To make rules of order and by-laws for the government of the Board, its members and committees, and general regulations to secure proper economy and accountability in the expenditure of the school moneys.

8. To continue the existing Free Academy, and organize a similar institution for females; and if any similar institution is organized by the Board of Education, all the provisions of this act relative to the Free Academy, shall apply to each and every one of the said institutions, now existing or hereafter established, as fully, completely, and distinctly as they could or would if it was the only institution of the kind; to distinguish each existing and future institution by an appropriate title; and to purchase, erect, or lease sites and buildings for each and all of the said institutions, provided that no additional institution shall be authorized or organized by the Board of Education, unless a majority of the whole number of members of the said Board shall vote in favor thereof.

9. To use and control the premises known as the Hall of the Board of Education, at the corner of Grand and Elm Streets, to direct the purposes for which the same may be occupied, and to make all the repairs, alterations, and additions in and to the same, which the Board may deem advisable, and to provide such additional sites and buildings as may be necessary for the purposes of this act, the title of which shall, in all cases, be vested in the Mayor, Aldermen, and Commonalty of the city of New-York.

10. To dispose of such personal property used in the School or other buildings under the charge of the Board, as the Trustees or Committees having the immediate charge thereof shall certify is no longer required for use therein; and all moneys realized by the sale of any such property shall be paid into the City Treasury, for the same purposes as the moneys raised under the sixteenth section of this act.

11. And for the purposes of this act, the said Board shall possess the powers and privileges of a corporation.

§ 3. It shall be the duty of the Board of Education:

1. On or before the fifteenth day of November, in each

year, to report to the Board of Supervisors of said city and county, an estimate of the amount over and above the sum specified in the fifteenth section of this act, which will be required during the year for the purpose of meeting the current annual expenses of public instruction in said city, for purchasing, leasing, and procuring sites; for erecting buildings, and for furnishing, fitting up, altering, enlarging, and repairing the buildings and premises under their charge; for the support of schools which shall have been organized since the last annual apportionment of the school moneys made by the Board, and of such further sum or sums as may be necessary for any of the purposes authorized by this act; but the aggregate amount so reported shall not exceed the sum of four dollars for each pupil who shall have actually attended and been taught the preceding year in the schools entitled to participate in the apportionment.

2. To apportion all the school moneys which shall have been raised for the purpose of meeting the current annual expenses of public instruction, to the schools entitled to participate therein by the provisions of this act.

3. To file with the Chamberlain of said city, on or before the first Monday of April in each year, a copy of their apportionment, stating the amount apportioned to the Schools under the charge of the Board of Education, and to the Trustees, Managers, and Directors of the several schools enumerated in this act.

4. To continue to furnish, through the Free Academy, the benefit of education, gratuitously, to persons who have been pupils in the Common Schools of the said city and county, for a period of time to be regulated by the Board of Education, not less than one year.

5. To supervise, manage, and govern said Free Academy, and make all needful rules and regulations therefor; fix the number and compensation of teachers and others to be employed therein; prescribe the preliminary examination, and the terms and conditions on which pupils shall be received and instructed therein and discharged therefrom; direct the

course of studies therein, and provide in all things for the good government and management of the said Free Academy; and purchase the books, apparatus, stationery, and other things necessary and expedient to enable the said Free Academy to be properly and successfully conducted, and to keep the said building or buildings properly repaired and furnished. And the Board, upon the recommendation of the Faculty of the Free Academy, may grant the usual degrees and diplomas in the Arts, to such persons as shall have completed a full course of study in the said Free Academy.

6. To appoint annually a standing committee of not less than five persons of their number, who shall, subject to the control, supervision, and approbation of the said Board, constitute an Executive Committee, for the care, government, and management of the said Free Academy, under the rules and regulations prescribed as aforesaid, whose duty it shall be to make detailed reports to the said Board of Education, and, among other things, to recommend the rules and regulations which they deem necessary and proper for the said Academy. The Board of Education may, at any regular meeting thereof, by a majority of all the members of the said Board, remove any or all the members of the said committee, and appoint another person or persons in place of the member or members of the said committee so removed.

7. To make and transmit annually, on or before the first day of February in each year, to the Common Council of said city, and also to the Secretary of the Board of Regents of the University of the State of New-York, a report signed by the President and Clerk of the Board of Education, and dated on the thirty-first day of December next preceding, which report shall state the names and ages of all the pupils instructed in such Free Academy, during the preceding year, and the time that each was so instructed, specifying which of them have completed a full course of study therein, and which have received degrees, medals, and other special testimonials; a particular statement of the studies pursued by each pupil, since the last preceding report, together with the books such student

shall have studied, in whole or in part, and if in part, what portion; an account or estimate of the library, philosophical and chemical apparatus, and mathematical or other scientific instruments belonging to such Academy; the names of the instructors employed in said Academy, and the compensation paid to each; what amount of moneys the Board of Education received during the year for the purposes of such Academy, and from what sources, specifying how much from each, and the particular manner, and the specific purposes for which such moneys have been expended; and such other information in relation to education in said Academy, and the measures of the Board in the management thereof, as the said Common Council or the Regents of the University of the State of New-York, may from time to time require.

8. To provide evening schools for those whose ages or avocations are such as to prevent their attending the day schools established by law, in such of the ward school-houses or other buildings used for school purposes, and in such other places in said city as they may from time to time deem expedient; and also a Normal School or schools for teachers, which shall be attended by such of the teachers in Common Schools as the Board of Education by general regulations shall direct, under penalty of forfeiture of their situations as teachers, by omitting to attend, which forfeiture shall be declared by the Board of Education; and to appoint teachers and furnish all needful supplies for the Evening and Normal Schools.

9. To furnish all necessary supplies, or make regulations for furnishing such supplies for the several schools under their care; but when such supplies are furnished by the Board of Education, they shall be obtained by contract, proposals for which shall be advertised for the period of at least two weeks.

10. To make and transmit, between the fifteenth day of January and the first day of February in each year, to the State Superintendent of Public Instruction, and to the Common Council of the city of New-York, a report in writing,

bearing date on the thirty-first day of December next preceding, stating the whole number of schools within their jurisdiction, specially designating the schools for colored children; the schools or societies from which reports shall have been made to the Board of Education, within the time limited for that purpose; the length of time such schools shall have been kept open; the amount of public money apportioned or appropriated to said school or society; the number taught in each school; the whole amount of money drawn from the city Chamberlain for the purposes of education during the year ending at the date of their report, distinguishing the amount received from the general fund of the State, and from all other and what sources; the manner in which such moneys shall have been expended; and such other information as the State Superintendent of Public Instruction may from time to time require, in relation to Common School education in the city and county of New-York; and the report which the Board of Education is hereby required to make, shall be held and taken to be a full compliance with every law requiring a report from the said Board, or any officer of the city and county of New-York, except the City Superintendent, relative to the schools in the said city, or any matters connected therewith.

§ 4. If the Board of Education shall neglect to make such Annual Report, within the time limited, the share of school moneys apportioned to the city and county of New-York may, in the discretion of the State Superintendent of Public Instruction, be withheld until a suitable report shall have been rendered.

§ 5. The Clerk of the Board of Education shall have charge of the rooms, books, papers, and documents of the Board, and shall, in addition to his duties as Secretary of the Board, perform such other clerical duties as may be required by its members or committees.

§ 6. All schools which have been organized under the act entitled "An act to extend to the city and county of New York, the provisions of the general act in relation to Common

Schools," passed April 11, 1842, and the acts amending the same, or organized or adopted under this act, shall be Common Schools called "Ward Schools," or "Ward Primaries," and each class shall be numbered consecutively, according to the time of their organization or adoption, and all such schools shall be under the supervision and government of the Commissioners, Inspectors, and Trustees of the ward in which they are located.

POWERS AND DUTIES OF SCHOOL OFFICERS.

§ 7. It shall be the duty of the School Officers, or a majority of them in any ward:

1. To certify to the Board of Education of the city and county of New York, whenever, in their opinion, it is necessary to organize one or more additional schools in said ward, with the facts and circumstances showing such necessity, together with the character of the school buildings required, and the number and class of scholars who will probably attend such schools, if organized, and to organize such schools as hereinafter provided.

2. To provide under such rules and regulations as the Board of Education may establish, the necessary books, stationery, and other essentials necessary to organize and conduct any school in their ward.

3. To examine, ascertain, and report to the Board of Education, and as frequently as may be, whether the provisions of this act in relation to the teaching of sectarian doctrines, or the use of sectarian books shall have been violated. And,

4. To notify the Board of Education of any vacancy in the office of any school officer of their respective wards, and to make nominations as in this act provided.

POWERS AND DUTIES OF COMMISSIONERS.

§ 8. It shall be the duty of the Commissioners of Common Schools in the several wards:

1. To attend all the meetings of the Board of Education; and if any Commissioner shall refuse or neglect to attend any

three successive stated meetings of the Board, after having been personally notified to attend, and if no satisfactory cause of his non-attendance be shown, the Board may declare his office vacant.

2. To transmit to the Board of Education all reports made to them by the Trustees and Inspectors of their respective wards.

3. To visit and examine all the schools entitled to participate in the apportionment.

4. They shall be *ex officio* members of the Board of Trustees in their respective wards.

POWERS AND DUTIES OF INSPECTORS.

§ 9. It shall be the duty of the Inspectors of Common Schools:

1. To inspect and examine each of the schools in their respective wards at least twice in each year, and oftener if necessary; and on or before the fifteenth day of October in each year, to make and transmit to the Board of Education, and to the Trustees of the ward, a report in writing, in which they shall set forth the condition of the several school buildings in use in their ward, and whether any, and if any, what repairs, alterations, or modifications of those buildings seem to them necessary.

2. Whether they are kept clean and in good order.

3. In what manner they are heated and ventilated, and how effectual the means used are in producing the result desired.

4. The studies pursued.

5. The progress of the classes in their different studies.

6. The punctuality of attendance of the scholars and teachers.

7. The order, attention, and general appearance of the school.

8. The length of each morning and evening session, and the number and length of recesses allowed.

9. The number and qualifications of the teachers, and such

other facts as in their opinion are important to insure the discipline or extend the usefulness of the schools.

10. In conjunction with the City Superintendent of Common Schools, to license teachers for their respective wards, and,

11. To examine and audit all accounts when duly certified by the Trustees to be correct.

POWERS AND DUTIES OF TRUSTEES.

§ 10. It shall be the duty of the Trustees for each ward, and they shall have the power:

1. To have the safe keeping of all the premises and other property used for or belonging to the Ward Schools and the Ward Primaries in their respective wards.

2. Under such general rules and regulations as the Board of Education may adopt, to contract with and employ teachers and janitors in the said schools, and conduct and manage the same, and furnish all needful supplies therefor, subject to the provisions of the third section of this act; and make all needful repairs, alterations, and additions, in and to the school premises; provided that if the cost of any such repairs, alteration, or addition, shall exceed the sum of two hundred dollars, the same shall be made by contract, pursuant to the twenty-fifth section of this act.

3. To procure, as may be necessary, blank-books, in one of which a statement of the amounts of all moneys received and paid by the Trustees, or otherwise, for or on account of each of the schools conducted by them, and of all movable property belonging to each school, shall be entered at large and signed by such Trustees; and, in one book, minutes of their meetings shall be kept; and in other books, the principal teacher of each school and department shall enter the names, ages, and residences, of the scholars attending the school, the name of a parent or guardian of each scholar, and the days on which the scholars shall have respectively attended, and the aggregate attendance of each scholar during the year; also the days on which each school shall have been

visited by the City and Assistant Superintendents of Schools, and the School Officers of the ward, and the members of the Board of Education, or any of them, which entries shall be verified by the oath or affirmation of the principal teacher in such school or department. The said books shall be preserved by the Trustees as the property of the school, and shall be delivered to their successors.

4. To make, at least five days before the first day of January in every year, or such other day as may be designated by the Board of Education, in the case of a school kept open after the twenty-fifth day of December, and transmit to the Board of Education, a report in writing, dated the thirty-first day of December, which shall be signed and certified by a majority of the Trustees, and which report shall state the whole number of schools within their jurisdiction, especially designating the schools for colored children; the length of time each school shall have been kept open; the whole number of scholars over four and under twenty-one years of age, who shall have been taught, free of expense to such scholars, in their schools during the year ending with the date of the report, which number shall be ascertained by adding to the number of children on register at the commencement of each year, the number admitted during that year, which shall be considered the total for that year: the average number that has actually attended such schools during the year, to be ascertained by the teacher's keeping an exact account of the number of scholars present every school time or half-day, which being added together, and divided by four hundred and sixty, or if less than a year, by the number of school sessions, shall be considered the average of attending scholars, which average shall be sworn or affirmed to by the principal teacher of the school; and a particular account of the state of the schools, and of the property and affairs of each school under their care; and the titles of all books used, with such other information as the Board of Education shall require; and for the purposes of this act, each department shall, whenever practicable, be considered as a separate school.

5. To hold as a corporation all personal property vested in or transferred to them for school purposes in their respective wards.

7. To meet statedly at times to be by them appointed, and to declare vacant, by the votes of a majority of the Trustees of the ward, the seat of any person elected or appointed as a Trustee, who shall refuse or neglect, without satisfactory cause shown by him to the said Trustees, to attend any three successive stated meetings of the Trustees, after having been previously notified to attend; and to notify the Clerk of the Board of Education, at least twenty days previous to any general election, of any vacancy that will exist in the school offices of said ward, at the expiration of their present year, with the cause or reason of such vacancy or vacancies.

OF THE CITY SUPERINTENDENT.

§ 11. The City and Assistant Superintendents of Schools shall take and subscribe before the Clerk of the Board of Education, the oath of office prescribed by the Constitution of this State; shall each hold office for the term of two years, and until his successor is appointed, subject to removal by the Board, on complaint, for cause stated; shall respectively receive such compensation as the Board of Education may designate, which shall not be changed during the term of office of any incumbent; and shall be subject to such rules and regulations as the Board of Education may establish. It shall be specially the duty of the City Superintendent:

1. To visit every school under the charge of the Board of Education as often as once in each year; to inquire into all matters relating to the government, course of instruction, books, studies, discipline, and conduct of such schools, and the condition of the school-houses, and the schools generally, and to advise and to counsel with the Trustees in relation to their duties, the proper studies, discipline and conduct of the schools, the course of instruction to be pursued, and the books of elementary instruction to be used therein; and to examine, ascertain, and report to the Board of Education, whether the

provisions of the Act in relation to religious sectarian teaching and books have been violated in any of the schools of the different wards of the city; and to make a monthly report to the Board of Education, stating which of the schools have been visited by him, and adding such comments in respect to the matters above specified, as he may consider necessary and advisable; and to transmit to the respective Boards of Ward Trustees copies of so much of such reports as relates to schools under their management.

2. Under such general rules and regulations as the Board of Education may establish, to examine into the qualifications of persons proposed as teachers in any of the schools under the charge of the Board, and to grant certificates, in the forms prescribed by the Board, to such of the persons so examined as may be entitled thereto; which certificates shall specify in which class of schools, and in what capacity, the persons to whom any certificate is granted are qualified to teach, and shall be evidence in respect thereto; to re-examine, whenever the City Superintendent may deem necessary, any of the teachers employed in the schools under the charge of the Board; and to annul, for any cause satisfactory to the City Superintendent, any license or certificate of qualification, to teach in the schools of the City of New York; but such action shall not be taken by him until he has given at least ten days' previous notice to the teacher and to the Trustees of the ward in which he is employed, nor until the teacher has been allowed a hearing; nor shall such action disqualify the teacher, until a note of the decision of the City Superintendent, stating the name of the teacher and the time when the license or certificate was annulled, has been signed by the City Superintendent, filed in the office of the Clerk of the Board of Education, and served upon the teacher: Provided, however, that every such teacher shall have a right of appeal to the State Superintendent of Public Instruction, and, in case such appeal is taken by the teacher within ten days after the note of the decision is served upon him, he shall not be disqualified until the action of the City Superintendent has

been confirmed by the State Superintendent of Public Instruction.

3. Generally, by all the means in his power, under the regulations of the Board of Education in respect thereto, to promote sound education, elevate the character and qualifications of teachers, improve the means of instruction, and advance the interests of the schools committed to his charge.

§ 12. The City Superintendent shall be subject to such general rules and regulations as the State Superintendent of Public Instruction may prescribe; and appeals from his acts and decisions may be made to the Superintendent in the same manner, and with like effect, as in cases now provided by law; and he shall make annually, to the State Superintendent of Public Instruction, at such times as shall be appointed by him, a report in writing, containing the whole number of schools in the city and county, distinguishing the schools from which the necessary reports have been made to the Board of Education by the Commissioners, Inspectors, and Trustees of Common Schools, and containing a certified copy of the reports of the Board of Education to the Clerk of the city and county, with such additional information as the State Superintendent of Public Instruction may require.

§ 13. It shall be the duty of the Board of Education, by general rules and regulations, to provide a proper classification of studies, scholars, and salaries, in such manner that, as near as practicable, the system of instruction pursued in the Common Schools, and the salaries paid to teachers, shall be uniform throughout the city.

OF THE SUPPORT OF SCHOOLS.

§ 14. Whenever the Clerk of the city and county shall receive notice from the State Superintendent of Public Instruction of the amount of moneys apportioned to the County of New York for the support and encouragement of Common Schools therein, he shall immediately lay the same before the Board of Supervisors of said county; and the Chamberlain of the said city shall apply for and receive the school moneys apportioned to the said county, as soon as the same become payable, and place the same in the city treasury, for the same purposes as the moneys raised under the sixteenth section of this act.

§ 15. The said Board of Supervisors shall annually raise and collect, by tax upon the inhabitants of the said city and county, a sum of money equal to the sum specified in such notice, at the time and in the same manner as the contingent charges of the said city and county are levied and collected; also, a sum of money equal to one-twentieth of one per cent. of the value of the real and personal property in the said city, liable to be assessed thereon, and pay the same into the City Treasury, to be applied to the purposes of Common Schools in the said city; and the Board of Education shall apportion the money so raised to each of the schools hereafter provided for by this act, except the Free Academy and the Evening Schools, according to the number of children over four and under twenty-one years of age, who were actual residents of the city and county of New York at the time of their attendance on such schools, without charge, the preceding year; and the average shall be ascertained by adding together the number of such children present at each morning and afternoon session of not less than three hours, and dividing the sum by four hundred and sixty; and if any school shall have been organized since the last annual apportionment, the average shall be ascertained by dividing by a number corresponding to the actual number of morning and evening sessions of not less than three hours each, held since the organization of such schools; and the sum apportioned to any schools, other than the Ward Schools, shall be paid to the Trustees, Managers, or Directors of such schools respectively, by drafts on the City Chamberlain, to be signed by the President and Clerk of said Board, and made payable to the order of the treasurers of said Trustees, Managers, or Directors.

§ 16. Said Board of Supervisors shall also raise and collect at the same time, and in the same manner, such additional sum or sums as the Board of Education, in pursuance of the provisions of the first subdivision of the third section of this Act, shall have reported to be necessary for the purposes therein mentioned. Such moneys shall be paid into the city treasury, and shall, together with the amounts apportioned to the schools under the charge of the Board of Education, be paid by the Chamberlain of the said city upon the drafts drawn on him by the Board of Education, signed by the President, and countersigned by the Clerk of the Board, and by the Commissioners, or one of them, of the ward for which the money is to be paid, except such sums as shall be drawn for purposes other than the expenses of Ward Schools, which shall be paid by said Chamberlain upon drafts drawn on him by said Board, signed by the President and Clerk, and countersigned by the Chairman of the Finance Committee of said Board, and all the drafts shall be made payable to the person or persons entitled to receive the same, except that the payment of wages and salaries may be made by pay-rolls, upon which each person shall separately receipt for the amount paid to such person; and in every case of payment by a pay-roll, the draft for the aggregate amount of wages or salaries included therein, shall be made payable to the Superintendent, Principal Teacher, or other officer designated for the purpose by the By-Laws of the Board of Education.

§ 17. If any of the said newly-organized Ward Schools, by reason of peculiar circumstances, shall be equitably entitled to a larger sum than they will receive under an apportionment made as aforesaid, then the Board of Education shall be authorized, and they are hereby required, to make to such schools such further allowance out of the school moneys as they, the Board of Education, shall deem just and proper.

§ 18. No school shall be entitled to, or receive any portion of the school moneys, in which the religious doctrines or tenets of any particular Christian or other religious sect shall be taught, inculcated, or practiced, or in which any book or books, containing compositions favorable or prejudicial to the particular doctrines or tenets of any particular Christian or other religious sect, or which shall teach the doctrines or tenets of any other religious sect, or which shall refuse to permit the visits and examinations provided for in this Act. But nothing herein contained shall authorize the Board of Education to exclude the Holy Scriptures without note or comment, or any selections therefrom, from any of the schools provided for by this Act; but it shall not be competent for the said Board of Education to decide what version, if any, of the Holy Scriptures, without note or comment, shall be used in any of the schools: Provided, that nothing herein contained shall be so construed as to violate the rights of conscience as secured by the Constitution of this State and of the United States.

§ 19. If the school moneys apportioned to the Common Schools, agreeably to the previous section of this Act, shall exceed the necessary and legal expenses of either of such schools, the Board of Education shall authorize the payment only of such sum or sums as shall be sufficient to provide for such expenses; and any deficiency in the sums apportioned to meet the necessary and legal expenses of public education in the said schools, shall be supplied by the Common Council of the said city, and they are hereby authorized and directed to raise by loan, in anticipation of the annual tax, such sum or sums as shall be necessary to meet such deficiency. And the Board of Education shall in all cases certify to the Common Council the cause of such deficiency, and that the same was unavoidable; and unless such certificate shall be made, the said Common Council may refuse to raise the sum required to meet such deficiency.

§ 20. The Board of Education shall require from the Executive Committees conducting schools by appointment of the Board, and from the Trustees, Managers, or Directors of the Corporate Schools entitled to participate in the apportionment of school moneys, a report in all respects similar to that required from the Trustees of each ward by the tenth section of this Act. And in making the apportionment among the several schools, no share shall be allotted to any school or society from which no sufficient annual report shall have been received for the year ending on the last day of December immediately preceding the apportionment.

§ 21. Whenever an apportionment of the public money shall not be made to any school, in consequence of any accidental omission to make any report required by law, or to comply with any other regulation or provision of law, the Board of Education may, in its discretion, direct an apportionment to be made to such school, according to the equitable circumstances of the case, to be paid out of the public money on hand, or, if the same shall have been distributed, out of the public money to be received in a succeeding year.

OF THE SCHOOLS ENTITLED TO PARTICIPATE IN THE APPORTIONMENT.

§ 22. The New York Orphan Asylum School, the Roman Catholic Orphan Asylum School, the schools of the two Half-orphan Asylums, the school of the Mechanics' Society, the school of the Society for the Reformation of Juvenile Delinquents in the City of New York, the Hamilton Free School, the school for the Leake and Watts' Orphan-house, the school connected with the Almshouse of the said city, the school of the Association for the Benefit of Colored Orphans, the schools of the American Female Guardian Society, the schools of the Society for the Promotion of Education among Colored Children, the schools organized under the Act, entitled "An Act to extend to the City and County of New York the provisions of the general Act in relation to Common Schools," passed April 11, 1842, or an Act to amend the same, passed April 18, 1843, or an Act entitled "An Act more effectually to provide for Common School Education in the City and County of New York," passed May 7, 1844, or any of the Acts amending the same, and including such Normal Schools for the education of Teachers as the Board of Education may organize, and the Normal School of the Public School Society for the education of Teachers, and such schools as may be organized under the provisions of this Act, shall be subject to the general supervision of the Board of Education, and shall be entitled to participate in the apportionment of the school moneys as provided for by this Act, but they shall be under the immediate direction of their respective Trustees, Managers, and Directors, as herein provided.

OF NEW SCHOOLS.

§ 23. Whenever a majority of the School Officers of any ward shall certify in writing to the Board of Education, that it is necessary to establish a school in said ward, with the facts and circumstances showing such necessity, together with the number and class of scholars who will probably attend such school, if established, it shall be the duty of the Board of Education, without delay, to investigate the subject, and to determine the expediency of establishing such school in such ward applying for the same. Should the ward officers, or any of them, deem themselves aggrieved by such decision, they may appeal to the State Superintendent of Public Instruction, who shall decide as to the propriety of the establishment of such school, and his decision, if adverse to the appellants, shall be binding for the term of one year.

§ 24. Upon a decision favorable to the establishment of a school or schools in any of the wards of said city, it shall be lawful for the School Officers of said ward to proceed to organize one or more schools, such as may be authorized by the Board of Education, and procure a school-house, by purchasing or hiring the same, or by procuring a site and erecting a building thereon, according to plans and specifications, and contracts which shall have been duly filed with and approved by the Board of Education; the erection of which said building, and the fitting up thereof, and the fitting up of any hired building, shall be done by contract, proposals for which shall be advertised for two weeks previous to deciding upon estimates thereon, unless such fitting up shall not exceed the sum of two hundred dollars; and the expense of establishing and organizing any school, as above-mentioned, shall be levied and raised pursuant to the provisions of this Act.

§ 25. The title to all school property, real and personal, purchased with any moneys derived from the distribution or apportionment of the school moneys, or raised by taxation in the city of New York, shall be vested in the Mayor, Aldermen and Commonalty of said City, but shall be under the care and control of the Board of Education for the purposes of public education; and all suits in relation to the same shall be brought in the name of said Board, and no contract or contracts shall be made by the School Officers of any ward for the purchase of any site, without the consent of the Board of Education, or for the erection, or fitting up, or repairing of any building, when such repairs shall exceed in amount the sum of two hundred dollars, as authorized in this Act, until a statement in writing of the amount required for that purpose shall have been presented to the Board of Education by said School Officers, and together with a copy of the working drawings, plans, and specifications of the work to be done, pursuant to the provisions of this Act, shall have been duly filed and approved of as herein required, and an appropriation shall have been made by the Board of Education therefor.

§ 26. The Trustees, Managers, and Directors of any of the Corporate Schools entitled to participate in the apportionment of the school moneys, may at any time convey their school-houses and sites to the Corporation of the City of New York, and transfer any of their schools to the Board of Education, on the terms and in the manner to be agreed upon and prescribed by the Board of Education, so as either to merge the said schools in the Ward Schools or adopt them as Ward Schools; and the same shall then be Ward Schools, subject to all the rules, duties, and liabilities, and enjoy the same rights, as if they had been originally established as Ward Schools.

OF THE DISCONTINUANCE OF SCHOOLS.

§ 27. Whenever, owing to any nuisance or other circumstances in the immediate vicinity of any school, or to the small attendance of scholars therein, or other sufficient reason, it shall appear to the Board of Education necessary and proper to discontinue such school in any of the wards of this city, the said Board shall give notice to the Trustees of said school of its intention to consider the propriety of such discontinuance; and in thirty days after such notice, may proceed to investigate the matter, and if a majority of the School Officers of the ward shall consent to the same, and if the said Board shall determine by a vote of a majority of all the members thereof that it is proper to close the same, it shall be the duty of said Board to withhold all moneys which may have been apportioned or appropriated for the support of said school, and the said school shall not thereafter participate in any subsequent apportionment of the school moneys. So soon as the same shall take effect, the Comptroller of the city shall be notified thereof by the said Board, and the said school-house and site may thereupon be used or disposed of, as a part of the general property of the city.

MISCELLANEOUS PROVISIONS.

§ 28. The Common Council of the City of New York are hereby authorized and directed to raise by loan, in anticipation of the taxes, when necessary, all moneys required for erecting, purchasing, or leasing school-houses, and procuring sites therefor, and the fitting up and furnishing thereof, and for alterations in, or additions to, the present school buildings, or required for any other of the purposes authorized by this Act.

§ 29. All expenses incurred for the support of Common Schools in the respective wards shall be certified by the Trustees of Common Schools in such ward, or a majority of them, and delivered to the Inspectors of said ward; and it shall be the duty of said Inspectors to examine and audit the same, and upon said Inspectors being satisfied of their correctness, to certify the same to the Board of Education. All bills audited and paid shall be filed with the Board of Education.

§ 30. No compensation shall be allowed to the Commissioners, Inspectors, or Trustees of Common Schools for any services performed by them, but the Commissioners and Inspectors shall receive their actual and reasonable expenses while attending to the duties of their office, to be audited and allowed by the Board of Education.

§ 31. Every School Officer who shall refuse or neglect to render an account, or to pay over any balance in his hands, at the expiration of his term of office, shall, for each offense, forfeit the sum of fifty dollars, which sum, together with said unpaid balance, shall be sued for and collected by the Board of Supervisors, who shall prosecute without delay for the recovery of such forfeiture, together with the unpaid balance; and in case of the death of such School Officer, suit may be brought against his representatives, and all moneys recovered, after deducting expenses, shall be placed at the disposal of the Board of Education.

§ 32. Every person in the employ of the Board of Education, and every School Officer, and every officer or teacher of a school or society, who shall willfully sign a false report to the Board of Education, shall, for each offense, forfeit the sum of twenty-five dollars, and shall be deemed guilty of misdemeanor; and every such person or officer, who shall willfully misapply any of the public funds committed to his care, shall be deemed guilty of embezzlement.

§ 33. The following shall be substantially the form of oath or affirmation to be made by the Teacher:

"A. B., of the City of New York, Teacher of No. department, being duly sworn or affirmed, declares and says, that to the best of (his or her) knowledge and belief, the average number of children, actual residents of the city and county of New York, at the time of attending said school, between the ages of four and twenty-one years, who attended said school or department, each school-time or half-day, from the day of to the first day of January, , was , said average having been obtained by adding together the number of scholars present each school-time or half-day, and dividing the total by four hundred and sixty, agreeably to the fifteenth section of this Act."

§ 34. In any suit which shall hereafter be commenced against the Commissioners or Trustees of Common Schools for any act performed by virtue of or under color of their offices, or for any refusal or omission to perform any duty enjoined by law, and which might have been the subject of an appeal to the Superintendent, no costs shall be allowed to the plaintiff in cases where the court shall certify it appeared, on the trial of the cause, that the defendants acted in good faith. But this provision shall not extend to suits for penalties, nor to suits or proceedings to enforce the decisions of the State Superintendent of Public Instruction.

§ 35. All children between the ages of four and twenty-one, residing in the city and county, shall be entitled to attend any of the Common Schools therein; and the parents, guardians, or other persons having the custody or care of such children, shall not be liable to any tax, assessment, or imposition, for the tuition of any children, other than is hereinbefore provided.

§ 36. The Free Academy in the City of New York shall be entitled to participate in the distribution of the income of the Literature and other funds, in the same manner and upon the same conditions as the other Academies of the State; and the Regents of the University of the State of New York shall pay annually to the Board of Education of the City and County of New York, the distributive share of the said funds to which the said Free Academy shall by law be entitled, and which shall be applied and expended for library books for the said Free Academy.

§ 37. The Clerk of the Board of Education is hereby authorized to administer oaths and take affidavits in all matters appertaining to the schools in the City and County of New York, and for that purpose shall possess all the powers of a commissioner of deeds, but shall not be entitled to any of the fees or emoluments thereof.

§ 38. No School Officer shall be interested in any contract, payments under which are to be made, in whole or in part, out of moneys derived from the School Fund or raised by taxation for the support of Common Schools. No teacher employed in any of the schools entitled to participate in the apportionment of the school moneys shall hereafter be eligible to the office of Commissioner, Inspector, or Trustee of Common Schools.

§ 39. The Superintendent of School Buildings shall take and subscribe before the Clerk of the Board of Education the oath prescribed by the Constitution of this State, and give such security for the faithful performance of the duties of his office as the Board of Education may direct; and the department under his charge shall be subject to such rules and regulations as the said Board may establish, one of which shall prohibit the performance by him of any work on other account similar to that performed under the regulations so established.

"All the ordinary appropriations made for the support and government of the Almshouse Department shall, before the same are finally made, be submitted by the Governors of the Almshouse to a Board of Commissioners, consisting of the Mayor, Recorder, Comptroller, the President of the Board of Aldermen, and the President of the Board of Councilmen; if the said Commissioners approve of the appropriation, they shall immediately report the same to the Board of Supervisors; if they shall disapprove of the same, they shall return them with their objections to the Governors of the Almshouse for reconsideration, and in case the said Governors shall, upon a reconsideration, adhere by a vote of two-thirds of all the Governors then in office to the original appropriations, they shall return them to the Commissioners, whose duty it shall be to report to the Board of Supervisors.

"The Board of Education shall also submit in like manner all appropriations, required by them, to the Commissioners named in the last preceding section, and said appropriations shall be subject to all the provisions of said section, so far as the same may be applicable."[1]

[1] The last two paragraphs are from another law relating to city affairs, but are here inserted for obvious reasons.

An Act relative to Common Schools in the City of New York.

Passed June 4, 1853.

§ 3. The Commissioners referred to in the seventeenth section of the Act entitled "An Act further to amend the charter of the City of New York," passed the twelfth day of April, one thousand eight hundred and fifty-three, shall approve of and report to the Board of Supervisors all appropriations submitted to the said Commissioners by the Board of Education, within twenty days after such submission is made, by a delivery of a statement of the appropriations required by the Board of Education, to the Comptroller, who shall immediately convene the said Commissioners to consider the same; or else the said Commissioners shall, within the said twenty days, return and file the same, with their objections, in the office of the Clerk of the Board of Education; and the provisions of the said Act shall cease to operate upon or affect, from and after the expiration of the said twenty days, any appropriation in respect to which the said Commissioners shall have omitted to take such action; or any appropriation to which the Board of Education, upon a reconsideration pursuant to said Act, shall have adhered by the requisite vote of two thirds which the said Commissioners shall omit to report, within ten days after the return thereof to them, to the Board of Supervisors. And the provisions of the said Act shall apply to such only of the appropriations required by the Board of Education as are required by law to be acted upon by the Board of Supervisors.

CHANGES IN THE SCHOOL LAWS.

On the 25th day of April, 1864, the Legislature of the state, then in session, passed an act relative to Common Schools in the city of New York, of which the following is an attested copy:

§ 1. The city of New York is hereby divided into seven School Districts, as follows:

First District—First, Second, Third, Fourth, Fifth, Sixth, and Eighth Wards.

Second District—Seventh, Tenth, Thirteenth, and Fourteenth Wards.

Third District—Ninth and Sixteenth Wards.

Fourth District—Eleventh and Seventeenth Wards.

Fifth District—Fifteenth and Eighteenth Wards.

Sixth District—Twentieth and Twenty-first Wards.

Seventh District—Twelfth, Nineteenth, and Twenty-second Wards.

§ 2. At every charter election in the said city, there shall be elected in each School District one Commissioner of Common Schools, who shall take office on the first day of January next after his election, and hold office for the term of three years; and there shall also be elected in each ward one Trustee of Common Schools, who shall take office on the first day of January next after his election, and hold office for the term of five years; and no School Officer shall hereafter be elected or appointed in the said city, except as provided by this act, and no person shall at the same time hold more than one school office.

§ 3. On the second Wednesday in January, one thousand eight hundred and sixty-six, the Mayor of the city shall nominate to the Board of Education one person for each School District as a Commissioner of Common Schools, and the said Board shall appoint or reject each of the persons so nominated. If any of them shall be rejected, the Mayor shall make a new nomination, and shall continue to nominate until seven shall be appointed by the Board. The person so appointed shall hold office until the first day of January, one thousand eight hundred and sixty-seven.

§ 4. On the third Wednesday in November in every year the Mayor of the city shall nominate to the Board of Education one person for each School District as an Inspector of Common Schools in the District, for the term of three years, from and after the first day of January then next. The Board of Education shall, on the first Wednesday in December, vote by yeas and nays upon the appointment of each of the persons nominated; and every person who shall receive the affirmative votes of a majority of the whole Board, shall be appointed. If any of the persons so nominated shall fail to receive the votes of a majority of the whole Board, the Mayor shall make a new nomination; and shall continue to nominate until an appointment shall be made for each District, in the manner and for the term prescribed in this section.

§ 5. If, on the second Wednesday in January next, there shall be in any School District more than two Inspectors of Common Schools in office by popular election, the Board of Education shall select two of them, and such of the said Inspectors as are not selected shall immediately cease to hold office. After such reduction in the number of Inspectors has been made, the Board of Education shall select by lot one of the two Inspectors in each District, in office by popular election, and the Inspector selected shall be an Inspector for the District, and shall hold office until the expiration of the term for which he was elected, and the Inspector not selected shall cease to hold office unless the Board of Education shall appoint him an Inspector for the District, in which case he shall hold office until the thirty-first day of December, one thousand eight hundred and sixty-six.

§ 6. Vacancies in school offices shall be filled as follows: If there shall be less than three Commissioners or three Inspectors in any District, every vacancy shall be filled in the case of a Commissioner until the same can be filled at a charter election; and in the case of an Inspector for the unexpired portion of the term in which the vacancy exists, in the manner provided by this act for the appointment of Inspectors; and if there shall be less than five Trustees in any Ward, every vacancy shall be filled by the Mayor and a majority of the Inspectors for the District in which the Ward is included, until the same can be filled at a charter election. Every vacancy in the office of a Commissioner or Trustee, occurring more than ten days previous to any charter election, shall be filled at the next charter election for the unexpired portion of the term in which the vacancy exists.

§ 7. The elections held by virtue of this act, shall be subject to the same laws and regulations in all respects, so far as the same may be applicable, as those which govern the charter elections in said city; but the ballots for School Officers shall be indorsed "School Officers, Number ," and deposited in a separate box. Every person voted for to fill a vacancy in a school office shall be designated in the ballot by the words "To fill a vacancy," written or printed immediately over his name; or, if there be more than one vacancy to be filled, the person to be voted for shall respectively be designated by the words "To fill vacancy of years."

§ 8. Every School Officer shall, at the time of his election or appointment, be a resident of the District or Ward for which he is elected or appointed, and every Trustee removing from the Ward for which he is elected or appointed, and every School Officer removing from the city, shall thereby vacate his office.

§ 9. The Board of Education shall be judges of the election and qualification of its members.

§ 10. Every person elected or appointed to a school office in said city shall, before entering on the duties of his office, and within fifteen days after the commencement of the term for which he is elected, or from the time of being notified of his appointment to fill a vacancy, take and subscribe, before the Clerk of the Board of Education, the oath of office prescribed by the Constitution of this State; and the school office to which any person who shall omit to take the said oath within the time and in the manner above described, may have been elected or appointed, shall be vacant at and from the expiration of the said fifteen days.

§ 11. The first section of an act entitled "An Act to amend, consolidate, and reduce to one act, the various acts relative to the Common Schools of the City of New York," passed July third, eighteen hundred and fifty-one, and so much of all other acts heretofore passed as is amendatory of the said section, are hereby repealed; but this section shall not affect the continuance in office of the present School Officers, nor their powers or duties.

§ 12. The schools in the several Wards shall be classified as Grammar, Primary, and Evening Schools, and teachers for the said schools shall be appointed as follows: Principals and Vice-principals, by the Board of Education, upon the written nomination of a majority of the Trustees of the Ward, stating that the nomination was agreed to at a meeting of the Board of Trustees at which a majority of the whole number in office was present. Other teachers, and also janitors, shall be appointed by a majority of the Trustees for the Ward at a meeting of the Board of Trustees. Any teacher may be removed by the Board of Education upon the recommendation of the City Superintendent, or of a majority of the Trustees for the Ward, or of a majority of the Inspectors for the District. The Board of Trustees for the Ward, by the vote of a majority of the whole number of Trustees in office, may also remove teachers employed therein other than Principals and Vice-principals, and may also remove janitors, provided the removal is approved in writing by a majority of the Inspectors for the District; and provided further, that any teacher so removed shall have a right to appeal to the Board of Education, under such rules as it may prescribe, and the said Board shall have power, after hearing the answer of the Trustees, to reinstate the teacher.

§ 13. Subdivision three of section two of the act entitled "An Act to amend, consolidate, and reduce to one act, the various acts relative to the Common Schools of the City of New York," passed July third, eighteen hundred and fifty-one, as subsequently amended, is hereby amended so as to read as follows:

3. To remove from office any School Officer who shall have been directly or indirectly interested in the furnishing of any supplies or materials, or in the doing of any work or labor, or in the sale or leasing of any real estate, or in any proposal, agreement, or contract for any of these purposes, in any case in which the price or consideration is to be paid, in whole or in part, or directly or indirectly out of any school moneys; or who shall have received, from any source whatever, any com-

mission or other compensation in connection with any of the matters aforesaid; and any School Officer who shall violate the preceding provisions of this section, shall be deemed guilty of a misdemeanor, and, upon conviction thereof, shall be punished by a fine not exceeding one thousand dollars, and imprisonment in the city prison not exceeding one year, and shall also be ineligible to any school office. The Board shall also have power to remove from office any School Officer who shall have been guilty of immoral or disgraceful conduct in any matter connected with his official duties, or which tends to discredit his office or the school system. If one or more School Officers or tax-payers of the city of New York shall present a written charge to the Board of Education, accusing any School Officer of a violation of, or a liability to, any of the provisions of this section, it shall be the duty of the said Board to cause the same to be fully investigated. All testimony taken upon any such investigation shall be under oath; and the Court of Common Pleas shall have power, upon the application of the Board Education, to compel any witness who may have been duly summoned, to appear and testify before the said Board or any committee thereof.

§ 14. The ninth section of the act entitled "An Act to amend, consolidate, and reduce to one act, the various acts relative to the Common Schools of the City of New York," passed July third, eighteen hundred and fifty-one, is hereby amended so as to read as follows:

§ 9. It shall be the duty of the Inspectors of Common Schools, or a majority of them, in their respective districts, to examine in respect to every expense certified as correct by a majority of the Trustees of any Ward in the District, and to audit every such expense which may be just and reasonable; and no expense shall be paid unless audited in this manner. They shall also examine, at least once in every quarter, all the schools in the District, in respect to the punctual and regular attendance of the pupils and teachers, the number, fidelity, and competency of the teachers, the studies, progress, order, and discipline of the pupils, the cleanliness, safety, warming, ventilation, and comfort of the school premises; and whether or not the provisions of the school laws, in respect to the teaching of sectarian doctrines, or the use of sectarian books, have been violated, and call the attention of the Trustees without delay, to every matter requiring immediate action. They shall also, on or before the thirty-first day of December, in each year, make a written report to the Board of Education and to the Board of Trustees, in respect to the condition, efficiency, and wants of the District, in respect to schools and school premises.

§ 15. Until the first day of January next, the Inspectors of Common Schools shall have the powers and duties now conferred upon them by law, except that the signature of one inspector shall be sufficient to audit any bill or claim.

§ 16. Subdivision two of section eleven of the act entitled "An Act to amend, consolidate, and reduce to one act, the various acts relative to the Common Schools of the city of New York," passed July third, eighteen hundred and fifty-one, as subsequently amended, is hereby amended so as to read as follows:

2. Under such general rules and regulations as the Board of Education may establish, to examine into the qualifications of persons proposed as teachers in any of the schools under the charge of the Board. Such examination shall be conducted by the City Superintendent of Schools, or such one of his assistants as he may designate, in the presence of at least two Inspectors of Common Schools, who shall be designated for the purpose by the by-laws of the Board of Education. Licenses shall be granted to those persons found upon such examination to be entitled thereto, which shall be in the form prescribed by the said by-laws, shall be signed by the City Superintendent, and by at least two Inspectors designated for the purpose, who shall certify that they were present at the examination, and concur in granting the license. The license of any teacher may be revoked for any cause affecting the morality or competency of the teacher, by the written certificate of the City Superintendent, and the

written concurrence of two of the Inspectors for the District in which the teacher is employed; but no such action shall be taken until at least ten days' previous notice has been allowed; nor shall it take effect until such certificate of revocation has been filed in the office of the Clerk of the Board of Education, and a copy served upon the teacher. It shall be the duty of the City Superintendent to re-examine any teacher upon the written request of any two Inspectors of the District, or three Trustees of the Ward, in which the teacher is employed. Any teacher whose license has been revoked as aforesaid, may appeal to the State Superintendent of Public Instruction, within ten days after service of a copy of the certificate of revocation by the service of a written notice of appeal upon the City Superintendent; and in case such appeal is taken, the teacher shall not be disqualified until the revocation is confirmed by the State Superintendent. The City Superintendent, in his annual report to the Board of Education, shall include a list of the licenses granted and revoked by him.

§ 17. Section twenty-three of the act entitled "An Act to amend, consolidate, and reduce to one act, the various acts relative to the Common Schools of the City of New York," passed July third, eighteen hundred and fifty-one, is hereby amended so as to read as follows:

§ 23. The Board of Education may, with the consent of a majority of the Trustees of the Ward, or without such consent, by vote of two-thirds of the Board of Education, discontinue any Grammar, Primary, Evening, or Colored School; and the said Board may also authorize the establishment of a new school, upon the written application of a majority of the Trustees for the Ward. It shall be the duty of the Board of Education to decide finally upon every such application within thirty-five days after the same is presented to it; and if the said Board shall omit to do so, or shall deny the application, and a majority of the Inspectors for the District shall certify that there is probable cause for granting the application, the Trustees may appeal to the State Superintendent of Public Instruction, whose decision in the matter shall be binding upon all the parties; and if adverse to the application, the same shall not be renewed during the term of one year next hereafter.

§ 18. The seventh section of the act entitled "An Act to amend, consolidate, and reduce to one act, the various acts relative to the Common Schools of the City of New York," passed July third, eighteen hundred and fifty-one, as subsequently amended, and subdivision four of section eight of the same act are hereby repealed, but this section shall not take effect until the first day of January next.

§ 19. The second subdivision of the tenth section of the act entitled "An Act to amend, consolidate, and reduce to one act, the various acts relative to the Common Schools of the City of New York," passed July third, eighteen hundred and fifty-one, as subsequently amended, is hereby amended so as to read as follows:

2. Under such general rules and regulations, and subject to such limitations as the Board of Education may prescribe; to conduct and manage the said schools; to furnish all needful supplies therefor, and to make all needful repairs, alterations, and additions, in and to the school premises.

§ 20. The Commissioners, Inspectors, and Trustees, elected or appointed in pursuance of the provisions of this act, shall respectively possess and exercise the powers and duties which the Commissioners, Inspectors, and Trustees of Common Schools now lawfully possess and exercise, except as is herein otherwise provided.

§ 21. This act shall take effect immediately.

The principal changes produced by this act may be thus enumerated:

First—The Board of Education is reduced from forty-four members elected by Wards, to twenty-one members elected, three from each of seven Districts.

Second—The Boards of Trustees are reduced from ten members, consisting of the Commissioners *ex officio* and eight Trustees, to five Trustees only.

Third—The Inspectors, instead of being two in each Ward,

elected by the people, will be three in each of seven Districts, selected by the Mayor and Board of Education.

Fourth—Vacancies in the office of Commissioner are to be filled by the Mayor and the Board of Education for the balance of the year; vacancies in the office of Inspector are to be filled by the Mayor and the Board of Education for the balance of the unexpired term, and vacancies in the office of Trustee to be filled by the Mayor and the Inspectors of the District embracing the Ward, for the balance of the year.

Fifth—A School Officer removing from the Ward or city, vacates his office.

Sixth—Principals and Vice-principals of schools are to be nominated to the Board of Education, in writing, by a majority of Trustees. Other teachers and janitors are to be appointed by a majority of the Trustees.

Seventh—Removals of teachers may be made by the Board of Education, upon the recommendation, either of the City Superintendent, of a majority of the Trustees of the Ward, or a majority of the Inspectors of the District. A majority of the Trustees may remove teachers other than Principals or Vice-principals, and janitors, on the approval in writing of a majority of the Inspectors of the District in which the Ward is located; but any teacher so removed may appeal to the Board of Education, who shall have the power to reinstate the teacher, after hearing the answer of the Trustees.

Eighth—The Board of Education have power to remove any School Officer for any conduct tending to throw discredit on his office or the school system. On complaint of any School Officer, or any tax-payer against any School Officer, the Board of Education shall investigate the matter, examine witnesses under oath, and the Court of Common Pleas may compel the attendance of any witnesses either before the Board of Education or any committees thereof.

Ninth—All bills passed by the Boards of Trustees shall be audited by the District Inspectors.

Tenth—Licenses to teach shall hereafter be granted by the City Superintendent or one of his assistants, in the presence of at least two inspectors to be designated for that duty by the Board of Education. Licenses may be revoked on a hearing and on ten days' notice, by the City Superintendent, with the concurrence of two Inspectors of the District in which the teacher is employed. The City Superintendent shall re-examine any teacher on request of any two Inspectors of the District, or any three Trustees of the Ward. Any teacher whose license is revoked, may appeal to the State Superintendent, and shall not be disqualified until such revocation is confirmed.

Eleventh—The Board of Education may, with consent of a majority of Trustees, or without such consent, by a two-third vote, discontinue any school, and may establish any school on the written application of a majority of the Trustees of the Ward. Such applications must be decided within thirty-five days after their presentation; and in case of failure to act, or denial of the application, on obtaining from the District Inspector a certificate that there is probable cause for granting such application, the Trustees may appeal to the State Superintendent, whose decision shall be final, and, if adverse, the application shall not be renewed for one year.

Twelfth—The limit of two hundred dollars to expenses of the Local Boards is abolished, and school repairs, etc., are to be made by the Trustees, under such rules and regulations as the Board of Education may establish.

An Act to erect the "Free Academy of the City of New York" into a College.

Passed March 30, 1866, by a Majority.

The People of the State of New York, represented in Senate and Assembly, do enact as follows:

SECTION 1. The Free Academy in the city of New York, heretofore established under the authority of law, by the Board of Education of the city and county of New York, and now under the supervision, management, and government of the said Board of Education, shall henceforth be a distinct and separate organization and body corporate, and be known as "The College of the City of New York," and, as such, shall have the powers and privileges of a college, pursuant to the Revised Statutes of this state, and be subject to the provisions of the said statute relative to colleges, and to the visitation of the Regents of the University, in like manner with the other colleges of the state.

SEC. 2. The members of the said Board of Education shall be *ex officio* the Trustees of said College, and shall have and possess the powers conferred upon, and be subject to the duties required of trustees of colleges by the Revised Statutes.

SEC. 3. All acts of the Legislature now in force in regard to the said Free Academy, and to its control, management, support, and affairs, and which are not inconsistent with the foregoing provisions of this act, shall continue in force, and are hereby declared to be applicable to the College hereby incorporated as aforesaid.

SEC. 4. This act shall take effect immediately.

An Act in Relation to the College of the City of New York.

Passed April 17, 1866, Three-fifths being Present.

The People of the State of New York, represented in Senate and Assembly, do enact as follows:

SECTION 1. The Trustees of the College of the City of New York shall annually, on or before the fifteenth day of November, report to the Board of Supervisors of the county of New York, such sum not exceeding one hundred and twenty-five thousand dollars, in any one year, as they may require for the payment of the salaries of the professors and officers of the said College, for obtaining and furnishing scientific apparatus, books for the library and students, and all other supplies therefor, for repairing and altering the College building, and for the support, maintenance, and general expenses of said College. And the said Board of Supervisors of the county of New York are hereby authorized and directed, in each and every year, to raise and collect by tax on the estate, real and personal, liable to taxation in such county, such sum of money, not to exceed the amount aforesaid, as may be reported to them by said Trustees, the amount so to be raised and collected to be in addition to the sums required for the purposes of Common Schools in the city of New York, under the act entitled "An Act to amend, consolidate, and reduce to one act the various acts of the city of New York relative to Common Schools," passed July third, eighteen hundred and fifty-one, and the various acts amendatory thereof. And the said Board of Supervisors are required and directed to raise and collect, in the manner aforesaid, for the Trustees of said College, in the year one thousand eight hundred and sixty-six, the sum of one hundred and twenty-five thousand dollars, for the uses and purposes aforesaid.

SEC. 2. It shall be the duty of the Trustees hereinbefore named, to select a suitable site upon the lands of the Corporation of the City of New York, north of Fortieth street in said city, for the future use of the College of the City of New York, and notify the Commissioner of the Sinking Fund of such selection, and such site shall not be sold, leased, or otherwise encumbered unless such disposition thereof is expressly authorized by some law hereafter passed.

TITLES OF SCHOOL ACTS RELATING TO THE CITY OF NEW YORK.

An act to direct certain moneys to be applied to the use of Free Schools in the city of New York. Passed April 8, 1801. Sess. Laws (Webster & Skinner's ed.), vol. 2, p. 253. Directs the school moneys apportioned to New York to be paid "to the Vestry of the Episcopal Church, the Vestry of Christ Church, the Trustees of the First Presbyterian Church, the Minister, Elders, and Deacons of the Reformed Dutch Church, the Trustees of the Methodist Episcopal Church, the Trustees of the Scotch Presbyterian Church belonging to the Associated Reformed Synod, and to the Trustees of the African School, and to the Trustees of the United German Lutheran, the Trustees of the German Reformed Churches, to the

Trustees of the First Baptist Church in the city of New York, and to the Trustees of the United Brethren or Moravian Church, each, one-eleventh part of all the money in the hands of the Common Council."

An act to incorporate the Society formed in the city of New York for promoting the Manumission of Slaves, and protecting such of them as have been or may be liberated. Passed February 19, 1803. Society formed 1785. School opened 1787.

An act to incorporate the Society instituted in the city of New York for the establishment of a Free School for the education of poor children, who do not belong to and are not provided for by any religious society. Passed April 9, 1805. Sess. Laws (Webster & Skinner's ed.), vol. 4, p. 265. Common School education from date of this law until 1842 was substantially in charge of this society, whose principal founder and promoter was De Witt Clinton.

An act to incorporate the Trustees of the First Protestant Episcopal Charity School in the city of New York. Passed March 14, 1806. Sess. Laws (Webster & Skinner's ed.), vol. 4, p. 378. This act incorporated a school to be kept instead of the Free School maintained for many years previous, under the care and management of the Corporation of Trinity Church.

An act for the further encouragement of Free Schools in the city of New York. Passed March 30, 1811. Sess. Laws (Webster & Skinner's ed.), p. 172. Gives to the Free School Society $4000 of the moneys arising from the excise duties then in the city treasury, and $1000 a year thereafter.

An act supplementary to the act entitled "An Act for the Establishment of Common Schools." Passed March 12, 1813. Sess. Laws, p. 38. The General School Act of 1812 did not apply to New York City. By this act the city was permitted to share in the distribution of the revenue of the school fund. The city was required to raise a sum equal to its share of such school money. The Common Council appointed school commissioners to receive and apportion it. It was to be paid "to the Trustees of the Free School Society in said city of New York, and the Trustees or Treasurer of the Orphan's Asylum Society, the Society of the Economical School in the city of New York, the African Free School, and of such incorporated religious societies in said city as now support or shall hereafter establish Charity Schools within the said city, who may apply for the same." The distribution was to be in proportion to the average number of children taught between the ages of four and fifteen years, but was to be paid to no society whose school had not been kept for nine months in the previous year. The children were to be taught free of expense. The Trustees of the several schools were to make to the School Commissioners reports similar to those of the Trustees of Common Schools, and the School Commissioners to the Superintendent of Common Schools. The public money was to be applied to the payment of teachers' wages. The Trustees of the several societies were declared inspectors of the schools of their respective societies.

An act respecting the Free School Society of New York. Passed April 5, 1817. Sess. Laws, p. 150. Granted $2000 out of the Excise Fund.

An act to incorporate the Hamilton Free School (New York), and for other purposes. Passed April 17, 1818. Sess. Laws, p. 163. The fourth section gives the Trustees of this school a share in the distribution of the Common School moneys.

An act relative to the common lands of the freeholders and inhabitants of Harlem. Passed March 28, 1820. Sess. Laws, p. 96. Directs the lands to be sold by trustees; $3000 to be paid to the Harlem Library; $3500 to the Hamilton School; $4000 to the Harlem School; $4500 to Manhattanville School; and, until such schools are established, the funds are to remain in trust in the hands of the Trustees, and placed on good interest.

An act relative to the Roman Catholic Benevolent Society in the city of New York. Passed April 1, 1820. Sess. Laws, p. 117. Requires the Commissioners of Common School Fund in the city to allow and pay to the Trustees of the Society their proportion of the Common School money.

An act to amend an act entitled "An Act relative to the General Society of Mechanics and Tradesmen of the city of New York," passed April 3, 1811. Passed January 26, 1821. Sess. Laws, p. 10. Permits the school of said Society to share in the distribution of the school moneys. Society was founded in 1784.

An act relating to Common Schools in the city of New York. Passed November 19, 1824. Sess. Laws, p. 337. Provides for the apportionment of school moneys to the city, and for the election of ten commissioners to distribute it; prescribes their duties as to making reports and visiting the schools, and repeals all former laws relating to the schools of the city.

An act incorporating the New York High School—exact title and date not known. The school was a pay school, and on the Lancasterian plan.

An act in relation to the Free School Society of New York. Passed January 28, 1826. Sess. Laws, p. 19. Name altered to "Public School Society of New York." The Society was also required to provide for the education of all children without regard to the sect or denomination to which their parents might belong. The Trustees were, by Section 3, permitted to charge a "moderate compensation adapted to the abilities of the parents of the children."

An act to amend the act relating to Common Schools in the city of New York, passed November 19, 1824. Passed April 8, 1826. Sess. Laws, p. 93. Increases the number of School Commissioners to twelve.

An act to provide for the building an Asylum for the Deaf and Dumb in the city of New York. Passed March 23, 1827. Sess. Laws, p. 76. Section 1 appropriated $10,000 for purchase of land and erection of buildings, provided the institution should raise an equal sum. The Secretary of State was to approve the site. By Section 2, the institution was placed under the supervision of the Superintendent of Common

Schools, and the directors were to file their consent under their corporate seal in the office of the Secretary of State.

An act to incorporate the Manhattanville Free School in the Twelfth Ward in the city of New York. Passed March 30, 1827. Sess. Laws, p. 103. This was essentially a Public and District School. The Trustees were annually elected by the freeholders of the village of Manhattanville. To receive $2500 from Trustees of Harlem fund.

An act to incorporate the Trustees of the Harlem School in the Twelfth Ward of the city of New York. Passed April 2, 1827. Sess. Laws, p. 119. A Public School, the Trustees to be annually elected by a vote of the freeholders of the village of Harlem. To receive $4000 from Trustees of the Harlem fund.

An act to incorporate the Trustees of the Yorkville School in the Twelfth Ward of the city of New York. Passed April 2, 1827. Sess. Laws, p. 114. This was also essentially a Public School, of which the Trustees were elected by the freeholders of the village of Yorkville. To receive $2000 from Trustees of Harlem fund.

An act further to amend an act entitled "An Act to incorporate the Trustees of the First Protestant Episcopal Charity School in the city of New York." Passed April 11, 1827. Sess. Laws, p. 315. Authorizes an increase of the number of schools and the number of trustees.

An act relative to deeds and mortgages executed or to be executed by the Public School Society of New York. Passed January 20, 1829. Grants the right to sell and convey real estate, and to mortgage and confirm all former sales and grants.

An act for the further support and extension of Common Schools in the city of New York. Passed April 25, 1829. Sess. Laws, p. 397. Authorizes the increase of the city school tax one-eightieth of one per cent.

An act for the further support and extension of Common Schools in the city of New York. Passed April 13, 1831. Sess. Laws, p. 164. Authorizes a tax of three-eighths of one per cent. on the valuation of the taxable property of the city for the purposes of Common Schools in the city. It is to be apportioned as provided in the Revised Statutes, Article 7, Chapter 15, Sections 117 to 127.

An act relative to the school connected with the Almshouse of the city of New York. Passed April 13, 1835. Sess. Laws, p. 54. Declares school entitled to its share of public moneys in any apportionment by School Commissioners, and places the school in charge of the Public School Society.

An act to extend to the city and county of New York the provisions of the general act in relation to Common Schools. Passed April 11, 1842. Sess. Laws, p. 184.

An act to amend an act entitled "An Act to extend to the city and county of New York the provisions of the general act in relation to Common Schools," passed April 11, 1842. Passed April 18, 1843. Sess. Laws, p. 290.

An act to amend the charter of the Public School Society of the city of New York. Passed March 23, 1844. Sess. Laws, p. 50.

An act more effectually to provide for Common School education in the city and county of New York. Passed May 7, 1844. Sess. Laws, p. 490.

An act authorizing the Board of Education of the city of New York to establish a Free Academy. Passed May 7, 1847.

An act to authorize the Board of Education of the city of New York to establish Evening Free Schools for the education of apprentices and others. Passed April 16, 1847. Sess. Laws, p. 82.

An act to amend an act entitled "An Act more effectually to provide for Common School Education in the city of New York," passed May 7, 1844. Passed May 11, 1847. Sess. Laws, p. 275.

An act to incorporate the New York Society for the promotion of education among colored children. Passed December 7, 1847. Sess. Laws, p. 425.

O

An act in relation to the Public School Society in the city of New York. Passed March 4, 1848. Sess. Laws, p. 81.

An act to amend an act entitled "An Act to extend to the city and county of New York the provisions of the general act in relation to Common Schools," passed April 11, 1842. Passed March 21, 1848. Sess. Laws, p. 147.

An act to authorize the Board of Education of the city of New York to establish Evening Schools for the education of apprentices and others. Passed March 25, 1848. Sess. Laws, p. 209.

An act to amend an act entitled "An Act more effectually to provide for Common School education in the city and county of New York," passed May 7, 1844. Passed March 27, 1848. Sess. Laws, p. 211.

An act to amend an act entitled "An Act more effectually to provide for Common School education in the city and county of New York," passed May 7, 1844. Passed May 11, 1849. Sess. Laws, p. 549.

An act to amend the charter of the Manhattanville Free School in the city of New York. Passed March 27, 1850. Sess. Laws, p. 147. Authorized to convey their real estate and improvements to the city. Became a Grammar School.

An act to amend, consolidate, and reduce to one act the various acts relative to Common Schools of the city of New York. Passed July 3, 1851. Sess. Laws, p. 734.

An act in relation to the school officers of the Twentieth Ward of the city of New York. Passed March 26, 1852. Sess. Laws, p. 130. Permits them to enter upon the duties of their office as soon as they take the oath of office required by law.

An act relative to Common Schools in the city of New York. Passed June 4, 1853. Sess. Laws, p. 629. Authorizes the Public School Society to transfer all its property and schools to the city.

An act relative to Common Schools in the city of New York. Passed March 31, 1854. Sess. Laws, p. 235.

An act relative to Common Schools in the city of New York. Passed April 15, 1854. Sess. Laws, p. 588.

An act to enable the schools of the Five Points House of Industry, and the school established by the Ladies' Home Missionary Society, to participate in the distribution of the Common School Fund. Passed April 12, 1855. Sess. Laws, p. 761.

An act to provide for the appointment of a commission to secure the more perfect establishment, government, regulation, and economy of Common Schools in the city of New York. Passed April 17, 1857. Sess. Laws, vol. 2, p. 528.

An act to continue the commission appointed to secure the more perfect establishment, government, regulation, and economy of Common Schools in the city of New York. Passed April 14, 1858. Sess. Laws, p. 318.

An act in relation to school libraries in the city of New York, passed April 13, 1860. Sess. Laws, p. 626.

An act to repeal an act passed April 16, 1860, entitled "An Act in relation to school libraries in the city of New York," passed April 13, 1860. Passed April 15, 1861. Sess. Laws, p. 194.

An act to enable the schools of the Children's Aid Society to participate in the distribution of the Common School Fund. Passed April 17, 1862. Sess. Laws, p. 455.

An act relative to Common Schools in the city of New York. Passed April 15, 1863. Sess. Laws, p. 193.

An act relative to Common Schools in the city of New York. Passed April 25, 1864. Sess. Laws, p. 822.

An act relative to Common Schools in the city of New York. Passed March 3, 1865. Sess. Laws, p. 94.

An act to erect the "Free Academy of the city of New York" into a College. Passed March 30, 1866.

An act to amend an act entitled "An Act to amend, consolidate, and reduce to one act the various acts relative to Common Schools of the city of New York," passed July 3, 1851. Passed April 2, 1866. Sess. Laws, p. 748.

An Act in relation to the College of the city of New York. Passed April 17, 1866.

An act relative to Common Schools in the city of New York. Passed April 9, 1867. Sess. Laws, vol. 1, p. 540.

GENERAL ACTS AFFECTING SCHOOLS IN THE CITY OF NEW YORK.

An act for the encouragement of schools. Passed April 9, 1795. Sess. Laws (Greenleaf) vol. 3, p. 248. This was the first general school law, passed in this state. It provided that there should be appropriated from the treasury $50,000 a year for five years, "for the purpose of encouraging and maintaining schools in the several cities and towns in this state, in which the children of the inhabitants residing in the state shall be instructed in the English language, or be taught English grammer, arithmetic, mathematics, and such other branches of knowledge as are most useful and necessary to complete a good English education." The first apportionment was made by the law, according to the representation of the counties in the Assembly; but it was provided that future apportionments should be made "in proportion to the number of electors for members of Assembly in each county." The Boards of Supervisors were required to apportion the money among the several towns according to the number of taxable inhabitants, as they should appear from the tax lists annually returned to them by the assessors. The Boards of Supervisors in the several counties in the state were also required to raise by tax a sum equal to the amount apportioned from the state treasury, except that the city of Albany was to raise a tax for only half the amount. In the city of New York the money was to be used for the support of Charity Schools, and all other schools, such as mentioned above, "whether the children taught in such Charity Schools shall be children of white parents, or descended from Africans and Indians." The inhabitants of the towns were required to elect not less than three nor more than seven persons to be Commissioners of Schools, to have the distribution of the money and the superintendence of the schools. The cities of Albany and Hudson, for the purposes of the act, were declared to be towns. The inhabitants of the towns were authorized to elect Trustees, and to associate together for the purpose of hiring school-masters and organizing schools. The Trustees were required to make, on the third Tuesday in March in each year, a return of the school kept in their charge, containing the name of the master or masters, the number of days he or they had taught, the names of the scholars instructed, and the number of days they have severally attended the school, and the time or times within which the school has been kept. The Commissioners were "to collect into one sum the whole number of days for which each and every scholar, that may have attended any one of the said schools, shall have been instructed therein, and to apportion the moneys allotted to and raised in that town for the purpose aforesaid, according to the whole number of days for which instruction shall appear to have been given in said schools, in such manner that the school in which the greater number of days of instruction shall appear to have been given shall have a proportionably larger sum." The money was paid to the Trustees by an order drawn by the Commissioners on the County Treasurer. The Commissioners were required to make to the County Treasurer an annual report of the condition of the schools, and the County Treasurer was required to transmit the same to the Secretary of State.

An act further to amend an act entitled "An Act for the encouragement of schools." Passed March 10, 1797. Sess. Laws (Greenleaf's ed.), vol. 3, p. 397. Ordered, that in the city of New York one-sixth part of the public money should be apportioned to the Charity Schools, and the other five-sixths "among the schools which in any wards in the city may be established and conducted in conformity to the said act." The inhabitants of the city were also granted the same rights, powers, and privileges as were granted the inhabitants residing in any parts of any towns in the state. It was also provided that no school in the state should receive any more money in any one year than should be required to pay the master or masters for the same year. The apportionment was made for the years 1796, 1797, 1798, but was omitted for the years 1799 and 1800. An abstract of the returns for the year 1798 from sixteen of the twenty-three counties shows a total of 1352 schools organized according to the act, in which 59,660 children were taught.

An act to raise a fund for the encouragement of Common Schools. Passed April 2, 1805. Sess. Laws (Webster & Skinner's ed.), vol. 4, p. 126. Appropriates the net proceeds of 500,000 acres of land first sold after the passage of the act, to be a permanent fund for the support of Common Schools. No distribution of the income was to be made until the interest should amount to $50,000 annually. This act laid the foundation of the Common School Fund.

An act for the establishment of Common Schools. Passed June 19, 1812. Sess. Laws (Webster & Skinner's ed.), p. 600. This was the first law for the organization of Common Schools. It was repealed in 1814, and superseded by an amended act. Repealed and revised in 1819. The revisers, whose work is known as the Revised Statutes, framed a new statute which took effect January 1, 1828, and which repealed all general laws on the subject of a previous date.

An act to appropriate the income of the United States Deposit Fund to the purposes of education and the diffusion of knowledge. Passed April 17, 1838. Sess. Laws, p. 220. The second section appropriates $110,000 annually for the support of Common Schools. The fourth section appropriates $55,000 annually to the purchase of books for school libraries. These appropriations have been annually made since the passage of the law. The surplus revenue has been bestowed upon colleges, academies, and literary institutions.

An act establishing Free Schools throughout the state. Passed March 26, 1849. Sess. Laws, p. 683. Submitted to the people, and ratified by large majorities in every county. Majority in the city of New York, 19,739.

An act submitting to the people at the next annual election the question of the repeal of the act establishing Free

Schools throughout the state. Passed April 15, 1830. Sess. Laws, p. 804. Majority against repeal in the entire state was about 25,000. The system was saved by the cities, and particularly by New York City and County, which gave a majority of 37,827 against repeal.

An act to provide for the care and instruction of idle and truant children. Passed April 12, 1853. Sess. Laws, p. 358.

An act creating the office of State Superintendent of Public Instruction. Passed March 30, 1854. Sess. Laws, p. 230. Created the Department of Public Instruction, and transferred to it the Superintendence of the Common Schools. The Secretary of State had been *ex officio* Superintendent from April 3, 1821, to April 8, 1854. There had been a State Superintendent from January 14, 1813, to April 3, 1821, when the office was abolished.

XIX.

ABSTRACT OF SCHOOL CENSUS OF THE CITY OF NEW YORK, 1867.

In November, 1867, the Clerk of the Board of Education, by means of circular letters and other agencies, instituted a series of special inquiries into the educational history and statistics of the city of New York, and its schools, public, private, and denominational. Besides the general and prompt response afforded by principals, trustees, and other officers, valuable assistance was obtained from Superintendent Kennedy, of the Metropolitan Police.

The inquiries embraced, among others, the following particulars:

The name and location of each school.

How supported.

The whole number of pupils taught during the year ending October 1, 1867.

Their ages, sex, color, and nativity.

The number of teachers employed, both male and female, and the number of years' experience in teaching.

The course of study.

The number of weeks the school has been opened, and the length of the daily session.

The average annual cost per pupil.

The number of volumes in the school library.

The approximate value of philosophical apparatus and of real estate.

Such other information, historical or statistical, as could be furnished.

These statistics relate to no less than 584 schools, and their collection and subsequent reduction to proper form involved much labor.

It is to be regretted that to many of these inquiries the replies were not sufficiently general or definite to allow their presentation in tabular form. Yet all the more important points have been covered, and the results are very valuable.

The total expense of each school has been found by multiplying the whole number taught by the reported average annual expense per pupil. The result may be somewhat in excess of the true amount, but is believed to be substantially correct.

Some apparent discrepancies in the statistics of the Public Schools are removed when it is remembered that the annual reports close with the 31st of December, while this special report includes the interval of one year ending October 1, 1867.

WHOLE NUMBER OF SCHOOLS.

Under control of the Board of Education	219
Corporate Schools partly controlled by the Board	36
All other schools	329
Total	584

PUPILS—HOW DISTRIBUTED.

Whole number reported taught in Schools of the Board.	224,416
" " " " all other schools	45,787
Total reported taught during the year	270,203

Among these there were:

In the Corporate Schools of the Board	16,567
In other Corporate Schools	5,213
Denominational Schools	31,490
In Private Schools of all kinds	27,058
In Day Schools	250,493
In Evening Schools	19,710

COLOR.

White pupils	267,770
Colored pupils	2,433

AGES.

Under 12 years of age	71 per cent	191,844
12 years of age, or over	29 per cent	78,359

SEX.

Male pupils	54 per cent	145,909
Female pupils	46 per cent	124,294

The nativity of the pupils of the Day Schools of the Board only is given; in the private and other schools it could not be ascertained:

NATIVITY.

Born in the United States	90¼ per cent.
" Germany	3¾ "
" Great Britain and Ireland	4½ "
" France	½ "
Born elsewhere	1 "

This statement does not properly indicate the nativity of the parents; a matter somewhat difficult to obtain, especially in the Primary Schools and Departments. In a Grammar School situated in the midst of a large German population recent inquiry showed that in the seven classes of one department the German parentage alone varied from fifty to eighty per cent. In other sections of the city other nationalities predominate; but in most instances, as the table above given would suggest, American parentage is most largely represented.

ATTENDANCE.

The following table exhibits the average attendance and the whole number taught in the several classes of schools under the supervision of the Board. The large proportion of pupils in the Primary Schools and Departments, when taken in connection with the course of study and the reported ages of pupils, throws much light upon the condition of a large part of those children who are the chief subject of the article on the "Vagrant Question."

	Average Attendance.	Whole No. Taught.
Male Grammar Schools	15,392	31,438
Female Grammar Schools	13,264	27,114
Primary Schools and Departments	52,198	129,900
Colored Schools	702	1,887
Normal Schools	406	1,000
Total for Public Day Schools	81,962	191,339
Corporate Schools of the Board	6,074	16,567
Total for Day Schools	88,036	207,906
Evening Schools of the Board—Males......4,716 / " " Females...2,763	7,479	11,877 / 4,633 — 16,510
Total for all schools of the Board	95,515	224,416

TEACHERS.

	Males.	Females.
In the Schools of the Board	360	2,044
In all other schools	901	717
Total number of Teachers.......4,022	1,261	2,762

COST.

Cost of	224,415	pupils in Schools of the Board	$2,950,000
"	45,787	" other schools	2,101,232
"	270,203	" all schools	$5,051,232

In this estimate the total cost of the Public Schools includes a large sum for the necessary new buildings, repairs, supplies, etc., while in the case of the private schools the cost of tuition only is given.

The following is the cost of tuition of pupils and care of the buildings in the schools of the Board:

Salaries of Teachers in Ward Schools	$1,497,180 88
" Janitors "	75,686 29
" Teachers and Janitors in Evening Schools	87,191 97
Salaries of Teachers and Janitors in Colored Schools	30,150 26
Salaries of Teachers and Janitors in Normal Schools	7,605 62
Total	$1,697,815 02
Gas and fuel for Ward and Evening Schools	83,024 03
Total for tuition, gas, and fuel	$1,780,839 05
Books, maps, stationery, etc., for all schools	$184,370 24

The total cost of the sites, buildings, and appurtenances at present under the control of the Board of Education has been a little short of $5,000,000. The present estimated value of this property is at least double that amount, or nearly $8,000,000. Several valuable pieces of property no longer needed for school purposes have been transferred, as by law provided, to the Commissioners of the Sinking Fund. These are not credited to the Board of Education as an offset to expenses.

The amount apportioned to each of the following schools is based upon the average attendance of the last year. This is the case with all schools participating.

CORPORATE SCHOOLS UNDER SUPERVISION OF THE BOARD.

Schools.	Sessions.	Average.	Whole Number.	Amount Apportioned.
New York Orphan Asylum	506	171	184	$1,151 28
Roman Catholic Orphan Asylum—				
Male Department	485	473	559	5,763 78
Female Department	484	354	397	
Protestant Half-orphan Asylum	570	145	310	1,601 46
House of Refuge	512	1,091	1,720	7,512 84
Leake and Watts Orphan House—				
Male Department	222	55	74	804 42
Female Department	466	39	52	
Colored Orphan Asylum	505	213	264	1,490 76
American Female Guardian Society and Home Industrial School	452	920	4,130	5,011 02
New York Juvenile Asylum	574	603	1,136	4,295 16
House of Reception of do	514	126	1,028	922 50
Ladies' Home Missionary Society.	454	352	1,834	2,022 12
Five Points House of Industry	510	413	1,095	2,627 28
Children's Aid Society	5,483*	1,051	3,702	6,900 30
Nursery and Child's Hospital	516	68	82	369 00
Total	....	6,074	16,567	$40,471 92

Among the schools not known as Public Schools there are the following:

Denominations.	Schools.	Male Teachers.	Female Teachers.	Pupils.	Reported Cost.
Catholic Free Schools	23	56	91	16,342	$142,909
Catholic Pay Schools	24	96	95	6,070	176,976
Protestant Episcopal Church	24	29	28	2,367	56,515
Other Protestant Denominations.	22	38	25	5,713	27,980
Children's Aid Society	13	3	26	3,702	18,510
N. Y. Female Guardian Society	7	...	16	4,130	48,527
Hebrew Schools, including Orphan Asylum	12	24	8	998	35,323
German Schools, Free and Private	25	86	33	3,641	102,383
Asylums not above given	7	25	51	3,267	368,000
Colleges and Corporate Schools for Adults	8	134	11	5,133	308,000
Other Private Schools	168	407	323	11,875	757,000

* In this case the aggregate of the thirteen schools of the Society is given.

Years.	Average Attendance.			Whole Number Taught.			Total Expenses.
	Common Schools.	Corporate Schools.	Total.	Common Schools.	Corporate Schools.	Total.	
1842	15,420	1,341	16,761	45,614	2,325	47,939	....
1843	18,017	1,450	19,467	56,927	2,458	59,385	....
1844	22,784	1,570	24,354	58,195	2,656	60,851	....
1845	24,124	1,571	25,695	68,450	2,740	71,190	$179,907 23
1846	26,491	1,584	28,075	74,158	2,827	76,985	220,704 16
1847	30,244	1,878	32,122	87,430	2,169	89,599	254,474 58
1848	33,239	2,125	35,364	91,303	3,742	95,045	289,325 53
1849	33,958	2,040	35,998	99,418	3,556	102,974	287,473 43
1850	38,009	2,046	40,055	103,798	3,565	107,363	361,417 95
1851	40,929	2,031	42,960	112,785	3,842	116,627	512,955 96
1852	42,588	2,008	44,596	123,786	3,451	127,237	505,452 57
1853	44,061	2,679	43,740	119,059	4,471	123,530	569,036 08
1854	42,887	2,503	45,390	123,528	5,080	128,608	776,973 38
1855	44,261	3,066	47,327	131,022	6,752	137,774	917,853 32
1856	44,608	2,997	47,605	128,205	7,517	135,722	1,023,354 36
1857	46,342	3,079	49,421	130,904	7,280	138,184	1,100,410 82
1858	51,431	3,488	54,919	139,441	7,613	147,054	1,126,613 00
1859	51,712	3,417	55,129	138,688	7,309	145,997	1,246,000 00
1860	55,050	3,455	58,505	145,870	7,168	153,038	1,314,052 00
1861	60,771	3,768	64,539	154,775	7,728	162,503	1,300,000 00
1862	74,598	4,135	78,733	179,975	10,050	190,025	1,358,435 00
1863	75,760	4,297	80,057	189,814	11,310	201,124	1,450,000 00
1864	80,220	4,753	84,973	195,623	12,461	208,084	1,787,000 00
1865	86,674	5,183	91,857	206,309	13,440	219,749	2,298,308 58
1866	88,442	5,483	93,926	212,267	14,636	226,903	2,454,327 54
1867	90,220	6,074	96,294	209,620	16,567	226,187	2,939,348 00

XX.

MEMORANDA—CHRONOLOGICALLY ARRANGED.

From 1614 to the Establishment of the Board of Education, 1842.

1614. New Amsterdam settled.
1633. Adam Roelandsen the first New York school-master.
1642. First efforts to build a school-house.
1659. Luyck's Latin School established.
1661. Evart Pietersen, sixth school-master, and last before the English occupation.
1696. William III. grants to ministers and Consistory of the Dutch Church the right to appoint the school-master.
1702. Free Grammar School founded, and built on the King's Farm.
1704. William Vesey, Episcopal missionary, opens a school for blacks.
1705. Lord Cornbury claims the right of appointing the school-masters.
1710. William Huddlestone, first master of Trinity School.
1732. First Free School for teaching Latin, Greek, and mathematics, established by law—Principal, Alex. Malcolm, gets £40 a year.
1754. King's—now Columbia College—founded.
1755. Nicholas Whelp, school-master, imported from Holland.
1764. Dutch Church has services in the English tongue.
1773. English language taught in the Dutch School.
1776. Schools closed by the war.
1783. Dutch Church School reopens in September.
1784. First receives the name of Charity School.
1785. Manumission Society founded.
1787. Its first school opened in Cliff Street.
1795. Clinton, in his message, recommends the establishment of Common Schools throughout the state.
Act appropriating $50,000 a year for five years.
1798. Teachers' Association—John Woods, President.
1802. Female Association established.
1805. One hundred and forty-one teachers in the city.
Act establishing the Common School Fund.
Act incorporating the Free School Society.
De Witt Clinton, first President of the Society.
Prof. John Griscom gives the first course of popular lectures on physical science ever given in New York.
1806. New York Orphan Asylum founded.
Free School No. 1 opened.

1807. College of Physicians and Surgeons chartered.

1808. New charter of Free School Society.

1809. No. 1 reopened in Tryon Row—permanent location.

1811. No. 2 opened in Henry Street on ground given by Col. Rutgers.

Trinity Church gives site for No. 3 in Christopher—now Grove Street.

1812. Fifty ladies instruct Free School pupils in various catechisms.

Act establishing Common Schools throughout the state, June 19.

1813. Act apportioning the school moneys, where distributed, among the schools of the city.

1814. First official record of pupils, preparatory to the

1815. First distribution of the income of the School Fund.

1817. Committee "to procure from England a teacher completely competent to teach the Lancasterian system."

Rewards and punishments by tickets of nominal value of one-eighth of a cent; prizes exhibited in glass cases, and labeled with ticket values.

Act passed permitting Society to expend surplus money on building new schools.

1818. Geo. T. Trimble elected a member, May 1.

No. 3 opened in the village of Greenwich, under Shepard Johnson.

Resolution that No. 4 shall be so built as to allow the separate instruction of girls.

Teacher Picton arrives from England.

Teachers ordered to institute special classes between 6 and 8 A.M. during four months each year for monitors and "high scholars"—abolished in less than a year.

Picton organizes St. Peter's School in Barclay Street on the Lancasterian plan.

Dec. 14, Lancaster in New York.

Fifty dollars' worth of books on history, voyages, and travels, for each school.

First Manual completed by teachers.

1819. Among the estimates are, salaries, $3600; three monitors' board, $550; their clothes, $300; rewards and prizes, $300.

Memorial to Legislature for $10,000, Jan. 19; get $5000.

Resolution that pupils shall repeat passages from tracts against use of ardent spirits.

Simultaneous examination of schools abandoned.

Death of John Murray, Jr., Vice-president, and one of the three originators of the Society.

1820. First vacation of three weeks in August.

Apprenticed monitors of Nos. 1, 2, and 3 too expensive; will average $200 a year; monitors in No. 4 cost only fifty cents a week.

"Resolved, that the three monitors be continued at $100 a year each until they can find other situations;" they are advertised as disposable in the New York and the Albany papers.

1821. Moffit and Sommerfield, of England, visit the schools.

Regular correspondence maintained with British and Foreign School Society, who continue as from 1805 to supply slates and other school material.

2000 copies of "Universal Non-sectarian Catechism" purchased.

Scripture lessons adopted.

1822. Lots purchased, and preparation made to build No. 5.

Bethel Free School complains that No. 5 will interfere with them. Remonstrance to Legislature as to extra privileges granted to Bethel School.

Register number, 2873, only one-third of them girls; Female Association has 760 girls; African Schools, 650 pupils.

Proposition to have some of the oldest and most meritorious pupils taught grammar, geography, history, and mathematics.

Schools closed on account of the yellow fever.

1823. Punishment with the rod abolished, Jan. 7; "After every persuasion has failed, a small leathern strap may be applied to the palm of the hand; and, if this also fails, the delinquent may be discharged by the Visiting Committee and 'by proclamation;'" that is, *a monitor* visits each class in turn and proclaims that A—— B—— is "turned out of school" for such and such an offense, or it is done before the assembled school.

March 1, Protest from No. 1 in relation to the strap; "palm of hand" amended to read "hand," and Committee of Supplies directed "to procure suitable straps for all the schools," male and female.

Teachers of No. 1 and 3 reported to have announced the strap order in a very improper manner; investigation ordered; report exonerates them.

Girls admitted to No. 1, and placed in separate drafts.

May 1, Picton of No. 4 protests against the strap order.

June 1, "Sections" appointed to each school; strap order repealed, and ratan reinstated.

Committee on Rewards and Punishments report advising a limited use of the rod, but that the chief dependence be upon rewards; $150 to be spent in "prizes" for this purpose.

Proposition from "middle-class citizens to be allowed to send their children for pay."

Freemasons and Fire Department have paid to date $3275 for the tuition of 200 poor children.

1824. No. 6 opened at Bellevue; Johnson and several monitors assist to organize.

Samuel W. Seton elected a member, and assigned to No. 3; makes "a very animated and appropriate speech to the children," and becomes chief annual speaker for 25 or 30 years.

Four hundred tickets for Scudder's Museum are presented by the Widow Scudder and her son; they are elected members of the Society; the tickets are given out to pupils as "prizes" to one in forty-five of the weekly attendance; they last for two or three years; a committee accompany the pupils to the Museum.

School Fund gives $7211.

New York Atheneum founded, "for the Encouragement of Popular Science and the Liberal Arts."

La Fayette visits No. 3 in October; grand parade and review of school children in the Park.

Whole number attending Free and Charity Schools during the year, 10,383; Free Schools, 6976.

Incorporation of New York High School Society; school to be on the Lancasterian plan; charter to expire in 15 years.

1825. High School for males opened in Crosby Street, near Broome, Dr. John Griscom and D. H. Barnes, Principals, with 200 pupils; 680 present in 1827, and 70 to 80 waiting for room; Introductory Department, $3; Junior, $5; Senior, $7 per quarter, fuel and stationery extra; 70 classical pupils; "mutual instruction in all branches;" disastrous effects upon many private schools; two Free School principals enter as tutors.

Borland and Forrest, 45 Warren Street, have 80 classical students.

1826. New charter, and new title—PUBLIC SCHOOL SOCIETY.

Pay system goes into operation.

Feb. 1, High School for Girls opened in Crosby Street, near Spring; terms, $3, $5, $7 per quarter; Junior Course includes "plain sewing, marking and cutting, and making of female dresses."

Establishment of the Executive Committee of Public School Society.

Disastrous working of the pay system.

Two permanent monitors appointed to each department.

Very large script alphabet first painted on the front walls of schoolrooms in Nos. 5 and 7; then of Nos. 3 and 8.

1827. Infant School Society; Mrs. Bethune, First Directress.

No. 10 opened in Duane Street—Junior Department instituted.

1828. S. W. Seton appointed General Inspector of Schools and Visitor of Parents.

Death of De Witt Clinton, Feb. 11, at Albany.

March 4, Samuel Demilt elected a member of the Board of Trustees; he was for many years a leading spirit in the government of the Society; member of Executive Committee, May, 1830; chairman of the Committee on Teachers till his death, May, 1845.

Abolition of tickets; Certificates of Merit soon after substituted; tickets had been given for sundry monitorial, police, and sanitary duties, and forfeited as fines for various offenses; $25 worth of books, penknives, scissors, toys, etc., had been given annually to each department; sold quarterly in school at auction for tickets; pupils often played in street till late, because "able to pay;" very worst boys often had most tickets, and purchased all the most valuable prizes; tickets often bought from boys of other schools; system frequently led to violence and dishonesty.

Colonel Henry Rutgers, second President.

No. 11, in Wooster Street, opened Oct. 27.

1829. Legislature gives power to mortgage; 5000 citizen tax-payers memorialize for a tax; passed law for tax of one-eightieth of one per cent.

School census of city taken.

Mr. Seton takes charge of the Depository, in addition to his other duties.

Female Association opens an Infant School in basement of No. 5.

Rutgers dies; Peter A. Jay, third President.

1830. Slates still imported from London.

1831. No. 12 opened in Seventeenth Street Jan. 1, burned to the ground on the 6th.

Primary Departments established.

Additional tax of three-eightieths of one per cent.

Roman Catholic Orphan Asylum admitted to participate in school moneys.

John Delamater elected trustee, and assigned to No. 3, Aug. 5.

Special Committee, Mr. Trimble chairman, "appointed to re-examine Boys' Departments Nos. 2, 4, 5, 8, and 9, with power to invite the principals thereof—one or all—to resign;" three lose their places.

1832. Pay system finally abolished.

Male High School building sold to Mechanics' Society.

Committee visit Boston; result, establishment of the small Primary Schools.

Common Council, by special ordinance, deny aid to poor families who neglect to send their children to school; ordinance posted throughout the city.

Cholera closes the schools; No. 4 a hospital.

Temporary school out of town at Sailors' Snug Harbor—Broadway and Eighth Street.

Manumission Society appoint a committee of conference for a transfer of their schools.

1833. Extension of course of instruction in upper departments; appointment of assistants.

Mr. Seton appointed agent—really a superintendent under another name, and keeper of Depository; total salary, $800.

Term Monitorial substituted for Lancasterian in the by-laws.

Evening Schools established, and the teachers of the Day Schools compelled to serve without additional pay.

First annual examination of Primary Schools began April 9.

Principals' salaries increased—Male Department, to $1000; Female Department, to $400.

No. 13 opened in May; No. 14 in November.

1834. Transfer of schools of Manumission Society, May 2.

1834. Public School Society have 49 principals, 28 assistants, 75 monitors; total salaries, $36,650.

Adoption of special report of Samuel Demilt, Chairman of Committee on Teachers and Monitors, advising a school for monitors; it finally becomes the Saturday Normal School August 1.

Teachers' Library established.

House of Refuge School, Colored School in Allen Street, and Colored School of Five Points apply for adoption by the Public School Society —applications refused.

1835. No. 6, the Almshouse School, removed to Long Island Farms; being out of the county, the Public School Society retain control by special act.

Male assistants ask increase of their salary from $500 a year to $600—application denied; Committee on Teachers and Monitors acknowledge in their report that it is a rather low salary for such acquirements, but think that the possibility of some day becoming principal at $1000 is sufficient additional inducement.

1836. The African Schools have, since the transfer, "greatly diminished in numbers, efficiency, and usefulness;" committee appointed to investigate; final report; one cause, the great "anti-slavery riots" and attacks upon colored population; many families had removed from the city; many children kept at home; they knew the Manumission Society as their special friends; knew nothing of the Public School Society; reduction of all Colored Schools but one to the rank of Primary had given great offense; also the discharge of teachers who had been long employed, and discontinuance of rewards and of taking home spelling-books; strong prejudices had grown up against the Public School Society; committee recommend a prompt assimilation of the Colored Schools to the white; the establishment of two more upper schools in a new building; a Normal School for colored monitors, and the appointment of a colored man as agent at $150.

Death of Lloyd D. Windsor, Assistant Secretary of the Society, and for 25 years Principal of No. 1, August 5, 1836; he was very highly esteemed.

Male assistant's salary raised to $700.

1837. Five hundred dollars appropriated for Teachers' Library.

Amon M'Vey, Superintendent of Repairs, etc., appointed Sept. 7; salary, $750.

Executive Committee learn that French is being taught in several schools; investigation ordered; classes found in nearly every building; classes supported by parents and pupils at $1 per quarter; chiefly taught after school-hours; unauthorized, therefore forbidden, and promptly suppressed; vocal music had a similar history.

1838. Lower classes first ordered examined; previously only the highest had been.

No. 16 opened in Fifth Street.

1838. Distribution of income of surplus Revenue Fund, and establishment of libraries.

Name of African Schools changed to Colored Schools.

Old No. 1 in Tryon Row torn down, and school reopened in new building in William Street (it has been recently again removed to Vandewater Street).

Joseph Lancaster again visits New York; asks and obtains use of room in No. 5 for lectures to teachers; proposes to the trustees that he shall "take forty Primary pupils who do not know their letters and teach them to read in from four to six weeks, using ten others as monitors; he will not disclose his plan, nor permit any one whomsoever to be present at any of his exercises with his pupils—report adverse. He was killed a few days after by being run over in the street; the Board suspended all business, and all the schools were closed to attend his funeral.

Application for a declaratory act as to the half-mill tax.

1839. Three pupils from Public Schools have free scholarship in Columbia College.

Property corner of Grand and Elm purchased for $19,500, June 27, now Hall of the Board of Education.

1840. Feb. 5, Monthly and semi-annual Certificates of Merit instituted.

Robert C. Cornell, President, died May, 1845.

Beginning of the "religious" controversy of 1840–42.

Expurgation of offensive passages from school-books.

Total salaries of teachers, $60,000.

Many documents in the controversy on religion and schools.

Resolution "that music is not one of the branches taught in the Public Schools, Sept. 5.

550 vagrant children brought to school by visitors in six months.

1841. Trustees' Hall completed.

Paying fire-monitors ceases; had previously received $5 a year and the ashes; wood the only fuel; schools heretofore chiefly swept, etc., by delinquents.

1176 Vagrant children admitted; 356 remain.

Section No. 5 asks that the female assistant may be permitted to teach girls of that school to sing; time, after school; no compensation asked—"declined."

Appointment of a committee of three to mark the performances of classes in examinations.

1842. First recorded comparative table of the "marking system," April.

Act of April establishes the Board of Education.

THE END.

www.ingramcontent.com/pod-product-compliance
Lightning Source LLC
LaVergne TN
LVHW010242110826
845151LV00004B/1370
9781425524227